P9-CEE-550

THE COUPLE'S SURVIVAL WORKBOOK

What YOU Can Do to
Reconnect with Your Partner
and Make Your Marriage Work

**DAVID OLSEN, PH.D., C.S.W. &
DOUGLAS STEPHENS, ED.D., C.S.W.**

New Harbinger Publications, Inc.

Publisher's Note

This publication is designed to provide accurate and authoritative information in regard to the subject matter covered. It is sold with the understanding that the publisher is not engaged in rendering psychological, financial, legal, or other professional services. If expert assistance or counseling is needed, the services of a competent professional should be sought.

Distributed in the U.S.A. by Publishers Group West; in Canada by Raincoast Books; in Great Britain by Airlift Book Company, Ltd.; in South Africa by Real Books, Ltd.; in Australia by Boobook; and in New Zealand by Tandem Press.

Copyright © 2001 by David Olsen and Douglas Stephens
New Harbinger Publications, Inc.
5674 Shattuck Avenue
Oakland, CA 94609

Cover design by Blue Designs
Cover image by Index Stock/ChromaZone Images
Edited by Kayla Sussell
Text design by Michele Waters

Library of Congress Catalog Card Number: 01-132283
ISBN 1-57224-254-X Paperback

All Rights Reserved

Printed in the United States of America

New Harbinger Publications' Web site address: www.newharbinger.com

03   02   01

10   9   8   7   6   5   4   3   2   1

First printing

To our wives, Cheryl and Janet, for the gift of long-term love, and marriage.

Contents

Acknowledgments

Many thanks:

To our clients who help us to refine and learn what helps couples to change.

To our graduate students who challenge us by constant questions to better understand ourselves and our work.

To my wife, Cheryl Olsen, for her patience, rereading, and constructive criticism of these chapters, and for cofacilitating the couple workshops that helped develop this material.

To Janet Stephens, my life partner, for her support, encouragement, and inspiration.

To Mary Barlow for her help with typing and computer formatting.

And especially to Kayla Sussell for her excellent editing, rewriting, and help clarifying our theories and making them readable.

Part I

CHAPTER ONE

Why Is This So Much Work?

Mary looked angrily at the clock and wondered to herself, "How many times in the past year has this happened?" Her son, Johnny, sat glued to the TV oblivious to the anger his mother was emitting and to another fight brewing between his parents. As soon as she heard the garage door open Mary rose from her chair, grabbed her purse, told her son to put his jacket on, and waited . . . grimly.

Her husband, Ralph, came into the house and Mary stood to face him. She said, "Where have you been? You told me you'd make a special effort to be here on time today! You're twenty minutes late . . . again! I can *never* count on you to keep a promise! Why do I put up with such disrespect?"

Ralph took a deep breath, let it out slowly between his front teeth, and then shouted, "Look, Mary, what do you want? I can't just tell my boss to get lost when he has a project in my face! I did the best I could! Every time I drop things to race back here to you and your whatever . . . I risk my job!"

Mary responded, "Your 'whatever' is a planned trip to the movies with your *family*! Remember? We planned it together! I can see you just don't care about anything! Ralph, where did we go so wrong?"

Mary remembers when things weren't always this way between the two of them. Perhaps Ralph does, too. Like most couples they started out with high hopes and ideals. Eighteen years ago, they were both thrilled to get married, convinced that their love for each other would conquer any problems they would ever face. But now they are disillusioned and full of despair. They feel stuck, unable to move beyond their anger and disappointment with each other and with their marriage.

What happened? How did they move from the optimistic idealism they began with to such negativity? What went wrong? Was it simply poor communication? Was it the absence of romance? The reality is not that simple. There are so many obvious, yet intricate, issues involved in a successful marriage. After spending eighteen years together trying to forge a marriage that meets their individual needs, Ralph and Mary know each other reasonably well. Nevertheless, their marriage is now seriously stuck. If they don't make some changes, they could easily become another couple filing for divorce.

Are the Odds in Your Favor?

Over the past thirty years the number of divorces in the United States has become mind-boggling. Half of all first marriages now run the risk of ending in divorce, regardless of the duration of the marriage (Gottman 1999; Bray and Hetherington 1993; Glick and Lin 1986). By the seventh year of marriage every other marriage ends in divorce. If a couple embarks upon either a second or third marriage (for either spouse), the odds are even more foreboding. Although remarriage is very common, the divorce rate is now approaching 70 percent in the first seven years of remarriage (Gottman 1999). The adults and the children in these families may all be casualties. Furthermore, the damage to children of divorced parents is enormous, as demonstrated by research recently published by Judith Wallerstein (2000) in *The Unexpected Legacy of Divorce*.

Wallerstein and her fellow researchers concluded from a twenty-five year study of children from divorced families that the children were indeed negatively affected by their parents' divorce. This became clear when these children were interviewed in their adult years and during their own marriages. "[I]n coping with the normal stresses in a marriage, adults from divorced families were at a grave disadvantage. Anxiety about relationships was at the bedrock of their personalities and endured even in very happy marriages. Their fears of disaster and sudden loss rose when they felt content. And their fears of abandonment, betrayal, and rejection mounted when they found themselves having to disagree with someone they loved. . . . They had a lot to undo and a lot to learn in a very short time" (Wallerstein 2000, p. 300).

So, what makes marriage so difficult? Is it that couples lack communication skills or is it the pressures of dual careers? Is it financial pressure or the lack of extended family support? Could it be gender differences? Are men really from Mars and women from Venus? Or are the politicians correct in saying that we are witnessing a breakdown of family values? We suspect that if ten couples were questioned about the reasons marriage is so difficult, ten completely different sets of answers would be given. Obviously, it is a complicated issue.

Too often, however, the reasons given for the rising divorce rate are simply speculative and reflect the biases of the person writing. Before the start of empirical research about family life, the opinions that most people expressed on the matter (even those of mental health professionals) were derived from experience or religious beliefs. In the early 1970s, the staff of the Timberlawn Psychiatric Hospital in Dallas, Texas, began an extensive study of psychological health factors in family life. This research group produced several books including *No Single Thread: Psychological Health in Families* (Lewis, Beavers, Gossett, and Phillips 1976). This began a trend to examine marriage and family life from a research perspective. Other research soon followed.

Healthy Marriage

Most recently, the work of John Gottman has continued the effort to understand, through research, what makes some marriages work, while others fail. Gottman used the data gathered from his clinic's study of hundreds of couples to determine what makes some marriages work, some fail, and which marriages can be rebuilt or repaired (Gottman 1999).

Gottman, a psychologist and the codirector of the Seattle Marriage and Family Institute, learned that, although communication skills and active listening are very helpful, they alone cannot create very successful relationships. He found that the factors that worked best were these: being true friends; yielding to the needs of the other at times; and understanding that a "win-win" solution sometimes requires tough choices.

In his recent book, *The Seven Principles for Making Marriage Work* (2000), Gottman sums up his findings as follows: Partners who understand, honor, and respect each other and their relationship are destined to enjoy a healthy and long-lasting marriage. Such partners are committed to maintaining a positive regard for each other, even in the midst of negative conflict. When these partners have arguments, they are about issues; not about each other's failings.

Of course this sounds good in theory, but it is difficult to achieve. Understanding, honoring, and respecting one another are values that most people applaud and try to teach to their children. Most people would agree with John Gottman about the importance of friendship in marriage. Yet the reality is that marriage is hard work, and these values are hard to live by inside the crucible of a marriage.

But a good marriage is worth all the work. People are learning that staying married can be good for one's health (with the exception of those marriages in which there is domestic violence). In Gottman's *The Seven Principles for Making Marriage Work* (2000), he references a convincing study done by Lois Verbrugge and James House of the University of Michigan, that determined "that an unhappy marriage can increase your chance for getting sick by roughly 35 percent and even shorten your life by an average of four years" (p. 4). Gottman's own research at the University of Washington has uncovered "preliminary evidence that a good marriage may keep you healthier by directly influencing your immune system, which spearheads the body's defenses against illness" (p. 5).

So why aren't people motivated to make their marriages work? Why isn't it easy? After all, isn't it common sense to do the things that further one's life enjoyment? Perhaps, perhaps not. Let's revisit Mary and Ralph to shed more light on some of the complicated issues in marriage.

After they arrived at the theater, Ralph sat sullenly throughout the entire movie, fuming inside, angry at the bind he thought he had been put in by Mary's expectations. Mary engrossed herself in the movie and their son's needs.

Ralph knew that he and Mary had worked on and improved their communication skills over the past year. He thought they had made some progress, especially since she had told him she understood why he sometimes needed to work late, mostly to ensure that he would stay in line for further advancement. He had even strained to learn active listening skills to demonstrate how committed he is to his marriage and its health. Nevertheless, this evening he felt misunderstood and disrespected. After all, if he didn't care about his family and marriage he sure wouldn't be working so hard at his job!

Even though Mary was able to attend to the film, she still felt frustrated and tense. Her neck was taut, her shoulders sore, and her heart felt broken. She had worked so hard trying to build a base of good communication with Ralph, especially this past year. She feared that they could easily go the way of both her sisters' marriages. Mary was committed to improving her marriage, but except for refining her listening and communicating skills, she had no clue as to how to do so. She sensed that all her efforts with Ralph were for naught. He just didn't understand how important family time was to her! Worse yet, she now believed that he really didn't care, either. That scared her and left her even more hurt and angry. After eighteen years of marriage, how could he still not know what family time meant to her? She began to wonder whether he cared about her at all.

What Mary and Ralph do not realize yet is that communication skills alone do not make for a better marriage. In fact, research has shown unequivocally that this is why so much of marital therapy has a relapse rate of 30 to 50 percent (Gottman 2000; Jacobson 1984; Jacobson and Addis 1993). Many marital therapists believe that improving a troubled marriage requires teaching communication and listening skills, as well as pursuing equality in household duties. But in studying more than 650 couples Gottman and his researchers found that successful conflict resolution is not what makes marriages succeed. They found that the key to a marriage's success lies in being respectful and caring friends (2000). It sounds almost too simple, yet if you think back to Ralph and Mary's struggle, you will recall that they each felt disrespected by the other.

What Makes Marriage Work?

So what really makes marriages work? Books about intrinsic gender differences aside, it turns out that men and women want very similar experiences within their couple relationship. They want sex and romance, passion and companionship. All of which are to be found in marriage if there is an underlying deep friendship of good quality. Believing that one's partner wants the best for us, as well as for themselves, somehow can give us the hope to move beyond the difficulties of the moment.

Another key to a strong marital relationship is having a transcendent value system, a belief in something greater than self. Believing that there are large themes at work in our lives can provide a depth of meaning and a purpose to marriage that can help us pursue connection with our partner, even through many frustrations (Beavers 1977; 1985).

Deep Friendship

Healthy marriages certainly do have conflicts, often in several areas, for example, parenting, housecleaning, sex, in-laws. Gottman found that despite significant differences in personality, avid interests, and even values, couples in happy marriages still reported high satisfaction with their relationship. What sustained them was deep friendship. That level of friendship allows safety and vulnerability even in the midst of conflict. But what is deep friendship in a marriage?

Friendship within marriage requires many skills, but there are two that are essential for a healthy marriage. The first, according to Gottman (2000), is that there must be a generally *positive* atmosphere in the marriage in both nonconflict and conflict situations. The second is that healthy couples who are deep friends can reduce negative affect; that is, they can reduce the emotional fallout from their conflicts by accepting each other's emotions and refraining from evaluating or judging them. Couples who are deep friends choose not to experience their spouse's emotions as personal attacks. Deep friends can quarrel with the understanding that the other's emotions are to be accepted; the issues are what must be negotiated. The partner is always valued and treated with respect.

Conflict and the expression of a wide range of emotion is an essential part of healthy friendship and healthy marriage. When marriage works, it works because conflict is faced and worked through, and feelings are expressed and understood. Healthy couples trust both each other and their relationship enough to not back away from the feelings that come with conflict, while continuing to respect each other throughout the duration of the conflict. In unhealthy marriage, this is not true.

In John Gottman's recent research (2000) he found that unhealthy marriages are characterized by the following behaviors:

1. Criticism (according to Gottman, criticism is more than a complaint about a specific action; it contains negative language about the partner's personality and character).

2. Obvious contempt is expressed routinely through conflict, and partners are necessarily defensive.

3. Patterns of stonewalling or avoiding the other person become routine. Conflicts are not only *not* resolved but they result in both partners feeling even more misunderstood and disrespected.

To illustrate this further, let's take a look at another couple's interaction, as it portrays an unhappy marriage in full operation.

Tom and Sarah

Tom was visibly angry. His face was red and he kept clenching and unclenching his fists on top of the table. Sarah looked at him and blurted, "What do you want me to do, stop buying the kids clothes when they need them? I don't know where you get off criticizing *my* spending when you have *no* trouble buying lottery tickets! And those stupid things you say we 'need' from the hardware store! I'm sick of this! We've had this same argument over and over, ever since we started living together! Frankly, I'm sick of you!"

Impatient to respond, Tom shot back, "You're damn right! I do think you waste our money on things we don't need. Both the kids have too many clothes. Their closets and the floors in their rooms are all overflowing with clothes. Just because you grew up in a cheap family where they didn't buy you anything doesn't mean you have to make up for lost time with our kids! We can't spend money like this! And, for your information, those lottery tickets cost the same amount every week. I plan my finances, not like you. You're always going off the deep end!" Not waiting for Sarah to reply, Tom stomped out of the kitchen, knocking over a chair.

Here, Tom and Sarah demonstrate the contempt and defensiveness so often found in unhappy marriages. For them to have a reasonable hope of improving their relationship, they would need to learn more about how their marriage works and doesn't work, what each partner needs from marriage, and, most importantly, whether they can ever become true, caring friends. It would be a huge undertaking, which some people (understandably) would balk at before deciding to begin.

Our Approach

Perhaps you have been wondering, "Why should I read yet another book on marriage? How can this workbook be any different from all the others?" Our answer is that this workbook is different because it will help you to change the interaction that exists between you and your partner *as a separate individual*. It does not require your partner's involvement either in reading the text or in doing the exercises. Rather, this workbook will focus on helping you to change *your* role within your marriage.

Self-Focus

So, where do we start on this journey toward long-term marriage grounded in deep friendship? In our experience there is one key factor that distinguishes healthy marriages from unhealthy ones. *That factor is self-focus.* What do we mean by self-focus? Stop for a moment and think about most couples who begin a course of couple therapy. Most know exactly what their problem is. Simply put, the problem is their partner. Most people naively believe that if they could change their partner, their marriage would improve. If they were really honest, they would say that they believe that if only their partner would change, all their problems would be solved. For them, a fulfilling marriage means a changed partner. They never focus on their own contributions to their marital problems.

In our combined fifty years of therapy practice, we have found that the most common misconception held in troubled marriages is the belief that the relationship would improve immensely if your partner would change significantly. To no one's surprise, including (perhaps) your own, this misconception is also held by your partner.

This workbook is different. It is intended to help you focus on your *role in creating a less than healthy marriage.* If your goal is to change your spouse, this book is not for you. If, however, you would like to experiment with changing your marriage by changing yourself, then this book will provide help. It will guide you step by step to examine your part in your marriage—to change what you can change and thereby to open up new possibilities for growth in yourself and your marriage. Self-focus means exactly what it says. If you read this book and do the exercises, you will be focusing on yourself—not on your spouse, your parents, or your children—only yourself.

What we are proposing is a clear method you can use to change how you operate in your marriage. It is based on the time-tested belief that we can change only ourselves, not our partners. *As you learn how to understand and change yourself as a marital partner, you will discover new depths of satisfaction and pleasure in your marriage.*

Assessment

So, where should you start in trying to create change? Begin on the simplest level possible. How is your marriage doing? How satisfying is it? Sometimes, doing an exercise can help to clarify your thinking. One simple exercise designed to open up your thinking is to rate your overall marital satisfaction on a scale of 1 to 10. The number 10 represents a wonderful marriage, while the number 1 represents a very painful and unsatisfying marriage.

First, rate your marriage yourself, and then ask yourself how your spouse would rate the marriage. (In our approach we want you to do all the exercises alone. Once you complete this book, and you have improved your self-focus, you may later inquire of your spouse how he/she would rate the marriage. This would be a checkpoint for your assumptions, rather than the beginning of an interaction between the two of you about marriage.)

This simple exercise will let you know how you view the marriage, and how similar (or dissimilar) your views of your marriage are. (Be careful: If you rate your marriage a 10, and you think that your partner would give it a 2, you have a lot of work to do!) Write the number in the space provided:

My marriage at this time is a _____ (1–10).

My spouse would think our marriage is a _____ (1–10).

Next, think back on what attracted you to your spouse. Was it the physical appearance, the sense of humor, or the capacity for responsibility? Was it how you felt when you were in his/her presence; a special feeling that you had only when your spouse was around? How did you describe your partner early on to your friends and family? Try to visualize some of your early dating memories and to remember some of the feelings you had back then. Zoom in on memories of what drew you together. Then come back to the present.

Are the same qualities still attractive, or has something changed? Too often what attracts us initially becomes a progressive irritant as we go through life together. For example, the man who is attracted to a carefree, spontaneous woman may refer to her after fifteen years of marriage as an "airhead." The woman who was attracted to a strong steady man, whose behavior was predictable, may now refer to him as "boring." Ask yourself if the qualities that attracted you initially are still attractive or have turned into irritants. We will talk more about how this happens in our chapter on marital interactions (see chapter 3).

After answering these simple questions, ask yourself another question. What are the strengths of your marriage? No matter how frustrating things may become, what is it that provides strength and stability? Try and assess what works and what does not. *Successful couples focus on their strengths and build on them.* Write your answers in the blank spaces.

1. What are the strengths of your marriage?

_____

_____

_____

2. What do you usually do to try to create change?

_____

_____

_____

3. What usually goes wrong when you try to solve problems?

_____

_____

_____

What Are Your Predictable Problems?

To take this assessment to a deeper level begin thinking about the predictable problems of your marriage. Most couples can usually identify several problem areas. It is important to know what those areas are (e.g., parenting styles, one partner working late every night, or arguments over money) around which you and your partner squabble, usually without achieving a successful resolution.

In couple therapy, most couples can evaluate the quality of their relationship by brainstorming about the chronic problems or conflicts that never seem to get resolved. You can begin in the same fashion by making a list of the types of problems that are most commonly associated with your fights or arguments. Remember, not all fights or conflicts are screaming matches. You may fight frequently by using a mutually agreed-upon silent treatment and withdrawal, or by a combination of both words and silence.

Toxic Topics

Basically, "toxic topics" are those that you and your spouse argue about constantly, usually with as much intensity as frequency. They are the topics you each know will lead quickly to a heated dialogue and dispute, seldom reaching a clear resolution. Some couples have several toxic topics, while others have only one or two. Note that these types of topics are found equally with happy or unhappy couples. Go through the partial checklist below and mark off the items that cause frequent fights. Remember, a problem should be noted when it is a topic of conflict, even if one partner states that the topic isn't an issue for him/her.

- Alcohol ____
- Children ____
- Drugs (illicit or prescription) ____
- Friends ____
- Finances ____
- Gambling ____
- Hobbies ____
- Internet use ____
- In-laws ____
- Music (performing or listening) ____
- Neighbors ____
- Pornography ____
- Sexual relationship ____
- Sports (watching or participating) ____
- Television ____
- Work ____
- Other _____

You may have noted the absence of "communication" as a problem area in the list above. *That's because simply improving communication skills does not significantly improve marriage.* When we communicate we do so either in an open, receptive fashion, which encourages a dialogue or debate, or we communicate in a closed, no-room-for-dialogue-about-it manner. It is either one or the other. Even open communication does not help us solve our problems fully because it does not affect the underlying beliefs we hold, nor does it have an impact on the predictable arguments we employ during our interactions.

So communication is not a problem area; it is simply a vehicle, broken or working, that can help us get to somewhere, or keep us stuck. Granted, if it is closed communication, it is a broken vehicle that needs repair. We still need to know what is important to us and whether we feel respected and honored by our mate. Solving problems such as those listed above demands a sense of shared purpose, a dedication to the relationship's improved health, and effective communication. These qualities will be addressed throughout this book.

Your Problems Could Increase

One problem is that when trying to solve these problems, a new problem is created. That new problem is your interaction or argument about the problem itself. We will explain this in detail in chapter 3. For the moment, however, it's important to recognize that the process of trying to solve these areas of conflict may create a new problem. In addition, your failed solutions may have become problems themselves. This dynamic arises from (1) not understanding your relationship interaction habits and (2) the underlying, unhelpful beliefs that contribute to your unproductive patterns of relating.

When both partners fight furiously about a problem like finances, each brings a set of beliefs about that issue into the quarrel. Those beliefs fuel the communication with strong opinions and intensity. (See chapters 4 and 5 for a discussion of these belief systems.) If finances are not an area of worry for one partner but they are for the other, the more verbal mate is likely to be deferred to by the more passive, or "unworried," partner. But if money was a toxic topic in both persons' families of origin, or in a prior marriage, there will be plenty of intensity coming from both partners, and even paying the phone bill on time can become an issue.

Examine Yourself

Part of any assessment requires learning to recognize that your unsatisfactory "solutions" and failed attempts at communication have become part of the problem. Before you can change yourself, you must begin to pay attention to what you do when you are trying to "fix" matters. What happens to your voice tone? What kind of body language do you communicate? How do you escalate the discussion, or make demands? Ask yourself the following questions and check the appropriate column:

Assessment Checklist

Do I ...	Yes	No
Maintain eye contact when talking or listening?		
Speak to my partner in a normal tone and volume?		
Use respectful language?		
Wait until my partner is done speaking before I respond?		
Show respect for my partner even if I am angry?		
Refrain from physical touch when I am angry?		
Stay in the discussion until we both agree the topic is resolved or tabled until another scheduled time?		
Stay on the topic?		
Show interest in discussing this issue until it is settled to both of our mutual satisfactions?		

Use this checklist frequently to *improve your self-focus.* We suggest that you place it where you will see it at least once a day. That could mean putting it on your desk at work, on your car's dashboard, on a mirror you look at frequently, on the refrigerator, or on the nightstand near your bed. The key is to look it over every day until it becomes a mental list committed to memory.

Even when you are not in a conflict with your partner, it will be useful to review this checklist after neutral, or even pleasant, discussions about your day, the people at work, or what's new in the world. The more practice you have with these observational skills, the more relaxed and focused you will become when you have an argument.

These observational skills will alert you to your role in the communication problems in your marriage. *It is the behaviors you each demonstrate, often activated subconsciously by a behavior of your partner, that triggers a response.* This dynamic exchange can be so rapid that we are rarely aware of what is happening until we review the interaction in memory later. This book will help you to better understand those rapid interactional cycles, and help clarify your role in them.

Assessment Is Only the Beginning

Although answering these assessment questions is helpful, *it is only the beginning of your task.* Much deeper assessment of the institution of marriage, as well as of your own relational issues will be covered in later chapters. Read each chapter carefully and always try to focus on yourself. The result will be worth it. Each chapter will ask you to take your assessment to deeper and deeper levels.

How to Read This Book

This book is set up in two parts. The first half (chapters 1 through 8) offers clear suggestions for understanding your role in your marriage in a variety of ways. By the end of chapter 8 you should have a new way of understanding your role in your marriage, and you will be offered clear principles by which you can effect the kinds of changes you wish to accomplish.

The second half focuses on specific problem areas of marriage and will help you apply what you have learned in the first part to your specific problems. We will look at the areas of conflict (chapter 9), intimacy (chapter 10), sex (chapter 11), parenting (chapter 12), remarried families (chapter 13), and money (chapter 14). In all of these problem areas we examine ways to help you to change your behavior, with the clear intent of changing and improving your marriage. Finally, chapter 15 provides a summary of the five principles of change that we believe can help you to create greater harmony in your marriage.

Using this workbook will take concentration and commitment. It will be demanding because any problem you may consider will touch on many levels of interaction and belief systems. Nevertheless, we trust that your reading and effort will be rewarded by greater self-understanding and empowerment in your relationship. It is never easy to focus on yourself. It takes self-discipline, and great concentration. It is tough work. However changing yourself and your behavior is the best way to improve your marriage.

CHAPTER TWO

Ten Myths About Marriage

Building a long-term marriage is a very difficult process. At the same time, the rewards for building a good quality, long-term marriage are enormous. Many scholars have speculated on the benefits of a successful marriage, some have even argued that marriage is good for your health. On the other hand, researchers like Judith Wallerstein (2000) have proved conclusively that the long-term effects of divorce on kids are devastating.

Although most couples would agree that building a long-term marriage is something they want to do, many have little or no idea of how to do it. Where can you find a blueprint that will show you how to construct a relationship of depth and quality? Many couples assume that their parents' marriages will provide a useful model for them. They often make this assumption without realizing what they are doing. Or, if their parents had unhappy marriages, young couples try to build their relationships on principles that seem to them to be completely opposite to those of their parents (see chapter 6). Still others couples turn to their churches and religious institutions for guidance. And many couples turn to popular culture for models of healthy marriage.

Before they are even old enough to think about marrying, most young people have been exposed to a variety of myths about what a good marriage should be. Movies, TV, and popular music carry the myths to teenagers hungry for popular culture, and the adolescents absorb the messages the myths carry without ever realizing it. Then, these myths become their models for good marriage.

The popular culture's myths are one type of potentially dangerous blueprint for marriage. They suggest not only the wrong kind of plan for building a good quality marriage, frequently they also promote life goals that are questionable at best. Such myths are half-truths that contain elements of truth and, as such, they can be extremely powerful.

Furthermore, people rarely question the veracity of these myths, choosing instead to think of them as eternal verities. Often, these half-truths can be summed up in a simple statement that describes what those who subscribe to the myths really believe about marriage. The myths may also become the standard by which we evaluate the health of our relationships.

Listen to the lyrics of popular songs, or the latest gossip about movie stars on one of the many talk shows. All of them reveal a number of myths about marriage. They include prescriptions about what marriage should be: what one's spouse should be like, what the level of satisfaction should be after marriage. Is marriage something to be barely endured or should it bring nirvana? Is it the closest thing to heaven, or a type of living hell? Is it designed to meet all of your needs? Listen to discussions at your gym, church, or social group, as well as to talk shows or pop music, and you will hear from believers in a great number of marital myths.

Life Means Constant Change

People buy into these myths because they are unable to see marriage for what it is, an ever-changing relationship between two ever-changing people. Life circumstances change, life cycle issues are a fact of life, and, as a result, marriage must also be adaptive and ever-changing. Myths promote simplistic ways of understanding marriage, without taking into account the changes that time inevitably brings. Those who believe that the myths are true enter marriage with all sorts of unrealistic expectations. Then they evaluate the health of their relationships against the impossibly high standards set by the myths.

If your goal is to build a good quality long-term marriage, it is essential to have a fact-based blueprint to build a relationship that will be strong enough to adapt and change and grow through the many problems and crises of life. A marriage firmly anchored in truth—not myth—is like a warm refuge in the midst of a storm. In contrast, a marriage based on popular myths may leave you stranded in the storm with a relationship that does not have strength or resiliency to survive. Consider some of the following myths about marriage. First ask yourself which myths apply to you, then think about how your belief in those myths may be hurting your marriage.

Myth No. 1: Changing a Relationship Requires Two People

Reality: The only person you can change is you! Many people believe that to create change in a relationship both persons must be motivated to change. Therefore, they believe that no real change can occur unless both parties are committed to work hard on their relationship. You can predict what happens next. The person who believes that the relationship needs to change spends most of his or her time trying to motivate his/her partner to change. In the end this becomes an effort to change the partner. "If you would just read this book, or talk to me more, or not go out with your friends, or share my recreational interests, or not call your mother so much . . ." The list goes on and on. In the end, the list becomes an agenda for attempting to change one's partner. The harder they try the worse things become.

Other people decide to strike and do no work on the marriage until their partner does what they determine to be an equal amount of work on the relationship. Their position is that there is no point in working on their part of the relationship if their partner is not doing at least an equal amount of work. This inevitably ends in a stalemate with the marriage more stuck then ever. "I won't work on this until he/she also does some work on it." As a result, a standoff takes place and no change takes place.

In both cases—(1) trying to change one's partner, or (2) not working on the relationship unless one's partner does his/her share of the work—the myth that to change a relationship requires two people has been accepted. What is obviously lost is the reality that the only person you can change is you, and that if you change your role in the marriage, the marriage itself will change. This does not mean that the marriage will always get better. It simply means it will change and will no longer be stuck. Our belief holds that you can change only yourself, and that by so doing you can work on your marriage even if your partner is unwilling to do so.

The reality of relationships is that if one person in a relationship changes, the relationship has to change for better or worse. Family systems theory teaches that in relationships, the sum is greater than the parts. That is, in marriage one plus one does not equal two. Husband plus wife create a third entity: the relationship itself (see chapter 3). Clearly, if one person in the relationship changes and acts differently, then the relationship will have to change as a result.

Jon and Diane

Jon and Diane had a very patterned way of relating. Jon was a highly successful physician who worked long hours. He was too busy to consider seeing a couple's therapist even though the marriage was less than satisfactory for both partners. Diane's response was to pursue her husband, to plead for more conversation, and to buy self-help books that she left on Jon's nightstand with bookmarks in them. She whined constantly about how unhappy she was and how neglected she felt. All of this had exactly the contrary effect. Jon worked longer hours than ever and Diane became progressively more unhappy.

At a friend's suggestion Diane began to get some counseling, and she began to look at her role in her marriage. She did not like what she saw. Realizing that she could not change Jon, she decided to change herself. She began taking some graduate courses and going out occasionally with her friends. She joined a community choir in which she found much satisfaction. As her friendships and social life grew, her time away from the house increased, and Jon began to get nervous. Their interaction had changed. Although he had complained about her constant pursuit of him, he began to be anxious about her time away from the house. He started wanting to do more things together. Their relationship changed. When Diane changed herself successfully, her role in the relationship changed and so did the marriage. This is the important principle this book is based upon. It is a one-person model of change. The more you can successfully change your own contribution to the marriage, the more likely your marriage is to change.

Myth No. 2: If I Just Try Harder, I Can Change My Partner

Although we've looked at the fact that change comes first by changing yourself, most people secretly harbor this second myth. They believe that if only they tried harder, or became more creative, or developed a new strategy they will be able to change their partner.

Most couples who have been married for any significant length of time will chuckle at this one. However, even as they chuckle, they may still entertain the fantasy that they can change each other. Secretly, most couples are convinced that if their spouse can be persuaded to change, then the marriage will change and they will be happy.

The obvious result of this is that they work harder and harder to change their spouse, offering him/her books and articles to read on timely mental health topics. Be honest, how many articles or books have you left out for your spouse, hoping that they would get it. We have listened to hundreds of couples who diligently presented their partners with the latest self-help literature in the naïve and misguided hope that their partner would change.

Those people who labor under the weight of this myth hope and pray for the "enlightenment" of their spouse. Down deep they are waiting for the day when their spouse "sees the light" and then becomes the ideal mate whom they have longed for. In short, they hope to convert their spouse into the fantasy person they would like as their mate. When this fantasy is articulated, it actually sounds pretty silly, doesn't it? Yet many couples buy into it and work hard to create this type of change.

Joanna and John

Joanna longed for a different type of marital relationship with John. She wanted a partner who enjoyed classical music, ballet, and her circle of friends. She also wanted deeper, more meaningful conversations with him. She longed to talk to John the way she talked to her women friends. John, on the other hand, loved football and rock music. His idea of a great night out was a Bruce Springstein concert, not the New York City Ballet. He didn't mind talking with Joanna, but he felt that whenever he did have a conversation with her, she always seemed to be disappointed. It always felt as if whatever it was she was looking for, he wasn't able to provide it. So, over time, John thought, "Why even bother trying?"

Joanna continued trying to change John. She begged him to go to the ballet with her, and occasionally he did, but then he would make terrible jokes about men in tights. She gave him articles to read on emotional intimacy, which he occasionally skimmed. The harder she tried to change him, the more distant he became. Eventually, John said to her, "If you are so unhappy with who I am, why don't you find another husband? I'm still the person you married, so why do you want me to become another person now?"

Now, Joanna must make a difficult choice. She can continue to try and change her husband, and probably become more frustrated, or she can focus on changing her own interactional style and possibly even her expectations of marriage. She has the choice of trying to change her husband or focusing on herself. In the end there is really only one acceptable choice.

The reality of relationships is the direct opposite of myth No. 2. *The only person you can change is yourself.* Only when this fundamental rule of relationships is accepted is there hope for a relationship to change.

Myth No. 3: My Spouse Will Be Everything to Me

When listening to the dreams of young couples as they plan their marriages and talk about their future life together, we hear some wonderful and perhaps grandiose expectations. Often, when they are asked in premarital counseling where they expect problems to emerge, they appear dumbfounded by the question. "Problems? Don't you understand? We are in love!" Their idealism is high and their expectations even higher. Together they will conquer any problem and create an ideal marriage. Unfortunately, the current divorce rate of over 50 percent indicates that at least half of these couples will be disappointed (Gottman 2000; Bray and Hetherington 1993; Glick and Lin 1986).

Myth No. 3 suggests that in the process of romantic spouse selection we can pick a partner who will be everything to us. Without being too disparaging about such idealistic expectations, think about what these couples are hoping for. They are hoping that their choice of a mate, in the midst of intense infatuation and high sexual energy, will provide them with a life partner who will be *everything* to them—sexual partner, best friend, nurturer of their children, breadwinner or financial supporter, housekeeper, nurse or personal attendant if they fall ill—this list could go on and on. Of course, that is a pretty tall order. Given the enormous cultural changes in the last century and the decrease in extended family support and community roots, the stakes are way too high. The odds of one's spouse being able to be "everything" to you are quite low.

However, for those who cling to this myth, the disappointment will be enormous.

Ordinarily, the course of a normal marriage is to move from high expectations and idealism to some disillusionment and finally, in the case of healthy marriage, to acceptance. For couples or individuals who cling to Myth No. 3, their experience of disillusionment will be profound. The more they cling to this myth, the more frustrated they will become. The more anxious and frustrated they become, the more they will work to change their partner. In the end, they work toward a type of fusion, wanting to do all of life's varied activities with their partner. Of course the harder they try, the more disillusioned they become, and the greater their disappointment.

What many people fail to realize is that Myth No. 3 fuels a belief system that causes them to interpret their marriage with increased negativity. Tom and Alison illustrate this problem all too well.

Tom and Alison

Tom, a well-dressed, successful businessman, whose extended family live in many different parts of the country, and with whom he has little contact, described with anguish how disappointed he was with his wife, Alison. "Before we married, I thought that she would be my best friend and that we would do everything in common. I thought we would share everything together, and be soul mates. I bought her an expensive bike for her birthday, hoping that we could take long bike rides in the country every weekend. She seemed appreciative, but she never wants to ride more than a few miles, and she is seldom in the mood to ride with me."

At first glance this seemed like a simple problem. A simple difference in interests. However, because Tom believed that he and his wife should be best friends, have all the same interests, and meet all of each other's needs, it felt like a significant problem. Tom interpreted her lack of interest in "serious cycling" as evidence that they did not have much in common after all. From there, they began to discuss other ways in which they were different. His conclusion was that, clearly, they could not be everything to each other and, therefore, they were not happily married.

Many couples struggle with myth No. 3. They expect (often without saying it) that they will be great sexual partners, have all of their interests in common, be soul mates, and share all of their interests on a deep emotional level. What they really are hoping for is that their partner will meet all of their needs, which is, of course, impossible.

Myth No. 4: My Partner Should Meet All My Needs

When you read that heading, it sounds ridiculous. How can your partner be expected to meet all of your needs?. Yet often, without realizing it, we become deeply hurt when all of our needs are not met by our partner, and often we are not aware of how powerful our expectations really are.

Although myth No. 4 seems similar to myth No. 3 (one's spouse will be everything to them), it actually moves to a deeper level. Often we believe that our relational needs are quite simple. We need companionship, sex, conversation, role sharing, or any number of combinations. It can be difficult enough to get some of those needs met in relationships.

However, some of our needs are not so obvious. Consider several examples: If you received little positive affirmation or validation while growing up, as an adult, often deep hurts and an internal emptiness remain. Such hurt and emptiness follow you into your marriage and, on some deep, barely conscious level, you may hope that your partner will provide you with the positive validations that you did not receive as a child.

Or, if you grew up in an abusive family, it is likely that you will have a strong need to feel emotionally and physically safe. On some significant level, you may long for a nurturing relationship where all your needs will be met, as if you were still a child. However, any degree of minor marital conflict may be interpreted by you as a sign that you are not really safe, and you might create emotional distance with your spouse as a result.

Or perhaps you were expected to be "perfect" when you were a child and you were never quite able to meet the expectations. You may have hoped for more balance in your marriage, only to find yourself in the same role you had as a child. You never quite measure up to your spouse's expectations, and it leaves you feeling as if your needs are unmet.

The problem, however, is that too often we are not aware of those needs, nor are we aware that we unconsciously expect our partner to meet them for us. The result can be deep disappointment, since the myth suggests that all of our needs should be met by our partner. Chapter 6, where we look at family-of-origin issues, will discuss strategies for working with these complicated problems.

Myth No. 5: Marriage Should Not Be a Lot of Work

Too often, couples begin their life together in love, with great idealism, and a strong sense of romance. They come back from their honeymoon, eager to build their lives together. Although they understand that there will be some problems along the way, many couples assume that most problems can be solved easily. They deeply believe that "Love will conquer all." They may think that building a relationship between two people from two different families, often with two different careers, and, of course, no training in how to be married is not a difficult task. How many individuals understand the complexities of choosing a life partner? Very few. When we teach students in graduate school couple therapy, they often tell us that they can't imagine marrying at all because there are so many things to think about.

Most couples do not realize that marriage moves through a series of predictable life cycle crises. Each of these crises presents opportunities for growth, as well as threats to the relationship. Think about the different types of predictable relationship life cycle issues that must be faced in a marriage. Each stage presents both challenges and opportunities for growth. All stages require adaptation, change, and good couple dialogue. These have been summarized in great detail by many authors, but most clearly by Carter and McGoldrick in their 1980 book *Family Life Cycle*. They suggest six stages for marriage.

The Six Stages of Marriage

The first stage of the family life cycle actually begins before marriage. It involves separation from the family of origin, the development of relationships outside of the family, and beginning the establishment of a career path. In essence it is establishing an individuated self apart from one's family. How well this is done has serious implications for marriage as you will see in later chapters (see, particularly, chapter 8).

Second, couples must separate from their families of origin and build their own separate couple relationship. This may seem much easier than it is. It means negotiating the expectations that each partner brings to the match from their family of origin such as who controls the money, gender-specific roles, whose career takes precedence, which religion (if any) will predominate, how vacations will be spent, and, of course, which family to visit at holidays. All of these are appropriate developmental issues that arise when two individuals from different backgrounds try to create a sense of "we." These are the first "crises" of marriage. Obviously, sorting out these complicated issues calls for quite a bit of work.

After the two people have formed a unique couple identity they may then be faced with a third developmental crisis or opportunity. Kids. What happens to the couple who have had years of vacationing together, adequate time to develop their own careers and pursuits, and time to hang out with friends when they are suddenly faced with the sleep disorder that follows the entrance of a baby into the family? When they actually have formed a sense of "we," another person enters the system—a helpless, very demanding person. Roles may become an issue. Whose life shifts the most? Who takes time off from work? What are the roles and rules about rearing children in the families of origin? Obviously, this can be a significant challenge for many couples and it certainly pushes them in terms of how they handle their roles.

A fourth major challenge occurs when the kids hit adolescence. With teenagers a whole new set of challenges appears. In our culture, at least, adolescents seem to need to challenge boundaries and rules, and they want to develop their own identities. They often push their parents hard at this point. At the same time, parents are frequently experiencing midlife crises and enormous career pressures. They seldom have sufficient energy for facing these issues squarely. This is often a time when couples struggle with what is left of their marriage. What is it that still holds them together? Do they still have and do they still enjoy each other's company?

In addition to all of these pressures, parents are aging and may begin to have health care crises. The "sandwich generation" takes on new meaning as couples in midlife may begin to feel sandwiched between their adolescents' and their parents' problems.

When the kids grow up and leave the nest, the fifth stage of marriage has arrived. During their kids' adolescence many couples long for the peace and serenity of the empty nest. They imagine the phone not ringing constantly, no more late night parties, no anxious listening at 3 A.M. for the car to come home. They imagine freedom. They think about how sweet it will be to make love without hearing their kids moving about the house, pulling all-nighters. Or perhaps they just look forward to catching up on sleep. But then the quietness hits. Where did the time go? Can we really be this old? After focusing on kids for so long, what is left of our marriage? What common interests do we still have together?

Clearly, there are a number of challenges at this stage. These include assessing the health of the marriage, and deciding how to build new interests, or ways of relating. This new stage also may involve renegotiating roles. A marriage can become more unbalanced as both partners readjust their career goals.

All too often as couples adjust to the empty nest and begin to enjoy it, a new crisis may develop. Someone moves back home. An adult child may return to do graduate work or maybe a relationship ended and they return home with a new baby. Maybe a career has not worked, and they need to recover and get a fresh start. Whatever the reason, the empty nest fills up again. And another set of adjustments must be made. When an adult child returns to live with his/her parents, difficult adjustments must be accommodated for all involved. Or, as we said earlier, an additional crisis may be the declining health of one or more parents. This may involve caring from a distance, making long-term care decisions difficult, or even having a parent move in for a while. This can put an enormous strain on the best of marriages.

Finally, as couples move into retirement age, a whole new set of issues appears. What to do with free time? What to do with so much time together? Financial struggles. Struggles with adult kids. Struggles to deal with sickness, aging, and in the end, death. The somber reality of love at this point is to love with the realization that the object of one's love will die sooner rather than later.

When examined briefly, these life cycle issues are a clear reminder that life is, in fact, "one damn problem after another." Does each life cycle transition mean a crisis? Not necessarily. It means that there is considerable work to be done at each stage.

The reality of marriage, contrary to the myth, is that it is work. Given the size of these life cycle issues, how can marriage not be work? When couples do not understand this, they are set up for increased disillusionment and stress. When couples accept this reality, they are better equipped to normalize the stresses of marriage, and to work more creatively at solving them.

Myth No. 6: Marriage Is a Constant; It Doesn't Change

Too many couples buy into the myth of a long-lasting, constant relationship. They assume that once they marry and work out some of the kinks and differences, then all will be smooth sailing ever after. This myth assumes that once a couple achieves a good marriage, and gets to really know each other, then they can coast.

The reality is that marriage and marital roles must shift constantly. As was just said, couples go through life cycle crises: they must deal with aging parents and growing children, they move through career changes and issues, health issues, and loss issues, and they must constantly adapt. A marriage must constantly change and adapt to cope with ever-changing life cycles.

Nothing stays the same. The only constant is change itself. This means that couples need to constantly shift and reinvent themselves. Those who buy into the myth that marriage is constant are in for a rude awakening. Healthy marriage requires debunking this myth and realizing that good marital health requires adaptation and change.

Jon and Sabina

Jon and Sabina's marriage illustrates this. When they first married, they both took on traditional roles. They married young and never questioned these roles. They assumed that since the traditional roles had worked well for their parents, they would work well for them, too. Jon pursued his career and Sabina stayed home and raised their three children.

Over time, however, Sabina began to feel confined by her role as a stay-at-home mom. She began to resent the friendships and social contacts Jon had through his work and the limited amount of adult conversation that she had at home. From time to time she would say to Jon sarcastically, "It must be nice to go to lunch with interesting people." To which Jon would respond, "Do you want the pressures that I'm under?", which would temporarily silence her. Although they had some tense moments, things worked relatively well between them. That is, until Sabina took some courses and then decided to go back to work.

Their "marital contract" had changed. Jon became threatened by her increased financial freedom and her lunchtime dates with coworkers. Sabina did well at her job and won several promotions, but her rapid success was even more threatening to Jon. She didn't need him in the same way that she had previously. Sabina, on the other hand, began to resent how their roles never really changed despite her new job. She still did 90 percent of the work around the house, and she often felt that when Jon finally did some ordinary household chores, he expected great applause. This couple has a strong marriage, with some real strengths. However, if they continue to believe the myth that marriage is a constant that does not change, they are in real trouble. At this point in their lives they have some adapting to do and they must renegotiate their earlier contract.

Myth No.7: Love Is a Feeling

If it is believed that love is only a feeling, there is a corollary that states, "When couples fall out of love, there is little they can do about it." This is one of the most destructive myths that couples can hold. What really happens when couples fall in love? Are they deeply in love with their partner early in their dating years? Probably not. In fact they barely know their partner. They are experiencing a high level of romantic infatuation, along with a healthy dosage of lust. Are these things negative? Obviously not. They are wonderful, but they do not last forever. In fact, when couples describe falling in love, they more often than not describe the feeling they receive as they perceive themselves loved, validated, and desired by their spouse. They may, in fact, be more "in love" with this feeling than in love with the person they are about to marry.

Too often they are in love with the feeling of falling in love. Mature love takes years, even decades to develop. It is grounded in taking the time to continually discover who the person we "fell in love with" really is. This takes work. The reality is that while love is a feeling, it is also an act of the will. Talk to couples who have been together for many years. Talk to them about the crises they have been through together and ask what sustained them. Waiting passively for the feeling of love to return will not sustain and deepen love. It will result in the relationship becoming even more distant.

Part of falling in love is enjoying the feeling that your partner loves and values you. It is seeing yourself as an idealized image through the eyes of your lover. While it lasts, this is a wonderful feeling. No wonder infatuation feels so powerful. You see your partner as close to perfect, and you are seen in the same way. However, as years go by, perfection fades noticeably. Irritants like too much TV or football watching, too much time with friends or time at work, those twenty extra pounds, clothes that never make it into the clothes hamper, etc., all take their toll. They begin to nag us and chip away at "perfection." You are no longer seen as perfect and obviously you do not see your spouse as perfect, either. The feeling of falling in love falls away. The great feelings of romance and passion are not the same. Sex starts to become a little boring. Your partner begins to irritate you more and more. At times you even wonder what attracted you in the first place.

It is easy to forget that this is a normal part of any relationship. Rather than passively moan about the loss of romantic feeling, now is the time to act. Ask yourself this: When things felt better, what was different? How did you show love to your spouse in the past ? *Without waiting for the feeling to return, begin doing more of what you used to do when you felt love, and see what happens.*

The reality is that although love is a wonderful feeling, it is also an act of will. Like anything worth having in life, a good marriage takes time, energy, and work. Professional athletes seem to act spontaneously with great feeling. Ballet looks effortlessly graceful and fluid. However, both disciplines require long hours of hard work and practice. When a batter hits a triple or a dancer executes a perfect entrechat, it is not spontaneous feeling that overtakes them. Rather, it is repeated, willful practice that allows their movements to seem so spontaneously beautiful. Similarly the "feeling" of being in love follows the work we put into our relationships.

Given that developmental changes are part of any marriage, and that fundamental changes do take place, it is unrealistic to assume that the feeling of "being in love" will last. Choosing to be loving, to adapt and to focus on changing yourself as the need arises, are the keys to keeping that loving feeling.

Myth No. 8: My Ideal Soul Mate Is Out There

Too often the myth of the soul mate follows the feeling that "I am falling out of love." This myth holds that "out there somewhere is my ideal soul mate. All I have to do is find that person, and I will fall madly in love and live happily ever after." Many women have a Prince Charming fantasy and, of course, their Prince Charming will be much more loving than their present spouse. This fantasy invests a high degree of idealization in the prospective Prince or Princess Charming. Again, the *solution to the problem is seen as outside the self*. When you believe this myth, rather than focusing on what you can do to change yourself within your current relationship, or what you might be doing that makes loving you difficult, your focus becomes finding your perfect soul mate. What is not so clearly stated is that your happiness is contingent on someone outside of yourself. It is little wonder that so few marriages which began as affairs last.

Paul and Liz

Paul and Liz had been married for eleven years. Although their relationship began with a whirlwind of traveling, exciting vacations, and passionate sex, those feelings had long since faded. Both were caught up in their careers, both worked long hours, and both missed their formerly passionate feelings. Unfortunately, both were "too busy" to talk about this with much depth, and each hoped that their next vacation would cure the problem. Liz, however, found herself daydreaming of meeting a new man who would sweep her off her feet, and make her feel special and loved. The more she thought about this, the angrier she became with Paul. After all, what was he doing to make her feel special? In fact, he hardly seemed to notice her.

Over time her anger caused her to distance herself from Paul even more and fueled her fantasy of one day finding her ideal soul mate, who would rekindle her passionate, romantic feelings. Then a coworker asked her out for a drink. She began thinking that he might be the one to help her find true love (again) and started fantasizing about a life with him. Meanwhile, she became more and more distant and resentful and irritated Paul even more.

For Liz, this myth has several real-life problems. First, the statistics indicate that 50 percent of first marriages fail, and about 70 to 75 percent of second marriages fail (Gottman, 1999; Bray and Hetherington 1993; Glick and Lin 1986). In other words, the odds of Liz finding her ideal soul mate are not supported statistically. The problem is that the myth of the soul mate keeps you from ever really looking at yourself, or at your own role in your marriage. For example, a person married to an alcoholic may long to find an ideal spouse, only to marry a second, and sometimes third alcoholic. When you look for a solution outside of yourself, you always lose.

Myth No. 9: My Marriage Will Be Healthy if It Is Like (or Unlike) My Parents' Marriage

If you grew up in a family without divorce or separation, you have one blueprint to consult when you embark on marriage. That blueprint is likely to be what you remember of your parents' marriage. If, on the other hand, as a child and youth, you lived in different households as a result of divorce and remarriage, you may have had several models. These models (or model) become a type of blueprint for marriage. You may have hated your parents' marriage—or divorce—and you may have vowed to do something different. Or you may have admired their marriage (or remarriage) and hoped that your marriage would be similar. Either way, while you were growing up, you began internalizing your model of marriage as a result of observing one marriage or several.

Marriage can become a blend of several models, yours and your partner's. Even in the best of circumstances, there can be a struggle between the partners to determine how much either set of their parents' marriages is to be emulated. Often, there is a battle about which set of parents is to be the model for the present marriage, and whose influence will be the strongest. On the other hand, there is often much about your parents' marriage that you wish to avoid. You might wish to build a marriage that would be the exact opposite of your parents' marriage.

The reality is that either imitating your parents' or stepparents' marriage, or trying to create the polar opposite, will be problematic. Usually, the facts are that even with the worst parental examples a new couple can find at least one small behavior worth borrowing from their parents. Even in abusive marriages there may have been occasions when a fleeting respect was present between the spouses, a respect that could be mirrored and expanded upon in your own marriage. And, on the other hand, even if your parents' marriage appeared to be perfect, it is not necessarily a model that will work for you.

Trying to create a marriage relationship that is the opposite of our parents' marriage rarely works. In our reactive attempts to build marriages that are opposite our parents' marriage, too often we find that despite our best intentions, we end up repeating familiar patterns.

Cathy and Carl

Cathy and Carl are good examples of a couple who were intent on building a marriage that was radically different from that of their parents. In the end, however, they began to repeat many of the patterns they so much wanted to break. Both grew up in what they defined as dysfunctional families, and they witnessed very strained relationships between their parents.

Cathy was quite clear that she did not want to marry a dominating, chauvinist like her father, who would force her to take care of all the emotional needs of the relationship. Carl was equally clear that he did not want to marry an overly emotional women like his mother. They were determined to build a radically different type of marriage. Although they got off to a good start, as their kids turned into teenagers, they started to observe some familiar behaviors. When Carl became stressed by all of his work-related pressures, he acted much like Cathy's father and became quite overbearing and demanding. As Cathy became more and more frustrated, and equally stressed, she became more emotional and angry. In short, their marriage began to resemble the marriages of their parents. This was even more depressing for both of them than the ordinary strains and stress of their marriage. They both wondered how they had reverted to the model they worked so hard to escape?

Finding a way to draw up your own blueprint for a uniquely satisfying marital relationship requires a great deal of work. We will look at that process in chapter 7 where we explore the movement from insight to change.

Myth No. 10: Only a Large Change Can Transform a Marriage

Too often, when a marriage begins to stagnate, or becomes overly conflicted, couples begin to think that myth No. 10 is true. They think that only a miracle will transform their marriage. They believe that only if their whole relationship changes, can they ever experience marital health. As a result, they hope for and work toward a total transformation. This process only leaves them more and more frustrated. It is like the person who decides to take up running as a way to lose weight, and enters a marathon as a first step. The resulting pain and discouragement of that premature enterprise may be enough to keep that person from ever running again! Obviously, if you want to get in shape, you will be coached to start slowly. You start by running and walking for fifteen minutes, and build up slowly. Attempting to run a marathon without prior training guarantees failure, discouragement, and pain. That is a no-brainer. Yet in marriage, we often begin trying to "run a marathon" before we have built up any strength or endurance. We forget to start small. In our desire for major transformation we want it all.

If you bought this book, the odds are good that you are hoping for some change in your marriage. We believe that this workbook can help you. But it will help only if you start by taking small steps. These small steps always include trying to change yourself.

Some of the couple therapists influenced by the theories of solution-focused therapy (O'Hanlon and Weiner-Davis 1989) begin with this standard question, "If while you were sleeping, a miracle occurred, and when you awoke, your marriage was miraculously changed, and was exactly as you would like it to be, what would be different? What would you notice?" Does that sound familiar? You have probably heard that question before in a variety of different forms.

But too many people stop there. They focus on whether the large miracle is possible that would totally transform their marriage. Sort of a marital lobotomy. As a result, they forget that the logical next question is *"What would you be doing differently* if such a miracle had occurred?" (Again, notice the focus is on changing yourself.) And what would be a way that you could do a little of that now, pretending that the miracle had happened?

Small changes lead to larger changes. Little successes lead to greater successes. The best way to change a marriage is one small step at a time. People do not run marathons by deciding to take up running and signing up to run a marathon the following week. They train one step and one mile at a time. Over time their fitness level improves and, at some point, they may be able to run a marathon. In a similar way, by focusing on small, progressive changes in your marriage, you can create an environment that will lead to larger and more profound changes. However, you can't get there in one step.

Exposing the Myths

All of these myths described above look for solutions outside of your self. They express the hope that either your partner will change, or that you should work harder to change your partner, or perhaps that you can find a more idealized partner. These myths are grounded in the beliefs that marriage should be easy, that once you work out your initial marital problems, your life will always be fine. They ignore the massive cultural changes that have made marriage difficult.

Exposing these myths means accepting the realities that marriage is hard work, life is one set of problems and challenges after another, and change is always guaranteed. It means giving up fantasies of falling in love or of an ideal Prince or Princess Charming, and recognizing where real change takes place—within yourself.

Marriage: A Changing Institution

We frequently forget the enormous changes that have taken place in the last century to the institution of marriage and the status of the family. These changes all have had a significant impact on the way in which we view both. Let us briefly consider some of those changes.

1. Our culture changed from a largely agrarian society to an industrialized, corporate society. In the older agrarian structure, people had more sharply defined roles. Both husbands and wives worked on the farm or in the family business within their defined roles. Extended family members frequently were available for child care and as alternate role models.

2. With industrialization, fathers left their farms for factories, and roles began to change. Men's and women's work roles began to look quite different than they did on the farm.

3. With corporate life, greater mobility was introduced to the family. Transfers to faraway places became common, and frequent moves became the norm. The result of this was to weaken the bonds of extended family. Families scattered all across the country, and often across the world. As a consequence extended family support became rare.

4. With the growth of feminist thinking over the last three decades women began making similar career choices as men. Today, with most women in the workforce, both parents work full-time and decisions about child care and whose career has priority have become important issues. Often there are no extended family members nearby to provide child care, or provide a break for the dual career couple. Due to these issues, tensions increase dramatically. Who stays home when the kids are sick? Who does the cooking, cleaning, school visits, etc.? Not to mention time to relax and simply be a couple. Many modern

couples are so stressed and guilt ridden about how little time they are spending with their kids that spending time as a couple gets frequently put on a back burner.

5. Add to this mix the pressures of aging parents in different parts of the country, corporate downsizing, the expectation that kids should be in as many enrichment activities as possible and that both parents should attend those extracurricular activities as often as possible, and the stress level indicators fly off the chart. Throughout all of these cultural shifts, the common denominator is change. Yet the same marital myths persist long after their usefulness.

Do these changes make marriage impossible? No, but it does make it a challenge. Our point in raising these issues, is to describe some of the modern context. Everything has changed. The postwar world is gone, and *Leave It to Beaver* families are an endangered species. In the twenty-first century, any attempt to return to those days is futile. Yet although these cultural changes are enormous and irreversible, the myths about marriage persist. They continue to influence young people just as if nothing has changed.

For marriages to succeed today, they must keep adapting to the changes that people encounter in their daily lives, whether these are cultural changes, life cycle challenges, or health or vocational crises. Using these myths as guides for a successful marriage has the same likelihood of success as driving with an antique road map. You will not arrive at your destination.

In the end, the only way to change your marriage is to change yourself. Look through the self-help literature. There are books, some of which are very helpful, that offer many different techniques for changing your marriage. What is often missing, however, is the most basic unit of change. You. The only person whom you can change is yourself.

This book will focus on how you can identify strategies to change yourself and thereby change your marriage. We will help you to change your role in different aspects of your marriage. But before taking those steps, throw away the old myths that lead only to frustration and pain. We will help you develop a map for changing your marriage by focusing on making changes in yourself.

To begin working on changing your marriage, you must first make an assessment of its quality. You did that in chapter 1. If you have not done that yet, go back and do it. After making your assessment, the second step is to examine the myths we have just explored. In the space provided below, answer the following questions. If you wish to explore these questions in depth, you may need to use another few sheets of paper:

1. Which myth or myths do you identify with? Why do you identify with them?

_____

_____

_____

2. Which myth or myths best describes the way you view your own marriage or partnership?

_____

_____

_____

3. When you first began to think about marriage, which myth best described your hopes for your future marriage?

_____

_____

_____

4. How has your marriage changed as you moved through the various stages of marriage?

_____

_____

_____

CHAPTER THREE

How Do I Keep Making Things Worse When I'm Trying So Hard?

Couples create predictable and patterned arguments over a number of issues. Unfortunately these patterns take on a life of their own, and too often individuals are not even aware of their roles in these patterns. Their predictable interactions can make change very difficult. How do marital arguments become so counterproductive? How do couples move from discussing a simple complaint to a full-blown argument that leaves both parties feeling wounded and discouraged? We will examine how these interactions develop as well as describing several couple patterns. We will then show you how to change those patterns, by changing your role in them.

In our experience, most couples are doing the best they can. They certainly do not want to argue, much less to be in unhappy relationships. They try to solve their problems, try to get closer, and often work at becoming better friends. Often, however, the harder they try to solve their problems, the worse the problems become. How can things get worse when you are trying so hard to make them better? How often have you said, "But I was trying to help solve this problem. All I've done is make you more angry"?

Many couples have been taught that all they need is training in communication skills. So they take a listening skills course, attend a workshop, or read a book. Yet no matter how many skills they learn, old patterns quickly return.

Think about your most common argument or fight. If you are like most couples, you have a predictable argument that escalates and leaves you and your partner feeling frustrated, discouraged and, at times, in despair about the future of your relationship. These arguments may be over a number of things. The reality, however, is that the original topic usually is not what you end up fighting about. The fight usually starts with something small, escalates to a variety of other issues, and then crescendos into a large crisis. Then you find yourself wondering in despair, "How did that discussion get so out of control? How did we start off arguing about something so small and wind up talking about ending our marriage?"

Bill and Alice

Bill and Alice provide a good example of this process. One evening as they were lying in bed watching the news, Alice commented to Bill, "I feel like I'm responsible for everything in this marriage. I'm responsible for the kids, the house, the cooking. I really need some help." Bill's response was, "I'm sorry you think I'm such a terrible husband! I can't do anything right."

Alice responded to that with disgust, "I can't talk to you about anything! You always get so defensive. Just forget it." Bill retorted, "I give up. Now you think I can't even talk to you. Don't you know how much pressure I'm under at work? What do you want from me. It seems I can't do anything right."

"What about my needs?" Alice replied. "You have no idea what I deal with every day. You're so caught up in your career. It must be nice to only have to worry about yourself." Bill replied, "Why don't I just quit? You should get a job that will pay enough to support us. You try it! You never want to hear about my struggles. I'm sick of this." At that point Alice grabbed her pillow and stormed out of the bedroom, shouting, "I'm going to sleep in the guest room!" Neither got much sleep that night.

What happened during that simple argument? How did it fly out of control so fast? Alice began with what seemed to her a fairly simple complaint. She wanted Bill to understand that she had too much to do and to respond to her wish for some help with household responsibilities. She feels overwhelmed by too much responsibility and needs some assistance.

Her complaint, however, is part of a larger theme that gets recycled periodically in their marriage. Like many couples they have never really resolved the "role issue" in their marriage. As a result, it remains a large unresolved issue. Complaints turn into arguments that easily tap into the large reservoir of emotion from such a large unresolved issue. Without realizing what they were doing, Alice and Bill escalated their argument until it got bigger and bigger. The result was that neither got much sleep that night, and both began the day feeling depressed. Their "attempt" to solve a problem only made the problem worse. Most of us, if we are honest, can relate to this. We know only too well how arguments like this can take on a life of their own.

From Complaints to Patterned Arguments

Too often when trying to make sense out of arguments that turned into blowouts, we have a simple answer for what went wrong. We think that it must be our partner's fault. If only our partner would change, or start therapy, or learn to communicate, then our problems would be over. We adopt a *one-person explanation* of the problem, which conveniently ignores our role and our contributions to the quarrel. Almost inevitably a one-person explanation assumes that the problem lies with the other person. Of course there are times when one person is responsible for the problem. For example, when there is domestic violence, clearly the person who commits the violence is more at fault, and in such circumstances, the victim needs to put safety needs first. However, in most arguments between couples the two people involved conspire together to make the problem worse together.

What most couples don't understand is that all couples create a patterned style of communication around difficult topics. This interaction frequently takes on a life of its own. This means that *all problems of communication are two-person problems.* When we use the term "two-person problem" we mean that the problem under discussion is created and maintained by both persons. Problems do not exist in isolation.

In a marriage there are no one-person problems. There are no saints and sinners, good guys and bad guys. Most problems are the fault of the two people. Even more important is the reality that the problem is *maintained* by both persons. Specifically, this means that the way they argue about the problem usually keeps the problem from being solved. Their argument is cocreated and unfortunately takes on a life of its own. Inevitably, both partners fuel the argument, thereby creating the patterned, familiar interaction. The term two-person problem refers to the fact that "it takes two to tango": both persons play a role in the argument. In marriage and in all significant relationships, one plus one does not equal two. In other words, there are the two partners, plus the communication pattern the partners create. *This communication pattern has a life of its own.* In the end it is the pattern that becomes the problem. The irony is that the pattern originally emerged in an attempt to solve a particular issue.

The Rules of Relationship Patterns

We believe that to create an effective change in a marriage, you must start by focusing on yourself. To begin this difficult process, you will have to change much of the way you think about relationships. As said above, many people believe that real change can come about only if their partner changes; they do not see what they contribute to the problem. In addition, they have difficulty stepping back from arguments and recognizing that the arguments are patterned, predictable interactions. To begin to change the way you understand your role in relationships consider the following set of rules as the beginning of learning a new way to view relationships.

Rule No. 1: All Communication Problems in Marriage Are Two-Person Problems

Understanding Rule No. 1 is essential to begin to look differently at your role within your marriage. Understanding this rule will help you to stop trying to change your spouse. It will also help you to see the communication problems in your marriage as a two-person problem. This in turn may help you to focus on your role in the problem.

When most couples begin couple therapy, they are convinced that they know exactly what the problem is—their partner. They do not understand that their interactions have evolved into a predictable pattern, one that maintains the problem they are trying to solve. Instead, they secretly (or not so secretly) hope that the therapist will realize that the main issue is their partner, and then proceed to help their partner to change (to their specifications of course). Or if they are reading a self-help book on marriage, their real fantasy is that their spouse will also read the book and then miraculously change. To that end they leave the book (open to pertinent pages) lying around the house, in the vain hope that their spouse will see it, read it, study it, and be transformed.

For any change to be effected, Rule No. 1 must be adopted. You must give up the fantasy that your marriage will improve when your partner changes. Obviously this is easier said than done because this fantasy dies hard. Real change in marriage begins only when self-focus, the ability to examine your own role in creating the problem, increases. This means that each person begins to look less at their partner, and more at what they themselves bring to the interaction. *Self-focus begins with the question, "What am I contributing to this problem?"*

This is, of course, a huge leap for most people. If you listen to the arguments of most couples, including your own, you will notice a familiar pattern. Usually, there is a "prosecutor/

defense attorney" type of debate. One person is the prosecutor, raising points about his/her concerns, while the other goes on the defense. They may switch roles back and forth, but the basic prosecutor/defense attorney pattern continues. Each partner is convinced the problem lies with the other. Obviously, once they start this prosecutor/defense positioning, there can be no winner. Neither can convince the other of his or her point of view.

If you are absolutely honest, you probably believe that the biggest problem in your marriage is the sole responsibility of your spouse.

So, being honest with yourself, complete the following sentence:

Our marriage would improve if my spouse would _____

_____

Suppose you had filled out the incomplete sentence with this phrase: "stop being so withdrawn and distant." So the completed sentence would read, "Our marriage would improve if my spouse would stop being so withdrawn and distant."

Now, using a completely different mindset, try to describe this same problem as a two-person problem using two-person language. Here is an example of how two-person language works: "When I nag, my spouse withdraws and grows distant." Observe that two-person language tries to include what both parties contribute to the interaction. More importantly, it helps you to identify what you are contributing to the problem. Since the only person you can change is yourself, stating things in two-person language enables you to understand those aspects of your own behavior that you can change. Only when you are able to understand and describe any problem as a two-person problem, will you be able to study your role and your contribution to the problem. When you accept this rule, and try to describe problems in two-person language, then Rule No. 2 makes sense.

Rule No. 2: Communication Patterns Are Bigger Than the Two People Who Create Them

What do you notice when you watch two very talented dancers dancing? Their fluid, graceful dance steps blend together. The dance they create actually eclipses the two individuals. It becomes its own entity. When you watch two very talented individuals dancing with each other, in the end you see the dance—not the individuals. The unit is bigger than its individual parts. If you see mainly the two individuals, then the dance is not very effective. In contrast, two skilled, graceful dancers create a third entity: the dance itself. If you watch ballet, you will see wonderful dances for couples where the man and the woman do entirely different steps, lifts, and leaps but the dance the two create is the sum of their separate parts. It is a whole entity that could not exist if only one of the dancers were on stage. Communication patterns are a lot like dances. Couples try to deal with an issue in their marriage that might be one of the big ones, like money, sex, in-laws, or parenting, or might be as minor as who takes out the trash. Too often, however, a patterned interaction forms around the issue they are attempting to resolve. For example, if you argue about who takes out the trash, you probably know exactly where the argument will go, and who will say what, and how it will end. Just as choreographers name the dances they create, so you could name this your "trash dance," or your "getting household chores done dance." You have a predictable pattern of communication that takes place whenever you try to solve a "simple problem" like taking out the trash.

As a result, the reality of any marital conflict is that it contains two problems: the issue itself, and the argument or interaction that occurs in the effort to solve the original issue. The *issue* can be anything that couples argue about, i.e., money, sex, in-laws, etc. The *problem* is the predictable, patterned argument that emerges as part of the sincere attempt to resolve the original issue.

The predicament the couple finds itself in is that this patterned argument makes it impossible to resolve the original issue. The more they try to solve the specific issue, the more they create a new problem, which is their interactional pattern or argument about the specific issue.

If this is confusing, think about any issue that you and your partner struggle with, for example, money. Gina and George cannot agree on balancing their joint checkbook. Gina argues that the checkbook should be balanced to the penny, while George often forgets to record the checks he writes, and argues that he can always call the bank to find out what the balance is. For Gina and George money is "the issue." However, when they try to resolve the issue, watch what happens between them.

Gina complains with a lot of agitation, "George, there are three checks missing from the checkbook! Can't you ever remember to record the checks that you write?" George responds, "Relax, we can always call the bank and find out the balance. You don't have to be so anal about this." Gina was already agitated, but the term "anal" upsets her even more." 'Anal'? If it wasn't for me, no bills would ever get paid on time. Anal? You are like a child, George! Grow up!" George swears under his breath, "Bitch! Can't you ever lighten up. I really don't need another mother." At this point the argument is off and running. Forget about the possibility of resolving the issue. The argument itself is now the problem. Their anger level, name-calling, and "parent-child" interaction is the problem. They now have two issues to deal with: the checkbook, and their inability to discuss it without escalating matters. Is this beginning to sound familiar?

Now think about your marriage and your repetitive arguments. Pretend that an argument had been recorded on video. (Imagine how embarrassing life would be if you had to watch your marital arguments replayed on video.) If you played the video back in slow motion, what would you see? What do you see yourself doing, and what do you see your partner doing? Take a few moments and in the space provided write down some of your observations.

_____

_____

_____

_____

If your arguments are like those of most couples, they follow a very predictable course. You say what you always say, your partner responds with what s/he always says, and the argument escalates to the same predictable end. As you watched this imaginary video clip of your arguments, was any new information ever exchanged? Was any creative variation to the argument ever achieved, much less any constructive resolution? Probably not. More often than not you can predict exactly what you are going to say as well as what your partner is going to say. Your responses to each other are totally predictable.

This of course provides further evidence for the truth of Rule No. 1 and Rule No. 2. Marital problems are created by both partners. Both George and Gina contributed to the escalation of their problem. And their argument took on a life of its own, which made the attempt to resolve the checkbook issue impossible.

Have you ever had one of those late-night marital arguments that escalate so intensely, so fast, that you can't even remember what the original issue was about? Rule No. 1 reminds us that both persons contribute to the problem, and Rule No. 2 reminds us that, in the end, the argument about the original issue becomes the problem itself.

How Do We Get Caught in These Arguments?

Why do you find yourself caught in the same predictable arguments with the people you care about most, with increasing frustration and distance? Certainly not because you are unintelligent, and usually not because you lack communication skills. So what is the problem?

The reality is that all relationships have particular communication patterns that become each couple's predictable, repetitive, and unique style of interacting. Thus a relationship has an interaction cycle that is larger than both people. In this cycle, the harder you try to change, the more you stay the same. More often than not, the solution you bring to the original issue actually becomes the problem. Part of what you want to be able to do is to step outside of your arguments and pretend that you are watching your quarrels on video to see exactly how you and your partner fuel your fights.

Only when you begin to recognize these patterns can you begin to *change your role* in the interaction cycle. In fact, with your "favorite" arguments, these patterns often take off without you! Once they get started, they are almost impossible to stop. It is like watching an energetic puppy running away from its owner. Every time the puppy slows down and the owner thinks she is about to catch him, the puppy runs away again. Round and round they go with the owner experiencing a lot of frustration. Trying to slow down and resolve one of your "favorite" arguments is much like that. Like energetic puppies, these arguments are almost impossible to catch.

What Do Your Arguments Look Like?

There are many types of marital arguments. To illustrate some of these types of arguments, listen to April and Allen's problem.

April is frustrated and hurt that there is not more emotional intimacy in her conversations with her husband, Allen. She wishes that she could spend as much time talking about the intimate aspects of her life with him as she does with her female friends. She wishes that when she did share with him that he would understand her completely, and encourage her to share even further. In fact, she is lucky when Allen grunts a response to a comment she might make while he is reading the newspaper. When she feels hurt and deeply frustrated she tries to solve the problem by pursuing Allen.

April:　Why don't you talk to me? Why can't we turn off the TV and just talk? Are those football games really more important than I am?

Allen:　Can't we just relax and watch TV? I've had a hard day. We can talk later.

As he distances himself, Alice responds by pursuing him even more and she becomes more critical and more emotional:

Alice:　Do you know how lonely I am living with you? Why do you have to be so insensitive?

As she increases the intensity of this interaction, Allen, of course, responds to her by distancing further and becoming angry himself.

Allen:　Stop nagging me. If you would just get off my back I would talk to you.

Round and round they go, each insisting that the other is the problem. Their pursuer/distancer pattern is now bigger than both of them, and they feel powerless to stop it. Their argument about the issue of closeness has now become the problem itself and has taken on a life of its own.

Their problem is a familiar one. They are trying to solve a problem. They both want a closer relationship. As they attempt to solve that problem they create a particular type of interaction pattern: the pursuer/distancer pattern.

Did they try to create this pattern? Did they want this pattern to arise? Of course not. Their pursuer/distancer argument is their failed solution to the problem of closeness and it has now become the problem. In fact, their pursuer/distancer pattern has not only become the problem, it guarantees that the real problem (creating intimacy) cannot be solved.

Does this pattern sound familiar? What is your most common fight or argument? Describe it below in detail. Try to describe the repetitions that take place in your most common fights.

_____

_____

_____

_____

Next, try and describe the way the argument that you just described escalates. What do each of you do that further escalates the quarrel. Try to write down your lines and those of your spouse. Remember, the best way to do this is to create some distance by pretending you are watching the argument on video. Pay careful attention to your role in escalating the argument. Try and fill in the following lines honestly:

The argument begins by talking about _____

_____

_____

I usually say _____

_____

_____

My spouse usually responds _____

_____

_____

My response to his response is _____

_____

_____

Finally, describe the predictable ending of the argument. For example, does it end with a satisfactory resolution, or does one partner blow up? Does it end with someone sleeping on the couch or storming out of the room slamming the door?

_____

_____

_____

As you went through this exercise, what did you learn? If you are like most couples, your lines were relatively predictable, and so were your spouse's. Rarely are there creative solutions to such arguments, and rarely do they end in any satisfactory way.

Remember, every relationship has a number of issues. Issues are simply a part of life. It is how we communicate about those issues that makes them better or worse. Our attempts to resolve these issues often result in a particular relationship pattern that emerges. To better understand your unique pattern and your role in that pattern, pretend that the argument has been videotaped and begin to recognize the predictable steps followed by the two of you. But always pay close attention to your specific role in the interaction.

Rule No. 3: Your Argument Has a Predictable Sequence and Pattern

In any team sport, good athletes must have a great sense of balance. Their particular positions on the team require others to play different positions so that the team can play together as a unit and balance each other. A football quarterback needs blockers or he will be tackled. A baseball pitcher needs a catcher and fielder, and so on. For a team to function and perform well together, they must balance each other out and be able to play smoothly together.

Balanced Relational Patterns

Family systems theory calls this kind of balance *complementarity,* which means that in a marriage the two partners balance each other (Watzlawick, Bavelas, Jackson 1967). There are a number of types of balanced relational patterns. Unlike team sports, in families, these patterns can be either positive or negative.

The Pursuer/Distancer Pattern

The first balanced relational pattern that April and Allen illustrate is called *the pursuer/distancer pattern.* In this pattern, one person pursues while the other distances. The pursuer is always asking questions like, "Can't we talk more? Why can't we spend more time together? Why can't we turn the TV off and just talk?" Not surprisingly, the distancer responds with increased distance, saying, "I need space. Why can't you get off my back and leave me alone?" Without realizing it, they balance each other. (Remember balanced relational patterns are not necessarily positive.)

For couples locked into this kind of pattern, change is impossible because the couples both balance and reinforce each other's position. That is, as long as the pursuer pursues, the distancer will always create more distance. Or as long as the distancer emotionally distances from the pursuer, the pursuer will keep on pursuing. As we said, it is a two-person problem. Both persons reinforce each other and together they create a relational pattern that is very difficult to change.

The Over/Underfunctioning Relational Pattern

Among couples, another frequently seen relational pattern is the *over/underfunctioning pattern.* Here, one partner overfunctions, while the other underfunctions. The overfunctioner is frequently frustrated and often complains, "I'm responsible for everything." Overfunctioners often feel that they are doing everything, while their underfunctioning partner does not pull his/her weight. The reality is that both partners reinforce each other's behavior. The more one underfunctions, the more the other overfunctions and vice versa. Without realizing it, they each reinforce the other, and the result is that the pattern continues. This is illustrated in Irene and Tom's story.

Irene and Tom: Irene loves a tidy house. Everything must be in its place, and she never slows down. She is constantly cleaning, organizing, and putting things away. Her husband, Tom, is her polar opposite. He drops his clothes wherever he happens to be when he takes them off, and he creates piles of disorder throughout their home. He is always just about to get organized.

Irene balances his checkbook, picks up his laundry, cooks his meals, and even organizes his clothing drawers. She complains of being tired and having to do everything. But she doesn't stop. Tom knows he should pitch in more, and occasionally he even tries to help, but when he does, Irene will often say things like, "Never mind. I'll finish up the dishes. Just do what you have to do." The more she overfunctions, the more he underfunctions. And, of course, the more he underfunctions, the more she overfunctions to balance him out. Each is convinced that the other is to blame and both would have great difficulty changing their behavior.

The Dominant/Submissive Relational Pattern

The *dominant/submissive pattern* is another example of a relationship balance pattern. This is often a gender stereotyped pattern, as well. The dominant person wants to control the relationship and the submissive person backs down and allows the dominant partner to have his or her own way. At least, this appears to be true on the surface. On another level, however, the submissive person often has control over less readily observed areas. For example, a dominant husband may bark orders to his wife and kids, and no one seems to challenge his somewhat hostile authority. It appears that his wife always gives in to him. However, the kids may come to her when they want something or when they need advice. So, as a result, the dominant father actually may have very little say in the day-to-day running of the household.

The Fight/Flight Pattern

Still another example of a balanced couple interaction is the fight/flight pattern. The "flight" person tries to keep things polite and calm, and avoid conflict at all costs. But her or his "fight" partner is ready to argue about almost anything. This becomes a difficult combination.

These are all examples of balanced relational patterns. In all of these patterns, both partners balance each other out in such a way that nothing ever really changes. They are all of course two-person problems that together create patterns bigger than either person's issues. In the end, these larger patterns prevent couples from resolving important issues, and wind up becoming the problem.

Now, go back and read the descriptions of the relational patterns again and try to figure out which pattern best describes your relationship. Note that it is possible for more than one pattern to be present. Then, after looking at the examples below, try to place your relational pattern into one of these categories. If there is not enough space in the blank table, use extra sheets of paper.

What I Do	What My Partner Does	Type of Relationship
I beg for help with the household chores. I do all the work around here, plus all the child care, plus hold down a job part-time.	My partner either ignores me or says that taking the kids to a movie on Saturday afternoon is plenty after putting in a 40-hour week.	Over/under functioning balance pattern
I want to visit my family who live in another state, but even though we have the money and the time, my partner won't let me visit.	My partner says that I'm needed here at home. That's it. End of discussion.	Dominant/submissive balance pattern

Drawing on these two examples, try and describe your relational patterns.

What I Do	What My Partner Does	Type of Relationship

Rule No. 4: Relational Patterns Reinforce Each Other

In all of the relational patterns described so far there is balance. The pursuer is balanced by the distancer and vice versa. The overfunctioner is balanced by the underfunctioner and vice versa. These finely tuned balances prevent any change from taking place. In the end, both sides balance each other so effectively that change cannot occur.

What is even more discouraging is that in addition to the type of emotional balances just described, these relationship patterns also reinforce each other. They follow a circular pattern of constant reinforcement. In other words, the harder the pursuer pursues, the more the other creates distance and vice versa. Not only do they go round and round, they end up reinforcing the *other's* position. The pursuer remains convinced that he or she must continue to pursue since the distancer is as distant as ever. On the other hand, the distancer is equally convinced that he or she must continue to create distance to escape the emotional pursuit of the pursuer.

This concept of relational reinforcement is sometimes difficult to understand. As an example, think of your house's heating system. It has a system of feedback loops designed to keep a constant temperature. The thermostat is set on a temperature. When the temperature drops, the thermostat sends a message to the furnace, which in turn kicks on and pumps out heat. When it reaches the prescribed temperature, the thermostat sends another message to shut off the furnace. Thus the temperature stays more or less constant. Family systems theorists call this pattern *homeostasis*. The system of feedback loops displayed by the heating system in your house keeps the temperature constant or at homeostasis.

In much the same way, people in relationships use particular feedback loops to retain the same emotional temperature. When the pursuer and the distancer do their dance, the one thing that is guaranteed is that nothing changes. All the communication skills in the world will not change those feedback loops.

Without wanting to, the pursuer reinforces the distancer's style of distancing. In the same way the distancer reinforces the pursuer's style of pursuit. The reality is, as difficult as this may be to imagine, both are reinforcing the behaviors they are trying to change. What is worse is the harder they try, the more they reinforce the specific behavior of their partner that they resent.

Parents know this pattern very well. They know that if a three-year-old throws a tantrum, and the parents buy candy to pacify the child, those parents just reinforce the exact behavior they want to change. Most parents are horrified if they see another parent reward a tantrum. What most people do not realize is that, in marriage, without ever intending to do so, we may end up reinforcing the very behaviors we dislike in our partner. The relational patterns that we have just described are good examples of this. Think about it: you are most likely reinforcing the very behaviors in your partner that you desperately are attempting to change!

As the pursuer pursues with more energy, without realizing it, s/he pushes the distancer to pull back further. As the distancer pulls back, without realizing it, s/he helps the pursuer to pursue further. Both reinforce the other's stance with predictable feedback loops. Remember the description of April and Allen's problem? They are a good example of the pursuer/distancer dance. April doesn't realize that her continued pursuit of Allen reinforces the very behavior she is trying to change. Her actions cause her husband to create even more distance from her. In the same way, Allen "teaches" April to pursue him more intensely by constantly distancing. This is a hard reality for most individuals to accept. They teach their spouses to continue doing the very thing that distresses them.

In much the same way, the overfunctioning person reinforces the behavior of the underfunctioning spouse. The more s/he overfunctions and does it all, the less the underfunctioner does. As any good parent knows, telling children to clean their rooms and then cleaning for them teaches them that they are not responsible for their own rooms. Similarly, the overfunctioning spouse teaches his/her underfunctioning spouse to do less, all the while becoming a martyr and complaining about all that he/she is doing. The behavior of each person is reinforced by the behavior of the other.

What could be more discouraging? The balance and reinforcement that is part of many relationships make it almost impossible to create change in a relationship. Unless you are able to think differently about your relationship, and see your role in reinforcing the behaviors of your spouse that drive you crazy, change will not occur.

To further illustrate this, think back once again to your most frequent fight. Think of how many times you have been determined to change, or tried to change your spouse. You may have even planned ways to change the way the conversation will go. Yet before you know it, you are caught back in the same old pattern. It is as if that pattern had a mind of its own. You are not sure how it happens, but it's as if you are playing a tape of what you always say, and the familiar argument is off and running like an old record stuck in a groove endlessly repeating itself. Unfortunately, these habits of relational balance and relationship reinforcement lock us into powerful marital patterns from which we want to escape but often feel trapped. Only by learning to recognize your patterns can you begin to change yourself and your role in that pattern.

In addition to these balanced complementary interactions, now let's consider two other types of interactions. These interactions are different because rather than being complementary, each partner employs a similar response to stressful situations. Both either escalate conflict or mutually avoid it.

The Rapid-Escalator Pattern

The rapid-escalator pattern describes the couple who reinforce each other by rapidly escalating their conflicts. With this couple, arguments escalate quickly and powerfully because each person fuels the conflict. Neither backs down on any issue and both continue adding more and more issues until the argument is a mile away from the issue that started it, and much damage has been done. This couple's quarrels can go from zero to 60 in a few minutes, and they require very little fuel to escalate.

The couple usually begins by arguing about a "small problem." But as their emotions are engaged, they begin to throw in more and more details about their various grievances so that the argument is soon out of control. Each person continues the escalation by adding more and more issues and/or personal attacks, and by increasing the emotional intensity and/or the decibel level. It can happen over the simplest things and proceeds with lightninglike speed to a full-fledged battle.

For example, Don promised Shelly that he would pick up a loaf of garlic bread to go with dinner on his way home from work. In the midst of the workday's details he forgot his promise. When he got home, Shelly was irritated, and snapped, "Can't you remember anything? I ask you to do one simple favor and you forget. Is it so difficult to remember a simple loaf of bread, when I have to cook the whole dinner?" To which Don responded with equal irritation, "I'm sorry, but I had a very busy, very stressful day. It's really not that big a deal." You can probably predict Shelly's angry response was, "I'm sure you don't forget what your clients need. My needs don't count for anything." Don, beginning to get louder, said, "Why do you always blow everything into such a big deal. You are so damned emotional!" Shelly, even louder, retorted, "Maybe that's because you never come through for me. How can I ever trust you with the big things if you forget something so little. What if I needed you to remember something really important? You can't even remember a loaf of bread!" From there they were off and running. Each brought up all of the failures of the other and the emotional temperature was at boiling point. A simple irritant escalated into a battle.

The Conflict/Avoidant Pattern

The rapid escalators represent one extreme. The other extreme is represented by couples who use the conflict/avoidant style to quarrel. In contrast to rapid escalators, the conflict/avoidant couple try to keep matters very polite. On the surface it may appear that these couples have a positive relationship, but that appearance is maintained at the expense of talking about difficult subjects. These couples create a pattern that keeps things calm on the surface but the price they pay for their politeness is that difficult issues are never resolved. The danger of this style of relating is that the underlying unresolved conflicts can result in a very polite but emotionally and even sexually distant relationship.

The opposite of love is not anger but indifference. Indifference is deadly for marital intimacy. Intimacy is built by dealing with conflict. The conflict/avoidant pattern winds up destroying intimacy. And too often the couples who are caught in this pattern are not even aware that they are damaging their relationship.

All couples have a pattern of relating to each other that is both unique and predictable. When things get tense, this pattern takes on a life of its own and is extremely difficult to change. The pattern often has complementarity or balance, and predictable feedback loops.

Now, in the space provided below, try to describe your favorite argument and how you and your spouse wind up reinforcing each other. If you need more space, use another sheet of paper.

_____

_____

_____

_____

_____

_____

_____

_____

_____

The Four Rules of Couple Relationship Patterns

Remember, the first step in creating change is to understand the four rules of couple relationship patterns and begin to recognize your own pattern, as well as understanding the unique but predictable part you play in this pattern.

1. There is no such thing as a one-person problem. All problems are cocreated.

2. Couples create interactional patterns that are bigger than both of them.

3. These patterns have predictable steps with built-in balances.

4. These patterns have feedback loops that reinforce each other.

Think about the implications of these rules. At its best marriage is hard work. In addition, marriage has a number of predictable life cycle issues as well as a variety of problems that must be worked through. Think about some of the so-called "big problem areas" of marriage such as money, sex, in-laws, parenting etc. All of these issues are hard enough to deal with in their own right. As couples try to resolve these problems, they will create a patterned interaction or argument around it. Then they have two problems: the original issue (money, sex, in-laws,) as well as the interaction that is created around the problem. In many ways their solution to the problem (their predictable discussion, argument, or fight) becomes the problem. The solution to the problem is more difficult to resolve than the original problem. In fact it often makes the original problem impossible to solve

Changing the Pattern

While reading this chapter you may have begun to get discouraged. Perhaps you saw yourself in some of our case stories. Maybe change for the better has begun to sound hopeless. We are certainly not promising you any magic solutions that will instantly create change in your relationship. Rather, we are about to outline several important steps you can take to begin to change *your role in your marital patterns*. We do not say that this will help you change your partner. Remember, the only person you can change is yourself. However, if you change your role, the pattern has to change. As you follow these steps, carefully consider how you can change your own patterns, roles, and responses. In the end, you will have changed your marriage by changing yourself.

Step 1

This step may sound like a review. Remember in chapter 1 we introduced you to the idea of assessing the strengths and weaknesses of your relationship? Although step 1 is about doing additional assessment, it is also a refinement of the more general assessment described in chapter 1.

The first part of effecting any kind of change is to learn to recognize the problem areas and patterns that have emerged around those problem areas. So step 1 begins by first clarifying the basic problem areas in your marriage. You must be honest about the problems that most frequently get you stuck because the second step will build on step 1.

List in order of importance the problem areas of your marriage. (Go back to chapter 1 and refer to the checklist of marital problems that you have already written.) Try and imagine how your spouse would rate the problem areas of your marriage as well.

Our Three Most Important Problem Areas

1. _____

2. _____

3. _____

Step 2

Step 2 is a little trickier. It is relatively easy to describe the problem areas of your marriage. It is more difficult is to try to visualize and categorize which interactional pattern or argument takes place around the problem areas of your marriage when you try to resolve them. Now you are going to try to look more specifically at how those patterns emerge when you take steps to work on the three problem areas that you have just described. Remember that there are always two issues: the original problem, and your attempt to solve the problem.

Think Video

The easiest way to visualize which interactional patterns are revealed in your arguments is to pretend that the arguments have been recorded on a video camera. When you are in a relaxed mood, imagine sitting in front of a video screen and viewing your fight on video.

Imagine watching yourself and your partner in slow motion engaged in your favorite argument. What would you see? Coaches frequently rely on video tapes to analyze their teams. They watch what their team does as well as what the opposing team does. They watch certain plays in slow motion, and from this they can isolate what individual players do wrong, as well as what the opposition is doing.

If you had a video of one or more of your fights or arguments, what would you see? What would you show in slow motion? What would you feel as you watched the video? Most of us would not be filled with an overwhelming sense of pride. Rather, we might even feel embarrassed.

In the space below, describe some of your observations as you visualize the "video" of your favorite argument in your mind's eye.

_____

_____

_____

_____

_____

_____

_____

Step 3

Step 3 takes discipline. As you continue to watch the "video" in your mind's eye, try to discipline yourself to *focus only on your responses*. Try to focus just on what *you* are doing that keeps the problem from being solved. As stated previously, too often we want to focus only on our spouse. We are convinced that s/he is the problem. As a result we lose self-focus and self-awareness, and we miss what we contribute to the problem.

So, as you watch the "video," zoom in just on your own personal responses. Watch it in slow motion and study yourself. What do you notice about yourself? As you watch the interaction unfold and see it escalate, what do you notice about how you respond both to your spouse and to the issue?

Do you become defensive? Do you attack? Do you generalize? Do you attempt to avoid the conflict by changing the subject? Do you try to use humor as a way to deescalate the conflict? Or do you try to fix the problem so quickly that you do not take the time to really listen to what your partner is saying?

Are you empathic as you respond? Do you maintain eye contact? Do you create an actual spatial distance and try to move away? Do you raise your voice and get overly emotional? Obviously there are a variety of responses that might be used. However, try to focus in on what you personally do as your interactions become intense.

Now, record some of what you notice about your responses:

These are my responses in the midst of arguments:

_____

_____

_____

_____

Finally, *describe as clearly as you can how your responses affect your partner*. For example, if you try to fix the problem, does it help your partner or make him/her become more frustrated. If you use humor, does it diffuse the conflict or make it worse? When you generalize away from the problem at hand and raise other issues, or bring up the past, does it make things better or worse? Keep replaying the "video" in your mind to better understand how you are affecting your spouse. In fact, how do your responses cause him/her to become more defensive?

Now, try and record how your responses affect your spouse:

My responses affect my spouse in the following ways:

_____

_____

_____

_____

Step 4

The fourth step is a very effective way to create change but it is contingent on the other steps being in place. Change cannot take place until you first understand these interactional patterns as well as your individual contribution to the pattern. When this is accepted, then the process of change can begin. As long as you hold on to the fantasy that the problem is the other, change will never happen. Remember, as you take these steps your only goal is to understand and then change your role in the pattern.

Step 4 is built on understanding your role in the pattern, and taking responsibility for your part in it. It means increased self-focus and self-awareness and a disciplined commitment to modify the ways you respond.

Constructive Confusion

The most effective way to modify the ways you respond is to *practice the art of constructive confusion*. What is constructive confusion? It is the attempt to confuse your spouse simply by not doing what you always do, and by doing something different and therefore confusing. As you reviewed your favorite arguments and observed your predictable responses, you probably began to realize that your partner's responses are greatly affected by what you say, as well as how you say it. So why not throw a curve ball and confuse your partner by doing something completely different?

The art of constructive confusion is based on the capacity to predict where the interaction is heading, recognize what we usually do, how our spouse responds to it, and then to do something completely different from what is expected. Understanding this gives us the capacity to create change through confusion. Rather than continue to argue, try confusing the pattern by doing something different than what you usually do. For example, if you usually are the pursuer seeking more time with your spouse, try developing more friends and not going after your partner. If you are usually the one who avoids conflict, try initiating a discussion about a touchy subject. If you are the distancer in the relationship, surprise your spouse by suggesting an after-dinner walk, or a relaxed cup of coffee to catch up on the day's events. If you attack or become defensive, try to just listen without responding, unless a response is absolutely necessary. And if a response is necessary, ask your spouse for more time to think about the issue before you respond.

Confusion Techniques

In order to provide constructive confusion, certain techniques can be quite helpful. It can be fun to watch the look of surprise and confusion on the face of your spouse while you use these techniques. Your spouse is used to you functioning in very predictable ways, and when you introduce change, he is not sure how to respond. Here are four confusion techniques. Think about how you can put them into practice.

1. The first technique is *to question as opposed to defend*. Our normal pattern during an argument is to defend ourselves. We mistakenly believe that if we go on the defensive, we will somehow convince our spouse of the validity of our position. If you have tried this, you know how futile it is. Defensiveness never works; it simply escalates the interaction.

   Rather than defending your position, try asking questions. When your spouse makes his/her point, try asking a question, rather than responding immediately. For example, "I'm not sure what you mean by that, could you explain it a little more?" Or, "I really want to understand what you are saying, could you say more about it?" This technique slows down the interaction and shows your spouse that you are really interested in understanding as opposed to defending. If your question succeeds in helping your spouse believe that you really want to understand more deeply what he is thinking or feeling, frequently the argument will diminish in intensity and might even move in a different direction.

2. The second technique is similar to the first. It is to paraphrase what your spouse has said and check to see if you are really understanding. Using this technique keeps the argument from escalating further. When you find the argument escalating and moving into generalizations, and you see yourself getting hooked or becoming overly defensive, try paraphrasing. For example, "It seems from your perspective as if our roles are unbalanced, and you feel that you are doing far more than your fair share. Have I understood you correctly?"

   If your spouse does not have a coronary attack, this is a very effective technique. Obviously it takes a lot of discipline. However, when you have begun to see where your arguments usually go and you recognize the predictable pattern of these arguments, then using some self-discipline is very desirable.

3. *A third technique is to stay on the topic.* If you have initiated a discussion, take responsibility to keep it on topic. In arguments, the tendency is to escalate or to generalize to a variety of topics. If your spouse responds to a comment of yours with, "So you're saying I'm a terrible father," your response might be, "No that is not at all what I'm saying. You are really a good father, but I worry that your work schedule is keeping you from spending enough time with our kids." If your spouse tries another escalation, "You really don't understand how much pressure I'm under," your temptation might be to respond, "Let

me tell you about pressure." Instead, you might respond, "You know I really want to understand the pressure you're under, but right now I just want you to hear my concern. I am worried that you are not spending enough time with our children."

In this example, the spouse who raised the initial concern takes responsibility to keep the discussion from escalating to too many other topics. Again, this takes great self-discipline. However, without it nothing will ever get done.

4. *A fourth technique it to take a time-out.* Sometimes, when an argument is getting too emotionally volatile, your best confusion technique is to say, "Right now I'm so defensive that I'm only going to make things worse. Can we take a time-out and come back to this later?" This brief time-out can save a lot of pain. It is far more effective than saying what you might say if you speak in anger. Of course, it also means you will come back to the discussion in the near future. Otherwise you are just avoiding conflict, and your partner will come to resent that. Taking a time-out is a way to slow down a powerful interaction, so you can come back to it later when you are calm.

Given what we have said about arguments being predictable, and escalating in predictable ways, one very useful exercise might be to develop a list of ground rules. What are ground rules? Think about the difference between a street fight and a boxing match. In a street fight, anything goes. Combatants hit anywhere they can, with any weapon they can find. There are no rules and anything goes. It is simply survival of the fittest. In contrast, although boxing may be a bit barbaric, there are clearly defined rules. There are places you can hit, and places you can't. There are time limits, a referee, and a ring in which the fight must be contained.

Couples sometimes fight like street fighters. They don't have rules, they hit "below the belt," they bring up the past, they rapidly escalate, and they certainly do not have time limits. Like boxers, they need ground rules. Here are some examples of ground rules:

- No arguing in front of the kids.

- No bringing up past issues

- No name-calling

- No intense discussions after midnight.

After you have understood how you and your spouse escalate a quarrel, you should make a list of ground rules that you and your spouse might agree to honor. If you have a hard time coming up with ground rules, ask your partner what you do that makes arguments so difficult. Then try to imagine what you can do differently. If you can establish some ground rules, write them down in the space provided below:

Our Ground Rules

1. _____

2. _____

3. _____

4. _____

5. _____

Finally, when making a request of your spouse, be concrete. Notice as your arguments escalate, that things get more and more generalized, and then become more and more difficult to resolve.

Using self-focus, ask yourself, "What do I really want?" Now, try and turn that into a positive behavioral request. For example, "Please stop nagging me" is not a positive statement. Asking, "When I'm describing my day, I would like you to just listen for ten minutes to help me unwind," or "I would like to take a walk with you for fifteen minutes after supper to catch up on both of our days." Or, "I would like to go out for dinner or a movie once a month without the kids."

Obviously all of this is a lot of work that will take a lot of discipline. Self-focus, and changing one's self, take an enormous amount of energy. In the end however, it is less work than living with the chronic pain of making problems worse and living with a less than satisfying marriage.

CHAPTER FOUR

Your Thinking Is Part of the Problem

There is no right or wrong position in couple arguments. As long as you try to *win* an argument, you will always lose. Perception is everything. That is, everything in communication is a matter of perception and interpretation. Interpretations are based on belief systems. This chapter will help you understand the key belief systems you hold, and show you how *those* beliefs affect and inform your interpretation of what your partner says to you.

As you probably figured out after reading the last chapter, changing the predictable patterns in your relationship is extremely difficult. Often, these patterns are so deeply ingrained that they have become resistant to change. In fact, sometimes it feels as if the harder you try, the more everything stays the same. The more you resolve to change your role in these patterns, the more you begin to realize how difficult the task is. If you experimented with the exercises in the last chapter, you probably became somewhat frustrated. Making change is not easy and creating lasting change is even more difficult.

As we explained in the last chapter, understanding your patterns of communication and your role within them is the first step toward creating change. However, we often ignore an important component of communication, which is our belief systems. Just as it is important to understand your role in communication patterns, so too you must understand how your belief systems may be part of your problem.

When we communicate, we do so based on what we see and believe. When we listen, we cannot help but hear everything filtered through our beliefs, which influence our interpretations of what we have heard. We see through our subjective beliefs, which then determine what we feel and say. Although initially this may sound complicated, the following short dialogue will show you how this works. Watch what happens in this "simple dialogue" between Tom and Ann.

Tom: Where's the checkbook?

Ann: Why are you always blaming me for everything? You are so unfair.

Tom: What is your problem? I just asked a simple question.

What went wrong in this "simple dialogue"? Why did it elicit such angry responses so rapidly? On the surface it appears that Tom asked a simple question that was answered with an angry response. Of course, no question is really a simple question. Perhaps he was not aware of his tone, or his look, or maybe he was reading the paper when he asked the question. Perhaps this is a long-standing argument between this couple. So one possibility for how this interaction became so heated might have been the way in which Tom asked the question.

On the other hand, Ann interpreted Tom's question through the filter of one of her beliefs. Ann's belief about Tom is that he blames and accuses her constantly, so she interpreted his question as blaming her for losing the checkbook. This belief led her to an interpretation that, in turn, produced her response. As a result, she heard an accusing and blaming tone which, in turn, made her feel angry and defensive. As stated previously, her interpretation may have been influenced by his tone, or his lack of eye contact, or by the fact that he was reading the paper. In any case, her response and anger were both the result of the interpretation she made.

No communication is pure: Everything is a matter of interpretation.

Thus, in this simple communication, any question or statement is interpreted (often automatically) through each partner's belief systems, which, in turn, fuel the responses. In any communication, no matter how simple it may seem, some interpretation is made. Any communication involves the following three-step dynamic:

1. The sender sends a message to a receiver.

2. The receiver's belief system affects his/her interpretation of the message.

3. This interpretation then determines the receiver's response to the sender.

Consider another example.

Ted got caught in a business meeting that went on longer than he had anticipated. He felt himself getting more and more tense hoping the meeting would end, so he could go home and have dinner with his wife, Angela. He considered calling, but he kept thinking that the meeting had to end soon. As a result, he arrived home almost an hour late wthout having called. Angela was furious when he arrived home and refused to talk to him. By way of a greeting, she said in an icy voice, "Dinner is cold, help yourself," and refusing to say anything else, she went to the bedroom.

Couple Interactions, Belief Systems, and Interpretations

Why is Angela so angry? Certainly becoming irritable when your partner comes home late is normal. However, why *so* much anger? Angela, without realizing it, interpreted Ted's lateness as rejection. She was saying to herself, "Obviously, Ted's work has a higher priority than our marriage. I can never count on him to come through for me." Ted interprets Angela's withdrawal as lack of sympathy for the pressures he is under at work. He resents this, and withdraws, setting up a cycle of mutual withdrawal and anger that lasts throughout the week.

Both parties drew their conclusions based on their interpretations or beliefs about the other. This couple is about to enter into a pattern of mutual withdrawal and resentment based on the interpretations each made about the other. These interpretations are based on beliefs each has about the other. Angela believes that Ted values his career more than he values her. Ted believes that Angela does not understand any of the pressures he undergoes at work.

One of the most difficult problems for couples is that they have a hard time accepting this fact: *When it comes to couple communication, there is no such thing as one "objective reality."* Couples can argue for days trying to get the other to accept their version of reality. They can go back and forth about what they "really meant," or what they "really said." There can never be any winners in this type of argument. Both partners continue to argue to prove what they "really said," or, at least, what they "meant to say." Think about the argument you have most often. If you are honest, down deep you believe that your position is the right one. You argue to prove your point and your sense of objective reality. The fact that communication involves interpretation and beliefs is completely ignored.

Hearing Through the Filters

Everything you hear, is heard through a filter. The filter is composed of your belief systems. Just as when you wear red sunglasses everything you see looks red, the filters in your mind determine what it is you hear and see.

The German philosopher Ludwig Wittgenstein illustrated this with a diagram of what he called "the duck rabbit." He would sketch a line drawing of a rabbit's head and ask his class to name or describe what they saw. Of course the class saw only a rabbit. But when he took the same drawing and turned it sideways, they saw a duck. His philosophical point was that the drawing was neither duck nor rabbit. What students saw was, in fact, determined by the frame around the drawing. If a vertical frame surrounded it, all that could be seen was a rabbit. If a horizontal frame was around it, all that could be seen was a duck. The frame determined what was seen. Or to state it somewhat differently, the students interpreted the line drawing based on the position of the frame. The frame served the same function that a belief system does. It created a context. In reality, the drawing was neither duck nor rabbit. The frame determined the interpretation in the same way that a belief system interprets "objective" facts.

Cognitive psychology suggests that we see nothing "purely" or "objectively." We see everything based on the conceptual frame—or belief systems—through which we make our interpretations. The question "Where's the checkbook?" is interpreted through the frame or belief "You're always blaming me." Coming home late is understood as rejection based on an interpretation that Ted's career has a higher priority for him than his marriage.

These powerful belief systems can make communication very difficult. What makes things even worse is that they often operate without our ever being aware of their presence. Angela did not think, "I am interpreting Ted's question in the context of my belief that he frequently blames me." She did not think when Ted came home late, "My belief system tells me that Ted values his career more than his marriage." These beliefs and interpretations start up automatically and they are seldom brought into conscious awareness.

Beliefs Operate Automatically

Cognitive psychologists tell us that these interpretations take place so quickly that we can say they happen automatically (Beck 1976; 1988). That is, they are not thought through, or consciously chosen, and so they appear to be automatic responses. Because they happen automatically they are seldom questioned or even thought about. They simply produce an automatic response. Did Angela take the time to ask, "I wonder what Tom really means by that question? I need to check that out." Of course not. She automatically assumed that he was blaming her. Her belief system started up instantly leaving her no time to question or reflect. Consider another illustration of how this works.

Mark and Donna

Mark was home sick with the flu. He asked his wife, Donna, if she could come home early from work to take care if him and to keep him company. When she responded that she couldn't due to an important business presentation, Mark became depressed. He interpreted her refusal as evidence that his needs are not important to her. He said to himself, "If I can't trust her to help me with this, what would happen if I really needed something?" This interpretation led him to anger and withdrawal.

Once again the problem was interpretation. Mark automatically made the assumption that if Donna really loved him, she would cancel all of her business meetings and come home for him. The fact that she would not cancel her meetings and come home became the evidence that she does not really love him. What is frightening is that he did not think this through. His belief and interpretation took over automatically. As soon as Donna said "no" to canceling her meetings, he automatically took her statement as evidence that his needs are not important to her. Worse, it became a trust issue, which then left Mark wondering whether he could trust Donna in the long term.

Before criticizing Mark too quickly, ask yourself how often you make similar interpretations. How often do you interpret certain actions of your partner's as evidence of lack of caring based on your own beliefs of what loving actions should be? Furthermore, how often do you check out your beliefs with your partner?

Unfortunately, your belief systems fuel interactions with your partner. Every statement you make is interpreted and vice versa. We are constantly interpreting—automatically—what our partners' actions or communication really means. As a result, communication patterns become more difficult to change. Our belief systems become a large part of our communication problems.

Challenging Your Beliefs and Interpretations

If your belief systems really are a large part of your communication problems, then how do you begin to create change? The answer is that, after (1) analyzing your problematic communication patterns and (2) changing your role in those patterns, the next step toward change is to (3) realize how you use your automatic beliefs to interpret what your spouse "really means" or what s/he is "really saying." As you have probably figured out by now, mind reading works very poorly in marriage. And, if you are honest, you will realize that you often misinterpret what your spouse says.

Deep change begins by exploring the way your belief systems and interpretations may be distorting communication. It involves accepting the fact that you are always interpreting what your spouse says to you on the basis of your belief systems, and that this can be part of the problem in your marriage.

The first step toward change is to accept the fact that you are constantly interpreting based on your belief systems. This in turn may mean that you must give up one of your favorite myths: the myth of objective reality. This myth takes as a given the notion that it is possible to figure out who is right and who is wrong, and who said which words exactly. We have listened to many couples struggle intensely trying to prove exactly what it was they said, as well as what they meant—all to no avail.

Trying to prove who is right and who is wrong is always a futile waste of time. The first step toward making real change means understanding that how you interpret what you hear is just as important as what has been said. You must start to work on understanding your own belief systems and taking responsibility for how your beliefs can distort communication.

Accepting that means asking yourself how you distort communication with what is called "distorted thinking." The term *distorted thinking* covers a variety of ways that we misinterpret events because of specific problems of interpretation. For example, Mark engaged in distorted thinking by concluding that his wife doesn't love him and will never be there for him because she would not cancel her meetings and come home to help him while he was sick. He jumped to some very large conclusions on the basis of very little evidence. His "distorted thinking" was the manner in which he came to his conclusion, without ever examining his evidence. He never stopped to question whether his wife's not canceling a meeting really was evidence for concluding that she did not really love him, and was not really trustworthy.

In the next section we will describe some of the ways that, like Mark, we use distorted thinking that only creates further difficulties in our relationships. What are some of these common errors in thinking? Cognitive therapists have been very helpful in describing some of the errors in thinking that distort marital communications.

Challenge Your Errors in Thinking

There are a number of predictable errors or distortions of thinking that are guaranteed to seriously distort communication. They have been summarized by Beck (1988) and Dattilio and Padesky (1990) in great detail. Here, we have summarized five of the most common errors in thinking that we see couples using. As you go through the list that follows, ask yourself which "errors" you most commonly use and which have caused the most problems in your marital communications.

Error No. 1: Catastrophic Thinking

In this situation, you jump to large, "catastrophic" conclusions on the basis of a simple statement or action. Although objectively the original statement does not merit the conclusion that is reached, the "catastrophic conclusion" is never challenged. For example, Angela arrived at a catastrophic conclusion when she assumed that her husband's lateness was evidence that he did not love her very much. Mark, too, used catastrophic thinking when he concluded that, because Donna would not come home to take care of him, it meant that she did not love him very much. In both of these examples, large conclusions were reached based on one example.

This type of thinking can become even more dangerous. Once you accept your conclusion uncritically, you will then proceed to communicate on the basis of your conclusion or belief. Almost inevitably, this will escalate the interaction, because it frequently catches your partner off guard. When Mark began to sulk and ignore his wife, believing that she didn't love him, how was Donna supposed to respond? She will most likely feel irritated or angry at his sulking and withdrawal. She may also feel attacked unfairly and respond accordingly. This will only make Mark feel worse, and they may soon have a discussion that can do a lot of damage.

Catastrophic thinking leaves very little room for discussion. It often leads one partner to jump to unwarranted conclusions, and the other partner feeling attacked and/or hurt or angry.

Error No. 2: All-or-Nothing Thinking

This error is an expansion of catastrophic thinking. For example, Mark concluded that if Donna cannot come home this time, then it means that she will *never* come through for him. Angela concluded that when her husband comes home late, it is evidence that she can *never* count on him to come through for her in really important matters. In both cases the data does not warrant the conclusion. They are using "all-or-nothing" thinking.

All-or-nothing thinking is characterized by thoughts like these: If it does not happen now, it will never happen. If my partner does not come through this time, s/he will never come through. If my partner forgets something, s/he will never remember, and so on. Again, this sets up arguments that in the end cannot be resolved, but will leave both parties worn out and debilitated. How in the world can your partner respond when you say, "I will never be able to trust you with the big things in life, since you didn't stay home from work when I was sick"? You know you are using all-or-nothing thinking when you find yourself using phrases like "you always" or "you never" frequently. These phrases, in turn, lead to black-and-white thinking.

Black-and-White Thinking: The problem with black-and-white thinking is obvious. It rules out anything between the two extremes. Things are either great or they are horrible. You either love me the way I want to be loved, or that means that you don't love me at all. Sex is either great, or it's horrible. You either come home on time all the time, or you are never on time.

Abstractly, it is easy to recognize this type of thinking. It is far more difficult to sort out in the midst of intense couple interactions. The woman who informs her husband that since he forgot once again to bring home some items from the grocery store for their family dinner, she will *never* be able to trust him again is engaging in black-and-white thinking. The man whose wife refuses to join him when he goes for long bike rides and then concludes that they have nothing in common is engaging in black-and-white thinking. Often, this type of thinking causes negative interactions between spouses to escalate and prevents them from discovering compromises. Frequently, it leaves one spouse feeling ambushed and attacked and this further fuels defensiveness. Soon, the couple will be caught in another counterproductive argument.

Unfortunately, we do this in so many subtle ways. We conclude on the basis of small pieces of evidence that our mates are not really trustworthy. We interpret specific criticisms as evidence that we are not truly loved. We experience small disappointments as evidence that we would be much happier married to someone else.

Error No. 3: Tunnel Vision

Tunnel vision is best illustrated in this story of a couple who had just returned from a ten-day vacation at an oceanside resort. When asked by friends how their vacation had been, they both reported that it had been horrible. When asked what had gone wrong, they described an argument they had on their way home, which had been the result of getting lost on the highway.

Both partners insisted that it had been the other's fault they had become lost, which had resulted in an argument that had grown more emotional and more intense. However, after being questioned further about how the rest of the vacation had gone, they reported that nine days of the vacation had been wonderful, relaxing, and romantic. The problem occurred on the drive home when they got lost. Without realizing it, they were engaging in "tunnel vision." All they could think about was their most recent fight. They could not see through a "wide angle lens" and recall that most of their vacation had been wonderful.

This happens too often. When we engage in tunnel vision we are able to focus on only one aspect of the relationship, usually a negative one. As a result, we lose the big picture. Successfully married couples have cultivated over the years their ability to tune into a broader perspective. They recognize that they have some problem areas, but when they evaluate their marriage, they use a more balanced perspective.

Tunnel vision forgets to look for strengths. Like the couple returning from vacation, people using tunnel vision can see only what is wrong. They forget that in every marriage there are many different aspects. They often fail to remind themselves of the areas of strength in their marriage and focus only on the problem areas.

Error No. 4: Poor Detective Work

Good detectives carefully gather all the evidence available at the crime scene before jumping to any conclusions. Poor detective work does the opposite. It forms strong conclusions on the basis of very little evidence. With this type of thinking, erroneous conclusions are reached in the absence of supporting evidence.

For example, the man whose wife comes home from a party an hour late concludes that "she must be having an affair." He does not ask why his wife was late, or talk with her about how the party went, or even disclose his fears. He jumps to a conclusion and then attacks his wife, who withdraws from him feeling hurt and angry. The more she withdraws, the more he interprets her withdrawal as evidence that she must be having an affair. His thinking has it that since she is so quiet, she must be feeling guilty. This leaves him more convinced that his conclusion is correct. This type of poor detective work can only lead to an unfortunate cycle of interaction that will inevitably cause both partners to feel distant from each other.

Some people have a tricky way of testing their spouse. They say little and thus create some distance. Then they wait to see if their partner notices that they are withdrawn. Or they hint at something they want for their birthday, and then watch to see if their partner picks up on their hint. When their partner fails whatever the test was, they use this as evidence that their spouse does not love them. Both poor detective work and setting secret tests for one's spouse will always result in greater distance and often painful arguments.

Error No. 5: Mind Reading

In this type of thinking error, spouses think they can read their partners' minds without needing verbal communication. Although most of the time we realize that this never works, more often than we care to admit we engage in this error. Often, when working with couples we encourage them to be clear with each other about what they really want, and they become indignant. A typical response would go like this: "After eighteen years of marriage I shouldn't have to tell him (or her) that. S/he should know."

This type of erroneous thinking is well illustrated by an account one couple gave of an argument that took place during a recent trip they took together. The husband had become very angry and agitated after they passed a rest stop. His confused wife asked him what was wrong. He angrily stated that they had just passed the last place to get coffee and then demanded to know the reason she had not stopped. She replied, "I didn't know you wanted coffee, you didn't tell me you did. " Her husband responded, "If after ten years you do not know when I want coffee, then you just do not know me very well." Translation: "If you love me you would be able to read my mind."

As a result of imperfect mind reading, couples end up attributing negative intentions to their partners. The man in need of coffee believes that his wife is insensitive and uncaring. And he responds to her on the basis of his beliefs.

We encountered another example of this type of thinking with a man who assumes his wife has ulterior motives when she is especially nice to him. He thinks, "I know what she is thinking. She really wants to go out with her friends for the weekend, so she is being nice for now. She has ulterior motives." He interprets her "niceness" as evidence that he is being manipulated and that his wife's kindness is motivated by ulterior motives.

Where Are Your Errors of Thinking?

If you are honest, you will see yourself in many of these examples. These types of thinking errors cause you to interpret, or more precisely, misinterpret much of what your spouse says or does. All too easily they can fuel powerful arguments and misunderstandings.

Now, take a few minutes to reflect before reading any further. In the previous chapter you tried to analyze and shift your role in your patterned and predictable arguments. Now try to think about which of these "thinking errors" you commit in your marriage. Which do you find yourself doing most frequently? Record your thoughts in the space provided below. Understanding your most frequent thinking errors could begin to shift your communication patterns.

_____

_____

_____

_____

_____

My Most Common Thinking Errors

Now that you have described your errors in thinking, take a little more time to describe how these thinking mistakes impact on your marital communications and add fuel to your miscommunication patterns. What exactly happens when you make these mistakes in thinking? How do they affect your partner? Write your responses to these questions in the space below:

_____

_____

_____

_____

_____

Thinking Errors Lead to Increased Communication Problems

These distortions in thinking all lead to communication distortions which fuel the counterproductive communication patterns between married partners. For example, _mind reading_ can lead to the belief that "My husband should know by now what I really want as a gift without me having to tell him." This, of course, will lead to disappointment, arguments, and emotional distancing. Most spouses are not talented mind readers.

Poor detective work, based on preexisting beliefs, will lead to distorted interpretations that impact badly on communication. The man who infers that his wife must be having an affair because she has come home late from work several times in the last few weeks will become more and more suspicious. He will then begin to question his wife with an undertone of hostility, which will of course cause his wife to distance herself, and will increase their problematic communication style.

The Problem Gets Bigger: Belief Systems

In addition to "errors in thinking" we have a number of powerful beliefs that lead to incorrect interpretations of our partners' behavior, and often to increased distance between the partners. Over time we form a series of beliefs about gender, about what good marriage is, about our spouses, as well as beliefs about ourselves, which all become filters through which we evaluate the health of our relationship. Obviously, these beliefs, when they lead to powerful interpretations, have the power to distort communication.

Beliefs About Gender

Some of your beliefs about gender can seriously disrupt a successful marriage. If you are honest, you acknowledge that not only are there gender-based differences between men and women, but that you have a particular view of the opposite gender. Often, your beliefs are not accurate. Your views emerge from a variety of places including your family, your schooling, your subculture, etc. Now, answer the following questions as honestly as possible about your feelings about the opposite gender.

- All men/women are _____

  _____

  _____

- The male/female style of communication is _____

  _____

  _____

- Men are mostly interested in _____

  _____

  _____

- Women are mostly interested in _____

  _____

  _____

- Women define a good marriage as _____

  _____

  _____

- Men define a good marriage as _____

  _____

  _____

- Men define good sex as _____

  _____

  _____

- Women define good sex as _____

  _____

  _____

After you completed this exercise, what did you discover about your gender-based belief systems? If you answered honestly and did not write only "politically correct" answers, you may have realized that you hold some strong, perhaps even biased, beliefs about the opposite gender. Listen to the many jokes made about men or women when you are in the company of those who are the same sex as yourself. Despite all the efforts of the women's movement and the gay movement, and despite all of the antidiscrimination legislation passed both by Congress and state legislatures, these old beliefs about gender are very powerful and often interfere with good communication between spouses.

Are we saying that men are from Mars, and women from Venus? No. We are saying that although there are some gender-based differences, it is the powerful beliefs about gender that disrupt marital communication. As Gottman's research indicated, men and women often want the same thing from a relationship. Seventy percent of both men and women said friendship was the main benefit they wanted from marriage (Gottman 2000).

Joe and Lisa

Joe and Lisa provide an illuminating example of how gender-based beliefs can deeply affect marriage. Joe believes that women are overly emotional and tend to not act logically. As a result, he backs away from any emotional subject when talking with his wife, Lisa. He is afraid that if he is too honest about what he is feeling, or if he allows a discussion to get "too emotional," that the discussion will quickly spin out of control. Lisa is frequently frustrated that they cannot discuss sensitive and important topics. Consequently, her frustration sometimes builds because of her need to hold things in for so long, and then she finally explodes quite emotionally. At that point, Joe stands back, and says, "This is why I don't talk to you: You are so emotional!"

He does not realize that he causes the very problem he most fears. By not ever talking honestly about what he is feeling, and by blocking Lisa from speaking honestly about her feelings, he causes her to become more emotionally explosive simply because she is so frustrated. The more frustrated she becomes as the result of not being able to express her feelings, the more likely she is to become emotionally explosive as the result of built-up frustration.

On the other hand, if Lisa holds the belief that men are interested only in their careers and sports, she will act on the basis of that belief. She may withhold information about her feelings, or about the children, because she believes that Joe does not really want to hear about these matters. This will fuel her frustration, for she will begin to feel as if she does not really have a partner. She will not share her needs with Joe, since she assumes that men are not interested in hearing about women's needs. As a result, when he watches sports, she resents it, since this proves her belief system.. Over time, this couple will become progressively more emotionally distant from each other and will have less and less emotional communication.

The problem here is not gender-based differences, but *beliefs* about gender that govern our behavior. The more we act on those beliefs, the more we create new problems and more distance between ourselves and our partners.

Previously, you listed some of your beliefs about gender. Now take a few minutes to describe how your beliefs about gender influence the way you communicate with your spouse.

_____

_____

_____

_____

_____

My Beliefs About Marriage

In addition to our strongly held beliefs about gender we have deeply held beliefs about marriage. Like our gender-based beliefs, beliefs about marriage also become a type of lens through which we evaluate the quality of our marriage. Again, these beliefs are learned from our families, schools, culture, religious institutions, and so forth. These beliefs become one more lens by which we evaluate the health of our marriages.

For example, if you believe that a good marriage means never having an argument, then every time you have an argument, it will serve as evidence that your marriage is in trouble. If your view of a good marriage is that it means having all the same interests, then when you discover that you and your spouse have different interests, that can become another piece of evidence that your marriage is not a satisfactory one.

There are many of these beliefs about marriage that we fail to discuss with our spouses. Some years ago, there was a line in a popular movie that went, "Love means never having to say you are sorry." If you hold that belief, then your marriage is probably in trouble. That line is, however, an example of how beliefs are popularized in our culture, and how they become another lens by which we compare and evaluate our own marriages.

There is a very popular belief that most of us are embarrassed to admit holding. Nevertheless, a lot of people think it is true and act on their belief. It can be summarized this way: "If you loved me, you would know what I am feeling. If I have to tell you, that means you really don't know me." This belief is illustrated nicely by the following story.

Irene and George

Irene and George were extremely discouraged. Irene was beginning to think that her marriage would never meet her needs. She explained that in the weeks before Christmas she had been feeling depressed thinking about her mother's death, and nostalgically wishing for the kind of Christmas she had experienced as a child. She felt hurt that George had never even noticed that she was feeling so down.

George, on the other hand, was confused. "How am I supposed to know what you are feeling if you don't share it with me? I'm not a therapist!" To which Irene tearfully responded, "If after all these years you can't be sensitive enough to know what I am feeling, what kind of marriage do we really have?" Upon hearing this, George became even more confused.

We hear dozens of variations of this couple's story every year. Too often when we coach couples to be more specific with each other about what it is they want, they respond by saying, "That sounds so cold and calculated. If s/he loved me s/he would know what I am feeling without me having to tell him/her."

There are a number of such deeply held beliefs about marriage. When we are honest, all of us admit to specific beliefs about what a good marriage requires. For some it is the absence of conflict; for others, the ability to be soul mates or best friends. Some people believe that a good marriage means sharing all the same hobbies and interests. And some believe that a good marriage can exist only if traditional roles are observed and maintained by the partners. Unfortunately, these deeply held core beliefs are often not discussed much before couples enter into marriage, and, as a result, they can cause great marital pain.

The reality is that these beliefs cannot help but become a type of conceptual grid through which you evaluate your spouse and the state of your marriage. You then act on the basis of your beliefs without discussing them with your spouse.

Now, list your beliefs about what constitutes a "good marriage."

_____

_____

_____

_____

A good starting point for effectively changing your marriage would be to do the following steps:

1. Identify your beliefs about marriage.

2. Have an honest dialogue with your spouse about your mutually held beliefs about what constitutes a good marriage, as well as your beliefs about gender.

3. Explore how these beliefs affect your communication patterns.

Beliefs About Your Spouse

Beliefs about your spouse are among the most dangerous or beneficial belief sets that can affect all of your interactions with your spouse. Over the course of your marriage and life together, you form beliefs about your partner, and then act on those beliefs as if they were true. Often those beliefs have not been examined or challenged, and they are rigidly fixed in your mind.

The danger here is that the way in which you view your spouse always has an element of truth. Once these beliefs about your spouse are formed, they are very difficult to change. Then, when you combine these "partially true" beliefs with your potential for errors in thinking, you may create a much more rigid emotional structure, as illustrated in the stories below.

Bob and Carol

Bob had been a fairly controlling kind of person in the early years of his marriage. Over time he mellowed, and he worked hard to change the controlling and unpleasant part of himself. He has actually made some significant changes within himself. However, Cathy, his wife, still views him through the lens of her old belief system. As a result she still holds back and does not share much of herself with him, because she believes that he is still trying to control her. She is not aware of how much he actually has changed. She continues to view him through her old lens and consequently does not allow herself to get too close to him.

George and Kim

George believes that his wife Kim is deeply disappointed with him. As a result, he sees her as someone who is never happy or approving, and who really would prefer a more successful husband. Consequently, he stays distant from her and is somewhat fearful. He takes it for granted that Kim will always be critical of him and so he never relates to her as a friend. It never occurs to him to take the risk of being vulnerable and sharing some of his fears with her.

All of us have our own variations of these beliefs. Who has not said or at least thought, "S/he knows what I really want, but refuses to give it to me"? "He is passive aggressive. He will always injure me." "She just wants to control me and tell me what to do." "If she knew who I really was, she would leave." The possibilities are endless. However, the danger lies in our tendency to communicate (or not communicate) on the basis of our beliefs. These beliefs have the potential to keep us distant from each other, to keep us cautious, angry, suspicious, and so forth. When you view your spouse through the lens of your beliefs about him or her, you will act accordingly. And, of course, you will communicate (or not) based on your beliefs about your spouse.

Beliefs About Yourself

Finally, we have beliefs about ourselves which are part of the relationship mix. How we view ourselves and what we believe about ourselves can influence marital communication. Without realizing it we often have a particular view of ourselves in our relationships. When we look at our marriage from some distance usually we have a picture of ourselves in that relationship. Marge, for example, described her husband as angry and distant. She said that he described her as controlling and bitchy. However, she believes that he is just an angry man who may have had a controlling mother. She views herself as an innocent, supportive wife who just happens to be married to an angry man. She cannot see anything that she has contributed to the problem. Her view of herself makes change difficult, since she really does not see anything to work on, other than changing her husband. In this way, Marge illustrates several problematic beliefs about the self that can cause difficulty.

First, if you believe that you are doing everything right, and that your spouse is the problem, then all of your work will be to change your spouse. You will not stop and think about what you might be doing that is a problem for your spouse. Rather, you will remain convinced that your spouse is the problem.

Second, gender roles may have an impact on the way you see yourself in the marriage. If your accept stereotypical gender roles, then you may believe you are acting appropriately, and you may not understand your spouse's frustration. For example, how many men still believe that their main role as husbands is to provide financially for their families? And how many men who believe that then feel frustrated when their spouse says they are not emotionally available.

Finally, some people are not in touch with their own needs and do not feel entitled to ask that some of those needs be met. If they are not even aware of their needs, or of what it is they want from their spouse, they will not ask for much. As a result, they believe that they are trying to be good husbands or wives, and then they feel like martyrs when their needs are never met. They never consider that they may not even have been clear about their needs.

Unfortunately, when self-focus and self-awareness are missing, unwanted and unacceptable parts of one's self may then be "projected" onto one's spouse and then attacked. For example, the man who is unsure about his own sexual impulse control will accuse his wife of having an affair. What is missing is more accurate self-assessment, and honest appraisal of the self. When we are not aware of our own issues, our own needs, and our own hurts, we often become bitter and attack our spouse for not meeting our needs. Thinking about the belief systems that we take for granted as givens, and our styles of interpretation, can help us to become more self aware.

Creating Change

Creating change means first understanding the power of your cognitive belief systems, and understanding how they cause you to interpret or misinterpret what your spouse is saying. When these interpretations are combined with errors in thinking there is a recipe for reactive communication.

To change means beginning to take responsibilities for your automatic assumptions and beliefs, to understand where they come from, how they cause constant interpretations, and how this has an impact on all of your communication. The process of change demands that you begin to understand the cognitive filters that you are constantly using to view your spouse. Without being aware of how your filters are used automatically, and often unconsciously, change is impossible. Simple communication skills will never be enough. Change begins with a clear assessment of the beliefs that form your filters in your marriage.

To better understand your grid of beliefs, through which you interpret much of what your spouse says, try to summarize your key belief systems. Spend a little time reviewing your answers to the questions we posed throughout this chapter. As you review, go back to the previous pages, and summarize your answers.

My belief system grid is composed of the following beliefs:

_____

_____

_____

_____

My beliefs about marriage are these:

_____

_____

_____

_____

My beliefs about gender are these:

_____

_____

_____

_____

My beliefs about my spouse are these:

_____

_____

_____

_____

My beliefs about myself are these:

_____

_____

_____

_____

As you summarize the key elements of your grid, try and visualize how it influences your style of communication with your spouse. Remember, it is not enough to understand this grid. The work of change requires that you begin to challenge some of your core beliefs, and open a dialogue with your partner about some of them. The work also means beginning to make some changes in the thinking errors that you commonly use.

The next chapter will begin to explore how to make changes in your belief systems in some very specific ways. It will explore how your belief system often interacts with your spouse's belief system, causing even more difficulty with your communication process.

CHAPTER FIVE

How Beliefs Reinforce Each Other

The problem with belief systems is that they end up reinforcing each other. In other words, you may end up "proving" your partner's beliefs about you to be true, even while you are desperately trying to help your partner see your point. This chapter will help you understand on a deeper level how belief systems and communication work. It will also introduce the idea of external and internal communication. Finally, it will introduce some steps for creating change.

By now, marriage may seem like more work than you ever thought it was. No wonder that 50 percent of marriages fail! To summarize what we have said thus far: First, marital partners create patterned interactions or arguments around specific issues in the marriage. This argument, or patterned discussion, often takes on a life of its own. Second, those patterned interactions are fueled by errors in thinking and by particular beliefs about gender, marriage, one's partner, and oneself. In this context, any issue whether it be money, sex, in-laws, or parenting, can result in an argument that can take on a life of its own. This argument is then fueled by belief systems that serve to further intensify the argument. Eventually, the argument becomes the problem, by making the original issue impossible to resolve.

What makes these arguments even more difficult to resolve is that *both partners have belief systems and these belief systems often reinforce each other.* In order to create change you must not only be aware of and challenge your own belief systems, but you must begin to be aware of your partner's belief systems. This makes change much more difficult because two sets of belief systems further complicate the problem.

The Struggle for Intimacy: Debra and Wally

To illustrate the way this works, let's look at Debra and Wally's situation. They describe their chief issue as a problem with intimacy. They struggle to grow closer emotionally, to achieve a more intimate marriage. As they try to solve the problem of how much time to spend together to create true intimacy, they drift into a patterned way of discussing the issue. As expected, with time, this pattern has taken on a life of its own. Debra's role in the discussion is to pursue and constantly ask Wally questions like, "Why can't we spend more time together? Do you always have to watch football? Why can't we ever just sit and talk?" This is Debra's solution to their problem. Wally's response is predicable: "Why can't you just give me some breathing space? If you would get off my back, then maybe I'd feel like talking to you. Just chill out, and back off!"

Not surprisingly, his response is met with hurt feelings and then with further pursuit by Debra. At this point, their interaction is entirely predictable: Debra pursues and Wally distances. The more he distances, the more she pursues. And the harder she pursues, the further he distances. Changing this interaction is not easy. The pattern is too well set.

For change to occur, they must be able to move to the next level: that of understanding their interaction. Both need to recognize that they each have strong belief systems that make their interactions more intense. Recognizing and becoming aware of these beliefs may help them to shift the nature of their interaction.

Debra was initially confused when she was questioned about her thoughts while pursuing Wally. She knew that her actions were not helping, but she had a difficult time understanding why she continued to pursue him anyway. She had to stop and think about what her thoughts were while she was engaged in pursuing.

In the midst of an argument, slowing down to try to articulate and understand your underlying beliefs is a very hard task. It requires conscious and intentional reflection. Like most people, Debra had never stopped to ask herself what her thoughts were while she pursued Wally. In time, though, she was able to access them. Then, she described how fearful she was that if she backed off, he would ignore her completely and she would become lonelier than ever.

Furthermore, she believed that having a good marriage meant doing everything together. So she believed every time Wally watched football, it meant her marriage was not working the way it was supposed to work. Thus, she had two beliefs that fueled her pursuit:

1. The belief that her husband would ignore her if she gave up pursuing him.

2. Her belief about marriage itself—that a good marriage requires the couple to do everything together.

Wally, after thinking through his beliefs, said that he believed a good marriage meant having time apart, as well as time together. He also believed that if he gave in too often to what Debra wanted, he would lose all of his freedom. Down deep he was convinced that she really wanted to control his life. Like Debra, Wally had two beliefs:

1. His belief that if he gave in and spent more time with his wife, she would then try to control every aspect of his life.

2. His belief that in a good marriage, both parties should have plenty of time apart to develop their own friends and interests.

When looking at the belief systems that are an integral part of Wally and Debra's interactions, it becomes clear why they are stuck. Each has a number of powerful beliefs about the other, and they have very different understandings of what goes into the making of a good marriage.

As a result of both of their belief systems, their pursuer/distancer pattern keeps going at an exhausting pace. Unless they can slow down and talk to each other about their underlying beliefs, and how those beliefs affect all of their interactions, it will be difficult to introduce any beneficial changes in their marriage.

For Debra and Wally, their pursuer/distancer pattern further confirms their belief systems. Debra believes more than ever that Wally really does want to stay distant from her, and, of course, Wally believes that Debra really wants to control every aspect of his life. The more they go round and round in their patterned interaction, the more both are convinced of the validity of their beliefs. Because they have not taken the time to slow down and discuss their different belief systems, their patterned interaction continues to do damage to their marriage.

When you look at this couple's attempts to resolve a common issue, it is easy to see how they first created this patterned interaction, which then became the problem, making the original issue very difficult to resolve. This interaction is fueled in turn by their beliefs, and in time their beliefs reinforce each other. Their beliefs form a type of circular interaction, in which each person ends up "proving" the beliefs about the other. After several arguments, Debra believes even more deeply that Wally will never pay attention to her, and Wally believes that Debra really does want to control him. Rather than challenge their belief systems, their predictable interaction confirms them, and in the end it produces stronger, more intense arguments, where their beliefs about each other become even more powerful.

Each Partner's Belief System Reinforces the Other's

The problem with belief systems is that rather than disprove each other, they wind up reinforcing each other. Debra and Wally illustrated this all too well. As stated earlier in the discussion of communication patterns, the more you work at changing communication, the more it seems to stay the same. Old patterns die hard. Similarly, we find that the longer this pattern continues, the more firmly each person believes in his/her belief system. How does this happen? We struggle with all of our energy to help our partner see us the way we want to be seen. Yet the harder we try, the more their view of us remains the same. How do couples who sincerely want to solve their problems wind up making them worse?

It is clear that the problem lies in the circular process that involves both belief systems and communication. Our beliefs reinforce the other's beliefs, so that each partner becomes even more convinced of the validity of his or her beliefs. What is clear from observing Debra and Wally is that in their marriage there are two sets of belief systems interacting, and the way in which they communicate serves only to "prove" those two separate sets of beliefs.

Beliefs Distort Communication

Remember Tom and Ann in chapter 4? They were the couple who had the "simple discussion" about their checkbook. We discussed the powerful belief systems that distorted the couple's communication in that interaction.

Let's look again at their "simple interaction."

Tom: Where's the checkbook?

Ann: Why are you always blaming me for everything? You are so unfair.

Tom: What is your problem? I just asked a simple question.

Now think about all the possibilities in that brief interaction. It turns out to be not so simple after all. There are numerous interpretations that can emerge from the discussion. Think first about Ann's interpretation. She was responding to a number of cues. She might have interpreted Tom's tone as blaming, or his scowl as angry, or heard blame in his question, or they may have had a long-standing continuous argument about the checkbook. Her response to Tom's question is of course fueled by her interpretation of what the question means. But her interpretation in turn may be part of her larger belief about Tom. If she believes he is basically controlling, or blaming and then hears a controlling tone, or sees a particular look, her interpretation will lock in. She will then respond based on her interpretation, which means she will respond angrily and with much irritation. If, in addition, she holds certain gender-based beliefs, she may believe that all men are controlling and blaming, and that they always expect women to know where everything is. This belief will deepen her resentment.

Ann, however, is not the only one who holds a belief system in this "simple interaction." Tom also has beliefs about Ann. He may believe her to be unorganized, or very sensitive, or too easily provoked. So, because he is most likely unaware of his tone, or of how his question comes across, he will be surprised by Ann's angry response. This in turn is filtered through his beliefs about her, and he will respond accordingly. He will treat Ann as if there were no grounds for her response at all, and he will become agitated and blaming; the very emotions that Ann felt in the beginning of their interaction. As with Ann, Tom may be operating on the basis of several beliefs of which he is unaware. First, he holds a set of beliefs about his partner as summarized. Second, he, too, may have some gender-based beliefs and conclude that Ann, like all the women in his experience, are overly sensitive and too easily hurt. These beliefs will influence how he responds to Ann.

Do you see how both partners successfully strengthened their partner's beliefs systems? Both are trapped by their interaction and by the belief systems that support it.

The "simple question" triggered a powerful interaction, in which both the belief systems and the interactional pattern of this couple became more intense. What is less obvious is that the longer this discussion goes on, the greater the possibility that multiple belief systems will be triggered. If their dialogue were to continue, it would become even more intense because there are really two levels of communication going on: the *internal and external dialogues*. The internal dialogue is the one that takes place inside our heads that we rarely share directly with our partner. Watch how the internal and external dialogues play out in the next section.

Internal and External Dialogues

For many couples, there are always two levels of communication going on: the internal and external. What does this mean? Simply put, the external dialogue is the obvious verbal dialogue that each person hears. In Paul and Debra's case, the external dialogue is quite clear. What is neither clear, nor obvious, is that they are also engaged in an internal dialogue. Remember, the internal dialogue is the conversation that takes place internally, inside each person's head.

Think about it. It is likely that in some of your most intense arguments you may have called your partner some very choice words—silently—in your head, but you never uttered one word aloud. This kind of internal dialogue is going on constantly. It consists of all the thoughts you have about your partner or about the subject that you are not talking about. Let's go back to the "simple question" about the checkbook as a way of understanding how this internal dialogue works.

Automatic Beliefs and Internal Dialogues

Tom: Where's the checkbook?

Ann's automatic belief and internal dialogue: *"He's blaming me for not knowing where the checkbook is. I can tell from his tone that he is angry. Where does he get off being angry at me for not knowing where everything is?"*

Ann's internal dialogue then determines her voiced response:

Ann: Why are you always blaming me for everything? You are so unfair.

Notice that her voiced response makes perfect sense based on her belief system and her internal dialogue.

Tom's automatic belief and internal dialogue: *"Oh brother. Here we go again. Why does she have to make everything such a big deal? I'm so sick of her blowing everything up into such a big deal! She is so damn emotional!"*

As with Ann, Tom's internal dialogue determines his response.

Tom's response: "What is your problem? I just asked a simple question."

Ann's automatic belief and internal dialogue: *"This is unbelievable. First he blames me, and now he's angry at me for calling him on it. I can't ever express any feelings without him getting angry. I am not about to put up with this!"*

Ann's voiced response: "I don't believe it. First you blame me, and now you get angry at me. Just forget it. I might as well never share any feelings with you. You can't handle it. You are just like your father—always angry and blaming."

At this point, the conversation is out of control. Tom explodes, throws down his newspaper, and yells, "You're sick. You blow everything out of proportion. I hate talking to you because you get so damned intense and emotional. Sometimes I just can't stand being with you." And with that he stormed out of the house and slammed the door.

Obviously, if their "dialogue" had continued, even more harm would have been done. What is clear is that during their discussion of a "simple question" there were really two dialogues going on simultaneously: They both were involved in internal and external dialogues as well as in their verbal exchanges.

The more powerful dialogue is the internal one, because that determines the external communication. In other words, your interpretation and internal dialogue determine what you say (or shout) aloud. Furthermore, the interaction that follows will "prove" each partner's beliefs about the other to be true. This further strengthens each partner's beliefs about the other, thus making meaningful change even more difficult to achieve.

Your Internal Dialogue and Your Beliefs About Your Spouse

We constantly form beliefs about our spouse, and all too often, our interactions and arguments wind up confirming our beliefs. By the end of their quarrel, Ann is absolutely convinced that her belief about Tom is accurate. She is convinced that he is angry, blaming, and impossible to talk to. After Tom storms out, her internal dialogue continues: *"This is ridiculous. I'm married to a hostile child, who blames me for everything. I guess I can never challenge him on anything because he will always blow up and storm out. I'm sick of living like this."*

Observe that her internal dialogue is all externally focused. She does *not* ask herself, *"I wonder if there was a better way to make my point so he would have been less defensive?"* Or, *"Is it possible that I misread his tone, or his intention?"* Because she does not ask those questions, her beliefs will grow stronger. Her internal dialogue helped to further strengthen her belief about her partner.

Tom also continued talking to himself while he drove his car faster than he should have. His internal dialogue went like this: *"I should have never married her. She is so intense and emotional. Everything has to be such a big deal. Give me a break, can't anything ever be simple. I can't keep living like this."*

Like Ann's, his dialogue is also externally focused. He does not ask himself, *"Did I sound blaming? Was my tone hostile? Why do I get so defensive so quickly when she challenges me?"* These are self-focus questions. Again, because he does not ask those questions his beliefs remain powerful.

Belief Systems and Couple Communication Principles

This "simple" couple interaction illustrates six principles:

1. **No communication is pure**. There are no simple questions or statements! All communication is filtered through belief systems. What you hear is determined by the filter through which you hear it. As we have said, that filter is influenced by beliefs about marriage, about gender, about your spouse, and about your self.

2. **Belief systems reinforce each other.** During intense couple communication each person is constantly listening through his/her own filter or set of beliefs. These interpretations and beliefs tend to reinforce each other and contribute to an even more intense interaction. The longer the argument continues, the more each partner is convinced of the validity of his or her position.

3. **Internal dialogues are as important as what is actually spoken.** As illustrated above, during actual conversations, the internal dialogues you have in your head, which are shaped by your belief systems, determine what you actually say aloud.

4. **As communication becomes more intense, more belief systems come into play**. This results in the creation of more intense internal dialogues. Notice in Ann and Tom's interaction how many more internal negative belief systems were triggered by their ongoing argument.

5. **At the end of an argument, we usually wind up proving our partner's beliefs about us to be right, and vice versa.** Both Tom and Ann at the end of their argument are more convinced than ever of the truth of their belief systems. Both would claim that the interaction with their partner confirms what they believe.

6. **Focus tends to be external rather than internal.** In these types of interactions, we focus mainly on our partners and on all of the things that they are doing wrong. We focus very little on what we might have contributed to the interaction. Rarely do we ask, "What have I contributed to this interaction?"

Steps to Change

Given the principles outlined above, how can you begin to change?

Step 1

The first step toward change is to accept the fact that *there is no objective reality, and therefore everything is a matter of interpretation*. Until this fact is accepted, no change is possible. Usually neither party is absolutely right or wrong. If the point of an argument is to find out who is right and who is wrong, then the argument will have no winners. Accept the fact that you are constantly interpreting what your partner really means.

Since everything is a matter of interpretation, give up trying to discover who is right and who is wrong. Rather, begin to look at your own interpretations and belief systems, and try to understand those of your partner.

Step 2

The second step toward change is to *begin to listen to your interpretations and belief systems*. This means beginning to tune into your internal dialogue and beliefs and asking yourself whether they are really "true." Remember the errors of thinking discussed in the last chapter. It is easy to form black-and-white views of your spouse. When you hear yourself saying things like, "S/he always...," or "s/he never...," or "You did that just to hurt me...," then it is time to begin to challenge the "truth" of your beliefs. These types of beliefs must be challenged, because matters are rarely "always" or "never." Look for a more middle ground.

Does your spouse "always" forget, or "never" try to meet your needs? Probably not. On a scale of 1 to 10, rate how often these irritants really happen. And when they do happen, are they really intentional? Too often, we believe that our partner is intentionally doing things to hurt or irritate us.

As you think about this, remember to listen to your internal dialogue. What are you saying inwardly about your partner? Think for a moment. When things become tense in your relationship, how do you view your spouse? Try and describe how your internal dialogue goes. In the space provided below, list some of your beliefs about your spouse that trigger a negative internal dialogue.

_____

_____

_____

_____

Now, try to challenge what you just wrote and come up with a more realistic assessment of your partner after challenging some of your beliefs and errors in thinking.

_____

_____

_____

_____

Step 3

The third step toward change follows logically. *Take responsibility for how your beliefs about your partner can distort your communications*. In other words, *focus on yourself*. Focus on what you believe about your partner, and the way your belief might be distorting communication. Take responsibility for your own beliefs, interpretations, and errors in thinking.

If you really believe that your partner is controlling, or overly emotional, or blaming, you will then always look at him or her through that lens. List some of the ways in which your beliefs about your partner influence the way you communicate. In other words, how do you speak to your spouse because of your belief systems?

_____

_____

_____

If you believe that your partner is not going to change, and is set in his/her ways, then your own beliefs become more rigid at the same time. If you believe that your partner is controlling, or emotional, or blaming, you will then always look through that lens. Now, try and challenge that lens. *The problem may not be your partner, but your view of your partner.*

It is easy to slip back into all-or-nothing thinking, and to accept an overly rigid view of your partner as true. Often, that rigid picture is not only inaccurate, it is also capable of creating more problems. It is important to begin challenging those pictures and replacing them with more realistic ones.

In the space below, try to change the picture you have of your partner. Try to challenge the negative picture by describing your spouse differently without using all-or-nothing thinking. If you have difficulty doing this, try to remember what attracted you to your partner when you first met. Now, in the space below, try to describe your partner differently.

_____

_____

_____

If that new picture were true, how would your style of communication change? What would be different? Would you be more open with your feelings? Would you be kinder and more helpful? Would you be more willing to have "emotional" discussions? Try and describe how you would communicate differently if your picture of your partner changed.

_____

_____

_____

Step 4

Recognize that your partner also has strong beliefs about you. Try and understand what those beliefs are. Just as you tend to see your partner through your own belief systems, so too your partner sees you through his or her own beliefs. Too often, rather than try to understand this, it is easier to get defensive and argumentative.

To go back to the checkbook argument, when Tom was accused of blaming Ann for losing the checkbook, his immediate response was to get defensive and then to counterattack. This is a natural response, but it simply inflames the situation, and, of course, it does little to change

Ann's belief system. If Tom could better control his defensive reaction, he might be able to ask Ann what he is doing that makes her think he is blaming her. In other words, he would try to *better understand her belief system about him.*

This is a critical step toward change. Rather than argue about whether or not he was "really blaming Ann" he would get much further if he would try to understand her subjective reaction to his question. In other words, if he would stay nonreactive and try to understand Ann's belief system, the escalating argument would soften and slow down. This is, of course, very hard work. It demands the ability to rein in your reactivity and defensiveness and work at understanding your partner's belief system. We will discuss slowing down reactivity and defensiveness in more detail in chapters 7 and 8.

Step 5

A final step toward change is to *understand that every issue is made more complicated by multiple belief systems.* We constantly make interpretations on the basis of our strong beliefs. As a result, every issue can become much more complicated. Not only do we have beliefs about gender, marriage, our partner, and ourselves, we also hold strong beliefs about a number of important issues that marriage inevitably entails. These issues include sex, money, parenting, in-laws, recreation, and conflict, for starters.

To create real change we must consider what our beliefs are about these major issues. Obviously, these are areas that have the potential to create conflict. What is not so obvious is that for each of these major areas we have beliefs not only about the particular issue, but beliefs about our partner in that area. In other words, *for every issue in your marriage you hold beliefs about that particular issue and you hold beliefs about your partner's relation to that issue.* As a result, intense conflict can arise in these areas.

Consider the issue of money. You may believe that money should be saved for future emergencies and never spent frivolously. You may also believe that your partner wants to spend money impulsively rather than save it. These two beliefs will provide powerful fuel for reactive arguments about money.

Rather than trying to explain your beliefs and trying to better understand your partner's beliefs, reactively you may try to control your partner's spending, which will inevitably cause even more powerful conflicts. It would be far better to explain the reason for your beliefs and to ask your partner to explain his/her beliefs. From there, the two of you could then explore grounds for compromise. (See chapter 9 for specific steps on how to do this.)

Putting Change into Practice

These steps toward change are not easy to put into practice. They require self-focus and self-awareness. Real change requires that you better understand your own belief systems and errors in thinking, and how they distort the way you communicate with your partner. Real change requires you to rein in your own reactivity and defensiveness and move toward better understanding of your partner's belief system about you. Finally, it means understanding that any marital issue causing problems in your relationship is fueled by a number of belief systems that the two of you hold.

When you read the following account of a couple struggling with their sexual relationship, look for the ways their belief systems, their views of each other, and their internal dialogues worsen their situation.

From the Checkbook to the Bedroom

Remember Tom and Ann and their argument over the checkbook? Picture them later that night going to bed still feeling somewhat tense. Their argument was over, but both were left feeling discouraged about their marriage and distant from each other.

Tom tossed and turned throughout the night intensely depressed about the state of his marriage. As he lay there, he said to himself, "If Ann really cared, she would initiate sex and break the tension between us. Why am I always the one to initiate sex? After being together this long, she should know what I want." These thoughts left Tom more and more irritated and discouraged. Notice that this was a completely internal dialogue.

He made no attempt to talk to Ann about feeling discouraged, even to indicate that he would like sex. He kept all of his thoughts to himself. After not sleeping well for a while, he woke up and tried to initiate sex with Ann. Ann responded with a few words. She said that she wasn't "in the mood." When Tom tried to initiate sex, Ann thought to herself, "This figures. He thinks we can make love without talking, and then everything will be fine. He never tries to talk anything out. He should know by now that I can't make love when things are tense and unresolved between us."

Unfortunately both of their dialogues remained internal, and their beliefs about each other became even more negative. They made no efforts to talk about what they were thinking. As a result, their day started off with both feeling tense, irritable, and misunderstood.

What Tom and Ann illustrate only too well is that your beliefs about your partner in relation to sex can move you into deeper trouble in the context of your overall relationship. Although gender-based beliefs and beliefs about sex itself are very important, as we will see in chapter 11, it is our beliefs about each other that do the most damage.

In our work, we hear a number of beliefs that couples have about each other in terms of their sexual relationship. The following lines are some of the beliefs we hear most frequently:

- "He always thinks that sex fixes everything."

- "She is never creative sexually."

- "He always thinks only of his sexual needs and never cares about mine."

- "She always needs to talk and talk and talk before we make love."

- "He thinks I should just be able to drop everything and make love on the spot."

- "She knows what I want but will never give it to me. "

As you read some of those beliefs, no doubt some seemed familiar. You may have said some of those lines to yourself in your own internal dialogue. Notice, however, the errors in thinking that are present. Many of these statements represent all-or-nothing thinking. Many use the words "always" and "never." None of these statements contributes anything to a deeper dialogue and understanding. They simply lead to increased polarization and deeper misunderstanding.

Obviously, as such beliefs about sex and about our partner's sexuality deepen the misunderstandings between us, they also make healthy sexual relating even more difficult. Furthermore, these beliefs create more and more emotional distance. Over time, couples begin to believe that their partners are *intentionally* not giving them what is desired, and are *intentionally* hurting them. Once you start thinking that your partner is intentionally trying to hurt you, you will become angrier and angrier.

Tom and Ann's Initial Steps to Change

To begin to make changes in their marriage, Tom and Ann would need to struggle with the steps toward change outlined above. For starters, each would have to relinquish their need to be "right" and for their partner to be "wrong." They would also have to accept the fact that there is no objective reality in their arguments. They both need to accept the fact that they each make interpretations about the other.

Change might begin with one or the other questioning whether their interpretation is on target, and looking for alternate ways of understanding their partner. Tom, for example, rather than thinking that Ann refused to initiate sex, might have thought, "I know Ann can't initiate sex when things are tense and unresolved between us. Although it would be great to have sex, I know that we have to talk first about our fight about the checkbook, and make sure the tension is resolved." If Tom were able to reinterpret Ann's sexual distance as her need for emotional closure, he would not feel so distant and angry. In reality, his interpretation was what made him feel so angry. The more he interprets Ann's behavior as intentional withholding the angrier he will become.

The next morning, Ann could have interpreted Tom's attempt to initiate sex differently. Rather than assuming that Tom tries to fix everything with sex, she could have tried to stay nonreactive, and come up with an alternative interpretation. For example, if she believed that Tom really wanted to close the distance between them, she could have said, "Tom, I really want to feel close to you. But I can't make love right now, because I'm still feeling distant. But I really want to feel close to you again. Let's try to talk more about what went wrong between us, so we can feel close again."

Change would involve not just learning to understand the way they make interpretations, but also would require them to shift their belief systems, and then respond to each other on that new basis. Obviously, that would take a lot of work.

Taking Change Further

The changes discussed above would be an excellent start to help Ann and Tom change their fundamental beliefs about each other. To create even deeper change would take even more work, and would require them to understand their internal dialogues about sex.

For any couple, sexual relating can become intensely complex since it involves not only sexual behavior but also both partners' beliefs about sex, and about each other. Although most people may want sex to be spontaneous, the reality is most of us do too much thinking before, during, and after sex. As a rule, so much thought hinders spontaneity! This was certainly the case with Ann and Tom.

The following section describes the internal dialogues Ann and Tom have with themselves before having sex, during sex, and after sex. Watch how both of their different belief systems are triggered.

Tom and Ann's Internal Dialogues Before Sex

Two days after the checkbook incident, Ann and Tom went to a favorite restaurant for a relaxing dinner. During dinner, Ann began to think, *"I know he will want to have sex when we get home. I hope I can relax and get work off my mind. We haven't been that close lately, and good sex would help close the distance between us. I know how important that is for Tom."* Meanwhile, Tom was thinking about how much he was enjoying Ann's company and he was feeling relieved that they are feeling closer again. He began to fantasize about the wild sex he hoped they would have later. At the same time, he began to remember that the checkbook argument had not been totally resolved, and he hoped that Ann was not holding that against him. He began to feel slightly tense, but said nothing. They continued to talk as they enjoyed their dinner, without either of them acknowledging their internal dialogue.

The stage was set. At this point, both of them could have talked a bit more openly about their internalized thoughts, which would have diminished the tension growing between them. But they didn't.

Tom and Ann's Internal Dialogues During Sex

As they drove home from the restaurant, Tom put his arm around Ann. "*There he goes,*" thought Ann, still feeling fairly relaxed. When they got into the house, Tom began to kiss Ann. "*Not so fast,*" she thought to herself. But she didn't say that to Tom. Ann tried hard to relax but she was thinking, "*I wish we could have a glass of wine and talk some more before rushing to the bedroom. Why can't he just hold me for a while without heading straight for sex. He's always in such a hurry.*" Tom began to feel the tension in Ann's body. He thought, "*Now what's the problem? Why can't she feel the same excitement that I feel? Why does she seem so tense?*" He continued trying to arouse Ann while beginning to feel more frustrated. "*What's wrong with me?*" he thought. "*Why can't I turn her on?*" At the same time, Ann was trying harder and harder to relax and to feel amorous, but what she really wanted was more talk and more genuine relaxation. As a result, she became even more tense.

They finally made love. Not surprisingly, it was a somewhat frustrating experience for both of them.

Tom and Ann's Internal Dialogues After Sex

After their lovemaking was over, Tom still felt frustrated and tense. He thought, "*Why does something that should be so much fun, seem so much like work? It feels like she can't ever relax and let go sexually.*" Ann, too, was feeling unhappy. She thought, "*I still feel a million miles away from him. I know he is frustrated with me and wants me to be more spontaneous. If he would just understand that I need to feel close in other ways before having sex. He doesn't understand that if he could be more affectionate when we are not sexual, and talk more about his feelings, things would be better sexually.*"

Of course you know how these inner dialogues ended. Both Ann and Tom finally fell asleep without saying a word about what they were really feeling, and as a result of their silence, when they did fall asleep, it was without feeling in the least bit loved or loving.

Further Steps Toward Change

Taking this theoretical discussion of how to change to a deeper level, Tom and Ann will have to find a way to talk to each other about their internal dialogues. To do that, both will have to challenge some of their beliefs about the other. Ann needs to talk about the pressure she feels coming from Tom and explain to him what she needs. Specifically, she needs to tell him to slow things down, and make sure things are resolved between them before trying to have sex. She needs to talk about the things she thinks about during her internal dialogues. She needs to find a nonreactive way to share those thoughts with Tom.

Ann could do this by taking responsibility for what she feels. By accepting the truth of her feelings and not blaming or attacking Tom she could share more of what she thinks, and feels, and needs. To do this would require her to discuss these matters calmly. And to do that, she would need to rein in her own reactivity and defensiveness. At the same time, she needs to try to better understand what Tom's beliefs are and what he is feeling.

Tom, in a similar way, needs to retain his reactivity and defensiveness and to talk more about his needs. He needs to be clear about his beliefs about sexuality and, if necessary, to challenge them. He needs find out from Ann what her beliefs about him are, and what she needs sexually. Finally, he may need to change his sexual behavior. He probably needs to slow things down, spend some more time in conversation and more time with foreplay to help Ann relax.

Both Tom and Ann need to understand the contents of all of their inner sexual dialogues about sex. They would be much better served by talking to each other out loud during each of the sexual stages rather than keeping it all locked up internally.

Changes in Your Relationship

What is true about sex is just as true for the other problematic issues within a marriage. Each of these problem issues can create strong belief systems and internal dialogues. Think about the key problem areas of marriage. Money, sex, parenting, in-laws, roles, intimacy vs. distance, common interests, etc. Each of these issues is a source of potential conflict and struggle. Fortunately for most couples, not all of these areas are problems. But those areas that are problems represent a number of belief systems that, in turn, take on a life of their own and grow into never-ending conflicts. Any one of these problem areas can trigger powerful arguments with equally powerful belief systems.

Take the issue of money. To be successful, every couple needs some agreed-upon way to handle money. This might include writing a budget, having a savings plan, figuring out who pays the bills, and who balances the checkbook. Should there be one checkbook or should each partner have separate checkbooks? At first glance, this would seem rather simple. Couples should simply talk about these issues and make their decisions accordingly. Yet, as we all know, life is not that simple. The reality is that a discussion about money (or any of the other problem areas) can trigger a set of interlocking belief systems. For example, talking about money can trigger the following belief systems:

- **Beliefs About money**: The meaning of money in an overall life plan; consuming vs. savings: what do we agree we should spend money on?

- **Beliefs About Marriage**: In marriage all money should be shared in one joint account; we should agree on all purchases; it is the man (or woman's) role to pay the bills.

- **Beliefs About Gender**: Women/men tend to overspend; are cheap.

- **Beliefs About Partner**: If I am not careful, he'll spend too much. She is so cheap, she will save every penny. He just wants to be in control financially.

These beliefs, of course, create powerful internal dialogues that then create external dialogues, which take on lives of their own.

To change means that you must become more conscious of the ways in which you interpret events, and the ways your interpretations lead to internal dialogues that you often withhold from your partner.

To change means taking the risk of becoming vulnerable about your internal dialogues, as well as your interpretations, and actually sharing the content of those dialogues and interpretations with your partner. If you can begin to do those two tasks, it will certainly help you to change and will undoubtedly help your relationship.

Five Rules to Aid Change

1. There is no objective reality in marriage. Everything is a matter of interpretation.

2. Take responsibility for your belief systems.

3. Understand how your beliefs distort communication.

4. Remember your partner also has beliefs, and your beliefs and your partner's beliefs can end up reinforcing each other.

5. Finally, remember to reveal your internal dialogues to your partner.

CHAPTER SIX

I Swear There Are More People Here Than Just the Two of Us

How many times did you say while you were growing up, "I will never have a marriage like my parents?" Or did you firmly vow, "I will never marry anyone like my father. . . ." Yet far too often, as adults, we replicate old, familiar patterns and wind up marrying someone who strangely resembles a parent in mannerisms, ways of relating, and perhaps even in appearance. This all happens despite our sincere intention to create a very different type of marriage.

Regardless of where and with whom you grew up, you are likely to hold deeply rooted beliefs as the result of your childhood experiences in your family of origin. And, if you grew up in a dysfunctional family, you may have developed very powerful, toxic beliefs. Unfortunately, most of us are frequently unaware of the power of these beliefs. We seldom even know what they are. Nonetheless, they can have enormous power in our lives. The fact is that such beliefs directly affect both how you view and relate to your partner, as well as how you view yourself within your marriage.

Childhood Beliefs About Marriage

Often, we're unaware of just how much our childhood beliefs affect the things we say and do. Yet these beliefs have a great influence on many aspects of marriage. Simple things, such as the manner in which you greet your partner after each of you returns home from work, may be laden with beliefs that you absorbed watching your parents greet each other at the end of the workday. You may find yourself greeting your partner in the very same way that your parents did.

Many of the beliefs that were formed in childhood have great influence over our views of how marriage should work. Here are some examples: "Discussing finances leads to fighting." "Only positive emotions should be expressed. If you are feeling negative, keep it to yourself." "Men should make all the important decisions." "Breaking things in anger is okay." "Trusting people leads only to getting hurt." "If I trust a woman she will leave me." "If I let my guard down, I'll get hurt." These are a tiny sample of the types of beliefs that we absorb from our family-of-origin experiences as children. The list could go on for pages and pages.

Your childhood beliefs become a filter through which you see the world, your spouse, and your marriage. This filter has the power to distort what you see in current relationships and especially how you view your spouse. These beliefs can easily lead to seeing your partner in negative or critical ways. For example, if you believe that men should make all important decisions, and your wife wants to share in the decision-making process, you may become anxious or irritated. If you believe that a good marriage means no conflict, and your spouse becomes angry with you, you may see your partner as unloving.

We absorb these childhood beliefs as we grow up by watching others: by listening to how family members speak to one another, and watching how they touch or do not touch each other, as well as by indirect messages that we may discern around the home. For example, an indirect message, based on a family belief, is sent to children when dinner is over and the father leaves the table without thanking his wife for making the meal and without clearing his own dishes. The message is that the wife and mother has done what is expected by both parents, and her work doesn't require a thank-you. (She doesn't protest out of fear or out of resignation.) From that subtle, nonverbal message a child might grow up believing that partners don't need to thank each other, nor should they expect gratitude. It also tells the child about gender roles and home duties.

Are you aware of all these beliefs when you are dating? Of course not. When you choose your future partner, often you are not mindful of anything but your fantasies of how great your marriage will be, or how it will differ from that of your parents. Most couples are convinced that their love for each other is enough to weather the ups and downs of marriage, and they are, for the most part, oblivious to the beliefs they bring into the marriage with them.

But after you are married, have you ever felt the uncanny sense that there are more than just the two of you in your marriage? Does it ever feel as if your words and actions have a familiar ring to them? Do you ever find yourself saying lines that you know you learned from one of your parents? Hitchcock's movies are nothing compared to the emotional horror you may experience when you find that you have chosen not only one person and his/her family influences . . . but you also married a facsimile of one of your own parents! This is not an uncommon experience. Therefore, it is important to understand how your childhood beliefs have drawn a type of internal relational map that guides you in your marital experiences, for better or worse.

Your Internal Relational Map

Murray Bowen and his followers found that we all formulate our identities and core beliefs based on the teachings of our families, whether biological or adoptive. In books like *Family Evaluation* (1988), Bowen and his followers stressed the importance of the emotional environment within the family. This environment helps us to create an "internal relationship map" that guides us in marriage. This map contains our beliefs about marriage, conflict, closeness, gender, marital roles, money management, and so forth. In effect the map is a template that provides you with a familiar pattern to use in your own marriage and family life. Often this internal map is never questioned, let alone understood. When the map is buried and not understood, it can leaves you frustrated and confused about why your marriage is not working the way you believe it should.

Part of understanding yourself and your partner is to begin to look at what your families taught you both about the key issues in marriage, as a way to understand your internal relational maps. There are many possibilities.

Historical factors in a family's life such as the traumas of divorce, the early death of a parent, and domestic violence are acute issues that will color a growing child's perspective about marriage. These traumas certainly will have an impact on the child's relational map. When that child becomes an adult and is considering marriage, he or she will have serious emotional reservations about the lasting and/or safe nature of marriage.

In the same way, a woman whose mother was left by her father for another woman will have serious questions about the trustworthiness of men in marriage, as well as potential guilt that she may be more successful in marriage than her mother was. These are deep issues that certainly can affect a person's internal relationship map for marriage. But there are many less dramatic examples of beliefs formed in childhood that can nonetheless disrupt a marriage. Don and Donna's marriage provides a good illustration of this.

Don and Donna

Donna was hurt and withdrawn because Don did not make a big fuss over her birthday. He bought her a gift and a card. However, in her family of origin, birthdays were a huge weekend event, with parties, lots of presents, and many people involved. In Don's family, birthdays were never a big deal. He was accustomed to receiving one gift and a thoughtful card, but these were placed on his bed during the day when he was not home, with no other recognition or fanfare. Birthday cake was optional and never really expected, even when he was a young boy.

Donna and Don were both operating in terms of their "families' different relational maps." So each person had different expectations for the same event and, as a result, frustration and hurt emerged, since they had never compared their expectations about birthdays, or any other matters they would find on their relational maps.

Your internal relational map contains within it your beliefs about how people should operate in many aspects of their marital relationships. The map guides you in dealing with issues such as balancing separateness and togetherness, closeness and distance, toxic topics, multigenerational patterns, as well as specific marital roles.

Separateness and Togetherness

Any successful couple must find a way to successfully balance separateness and togetherness in their life together. This is easier said than done. The more successful a young person is in achieving a graceful emotional separation from his/her family of origin, the more successful that young person will be in forming a healthy marriage that balances separateness and togetherness. This is because she or he will have met the conditions necessary for developing autonomy, yet will still be capable of giving and receiving in an intimate relationship.

However, when the developmental markers of childhood and youth (e.g., self-esteem, independent, and responsible behavior) have not been fully met, there is either an overreliance on the family of origin to act as the emotional shelter from the challenges of adult life, or an environment against which the person continually rebels. In these cases, separation from the family of origin is not easy.

The ability to be separate is an important quality for an individual to have in an intimate relationship. In Khalil Gibran's classic book of poetry, *The Prophet*, the two people in a marriage are compared to the separate strings of a lute as a symbolic reminder that for there to be a meaningful togetherness, there must be two separate beings seeking meaningful connection. Our clinical practice has shown us that the more we were allowed to be individuals within our families of origin, the greater the likelihood that we will seek a partner who can encourage both our need to be separate and our healthy need to be intimate.

How Did You Establish Your Separateness?

When we are ready to leave home, regardless of our age, our leave-taking is often part of a larger "script" that was written before our time. Think about the members of prior generations in your family of origin. How did they leave home? How did they break away? Did they join the military to get away from home before starting a family of their own? Did they go to college, graduate, and rent their own apartments after graduation? Or maybe they had to get married first before they could leave home?

Then there are adult children who relocate to take a job 3000 miles away, their first time out of their hometown. Some young women become pregnant and their parents help out both of the young parents by allowing them to live together in one of their family-of-origin's homes until the baby is born. Sometimes, grandparents continue to do daily infant care while young single mothers finish school or work. Some young people move into apartments with other young people and start professional jobs, vowing to their parents that "I'll never become a mother!" (or "father" as the case may be). These are simply a sample of the many scenarios available for leaving home and breaking away from your family of origin. There are many other possibilities. Separating from our parent(s) is different in every family.

Men and women may even have different expectations as to how their family will accept their effort to leave and be on their own. Young adults who leave home abruptly, embroiled in conflict, and who move miles away, and stay out of touch actually do not leave home emotionally. They may be so stuck that, while they deny having any feelings for their family, they can pursue an attachment with another young adult with great energy. They may actually seek out someone who left home very differently, like someone who moved just across the corner from Mom and Dad, thereby marrying into another family system that may have its own separation problems.

Sometimes we may choose someone because their family *appears* to be warmer and more loving than our own. When that happens, it may mean that we have some unconscious expectations of marriage and what it will provide for us. One common hope among newlyweds is that their new in-laws will become substitute parents who will finally love and accept them unconditionally, unlike their families of origin.

The ways in which we separate from our families of origin, as well as the ways in which our families model the balancing of separateness and togetherness, provide not only internal relational maps, they shape our interactions as well. They may cause us to pursue more emotional connections, or to distance ourselves emotionally, as a way to avoid closeness. Or they may cause us to look to our in-laws for the kind of emotional sustenance that we didn't receive at home.

Martha and Mitch

Martha came from a family of three daughters, raised by an alcoholic mother who worked long hours on the second shift at a local factory. As she was the youngest daughter, she never knew her father as he left the family when Martha was eleven months old. She was raised primarily by her maternal grandmother who lived in her mother's household. Martha married Mitch when they both graduated from high school at the age of eighteen.

Mitch came from a very different family in the same town, one notable for its extended family gatherings at holiday time, and for the longevity of Mitch's parents' marriage. Mitch's mother was the central figure in his family of all boys. Martha was welcomed into the family after their marriage, without question. To her, her new family felt as though she had found the mother she had longed for, and the family where she belonged.

However, as the years progressed, Martha soured with the realization she did not yet feel the specialness in Mitch's family that she had always lacked in her own. She lived within the closeness of a tight family system, yet she still felt emotionally empty inside.

Mitch could not understand what her problem was and why she seemed withdrawn and sullen at family gatherings. She was unable to describe what was affecting her, especially as their own youngest child, a daughter, had just turned two years old. Martha's family map was clearly having an impact on her, while Mitch's map gave him no clue as to what was missing in Martha's life. He couldn't tell that her feelings of not being loved and special in her own family were part of her internal relational map. And his family's warmth and friendliness wasn't the answer.

Martha's difficulty with separateness, as well as her early losses, affected her ability to separate emotionally from her family of origin. She married Mitch and joined his family in search of an emotional bond to compensate for what she had lost early in her life. But she had not resolved her childhood pain well enough to separate in a healthy fashion from it. She then sought closeness with Mitch's family, but her needs for closeness were excessive, and their ordinary day-to-day affection wasn't enough for her, which left Mitch frustrated and feeling the need to defend his family.

Family Myths

Internal relational maps not only guide us in negotiating separateness and togetherness issues, they also provide many of the myths and beliefs we have about how to be a family. Everyone's family has myths (or half-truths and legends) about marriage and close relationships. For example, in some families, a good marriage means there is never any fighting, or everyone shares the same interests. Here are some other examples of myths in families: "Adult children should always phone their parents at least weekly to stay in touch." (Just consider how this might cause conflict between you and your partner if your phone bill is sky high.) Or, "Men should be the breadwinners," or "Every Sunday we have dinner together as a family."

Now, think about what you learned from your own family of origin. Take the time to write down some your family myths that quickly come to mind.

My Family Myths About Relationships

1. _____

_____

_____

2. _____

_____

_____

3. _____

_____

_____

Over time, many of your family myths should be outgrown and challenged so that you and your partner can begin to create new possibilities and new belief systems. As you mature and develop greater emotional separateness from your family of origin, there is a healthy need to replace outdated family myths with lessons created from your own experience. Over time, you and your partner need to carefully redesign your own beliefs about what constitutes a good marriage so as not to be held captive to beliefs you both inherited from your families of origin, beliefs that you may have outgrown.

Pursuit/Distance

We have discussed the family-of-origin influences you carry into your marriage. We have also discussed how your ability to separate emotionally from your family of origin, while still staying connected to them, has a direct bearing on your internal relationship map. The more you have been able to separate emotionally and be your own person, but still stay connected, the easier it will be for you to balance closeness and distance in your own marriage.

On the one hand, if you grew up in a family that made it difficult for you to be your own person and to have your own identity and values, the more difficult it may be to be yourself in your marriage. On the other hand, if you felt hurt or unloved in your family of origin, then you may become anxious that you will be hurt in similar ways in your marriage. In either situation, creating intimacy may be a problem for you in your marriage.

If you were not allowed to be your own person while you were growing up, that is, if your autonomy was not encouraged, then you will tend to distance yourself from your spouse if s/he gets too close to you, for fear of losing yourself and your individual identity. If you felt unloved while growing up, you might pursue your partner with more fervor to try to find the love that you missed in your childhood. In both cases, anxiety becomes the fuel that moves you either toward distancing or pursuing. Both are attempts to deal with old family-of-origin issues.

When anxious, people who equate too much closeness with the fear that their individuality will be engulfed will tend to create distance. They will worry that they cannot express different opinions or even hold different interests from their partner without feeling guilty or disloyal. In a similar way, those who are pursuers become anxious when they fear that they do not have enough closeness with their partner. Anxiety moves you either to pursue or to create distance, depending on the family-of-origin issues you bring with you.

Anxiety Is a Part of Life

When you become anxious, you are more likely to engage in one of the interactional styles described in detail in chapter 3. Anxiety can motivate you to pursue or move away. It can cause you to overfunction, or to avoid conflict. It can fuel intense discussions. But in all of these scenarios, the family-of-origin relational map is the key influence on your beliefs about pursuit and distance in your current relationship. It is important to recognize these historical roots of your pattern of pursuit or of distance.

Keep in mind that if you chose someone who is your opposite in interaction style, that was no coincidence. In fact, your partner's style may be somewhat reminiscent of the style your parents had, especially the parent you might have had the most difficulty with over the years. Marriage can be a way of continuing our family life all over again!

Take some time to review your own family history. Which of your family members tended to pursue? Which family members tended to create distance? Was there a gender pattern involved? What beliefs about closeness did your family communicate to you? How did your parents deal with the growing autonomy of their children? Spend some time thinking about how this complicated issue of pursuit and distance was handled in your family. If you can't answer these questions right away, do some research. Ask your parents about these issues, or your siblings. Then, when your have arrived at some answers to these questions, write them down in the space provided below.

_____

_____

_____

_____

_____

Gender Issues

How you perceived the different roles that men and women played in your family—and in the world—when you were young has a major effect on the manner with which you function in your marriage today. Think back on the gender roles in your family as you were growing up. What were you taught about men and women's expected behaviors? Were the women the steady, functionally stronger members, especially in their marriages? Were men seen as those who made the major decisions such as where to live, what cars to purchase, how money was to be handled, and so forth? Which parent had the most power in your parents' marriage, and what did that teach you about gender roles? Who did you go to when you needed to make a decision about something important? Who did you seek out when you needed to talk about something troubling? Who were you closest to? The answers to all of these questions helped to form your beliefs about gender and gender roles.

Of all the parts that make up your internal relational map, the components of gender bias and gender expectations are a major influence on the role you play in your marriage. The question that must be asked, however, is this: Are you and your partner comfortable with your gender-determined roles and responsibilities? Do these roles fit your present circumstances? If not, what would you change in your beliefs and behaviors as a wife or husband? Too often, in unhappy marriages, the problem lies with old gender-based roles that no longer fit the circumstances of the couple's modern lifestyle, and need to be challenged and changed.

Family Roles

Every family finds a way to assign roles to its children. Some are gender-related and some are not. Roles like the "rebel," the "scapegoat," and "the good child" are all fairly common.

Overfunctioner/Underfunctioner

In some families the role of overfunctioner often falls on one child. If that was your role, as you know too well, old roles die hard. As you are now considering how you choose to act as a wife or husband, and are also thinking about how your beliefs were shaped by your family-of-origin messages about gender roles in marriage, try to consider whether you do more than 50 percent of the "work" in your relationship.

By "work" we do not mean the physical work of housework, parenting, or earning the family income. Work also includes taking responsibility for the emotional issues in marriage and the marriage's emotional health. Who makes sure you both spend time together? When there are problems, who raises the issues to discuss? Who functions as the emotional thermostat in the family, taking responsibility for everyone else's relationships?

When you think about your family you can probably remember that some adults were known for being hard workers. Others may have been known for being lazy. Often, one person was responsible for the emotional well-being of the family. Is this true in your marriage? Is one person responsible for everyone else's emotional health?

Sometimes spouses share jobs and roles equally. They may have worked out such a marital agreement to suit their needs. Other couples may have a more traditional division of labor and roles, with the woman attending to the home (inside) and the man attending to the larger world (outside). Either model can work well so long as it is the configuration that both partners want and have chosen intentionally. However, when one person ends up routinely doing more than the other partner, there is an imbalance that can lead to serious problems.

When there is such an imbalance in how responsibility is distributed, one partner is referred to as the "overfunctioner" (the one who carries more responsibility) and the other as the "underfunctioner" (the partner who does less). The tendency to be an overfunctioner or an underfunctioner often emerges from your family influences. For instance, if you were raised in a single-parent family, with your father either deceased or uninvolved, you may have been asked by your mother (especially if you were the oldest) to watch your younger siblings when your mother was working. Or perhaps you prepared meals when she was too tired after the day's work. By necessity, you may have been operating as a young adult before you reached your teens. In your family of origin, you overfunctioned for the benefit of the family. Unfortunately, you may be stuck in that role and, as a result, you may be having a difficult time in your present marital relationship.

For example, if you married a man who was the youngest of four siblings and the only son, even though he may be terrifically successful in his career, he may not assume much responsibility at home. In fact, he may act just as he did in his family of origin, with the expectation that the women in the family are *supposed* to take care of such matters as cooking the meals, cleaning the house, taking care of the children, etc. If this is the case, it will, of course, reinforce your role as the family overfunctioner.

The overfunctioner/underfunctioner division becomes a more serious issue if the underfunctioner is chronically ill, chronically underemployed, or addicted to drugs or alcohol. In such families, regardless of the cause for underfunctioning, it causes great distress and exhaustion for the overfunctioner. If there are also feelings of obligation or guilt that carry over from your family history, or from your partner's family, those feelings can significantly impair your efforts to change your role to become less of an overfunctioner.

Other Patterned Relational Types

We have noted that there are various other role patterned relational types in addition to *overfunctioner/underfunctioner*. Role behaviors are not defined by gender, but you may note that in your own family of origin many of the men or women tended to operate within predictable roles in their marriages. Other types we should look at briefly now are the *dominant/submissive* couple, the *fight/flight* couple, and the *pursuer/distancer* couple.

Dominant/submissive couples developed their patterns of interacting usually from the first day of their relationship. If you or your spouse came from a traditional family structure with the father deemed as the leader and decision-maker of the family, either of you may be comfortable with that pattern repeated in your marriage. When you both agree with, say, the husband as the decision-maker, and the wife as the sustenance provider for the family, deferring to the husband on decisions in a submissive manner, then there can be a sense of balance and compatibility to your marriage. Many couples are comfortable with this style as it is also supported by their church beliefs and practices. Others are at ease with it as the roles are clear and there is no pressure for the partners to negotiate needs or conflicts.

Fight/flight couples operate from a pattern of conflict engagement and deferment. You may be the partner who engages your spouse in a fight to settle a disagreement or anything else. You may have even learned from observing your parents or grandparents that fighting fairly is sometimes important for a major problem to be fully resolved. However, if your partner came from a family where quick exits from conflicts were the preferred pattern for coping with tense relationship dynamics, then you and your partner have a type of marriage that very likely frustrates you. The more you engage in conflict to reach a "healthy" agreement on an issue, the more your partner may seek a "healthy" solution by fleeing before someone is physically or emotionally hurt (as may have occurred in your partner's family).

Pursuer/distancer couples have a more common relational pattern that they learned from their family experiences. You may be either the pursuer or the distancer, but what motivates your behavior is your anxiety (about impending conflict, or about possible intimacy, and so forth), while the behaviors were learned from family observation over many years. Your pursuit may take the form of seeking out your spouse for a "meaningful, heart-to-heart discussion," or it may be in the form of critical comments to your spouse about his/her actions or statements. Your partner's distancing may take the form of changing the subject during a conflict, shifting attention to watching television during a discussion with you, calling or visiting a friend at a time of potential tension between the two of you, or engaging in a solitary activity (e.g., reading) to create distance from the tension and to calm himself/herself. Unlike the *flight* partner described in the paragraph above, the motivation for the distancer is to reduce inner anxiety rather than solely to avoid conflict. Anxiety can arise in either the pursuer or the distancer even when there is complete silence between the partners while in a room together.

In all of these couple relational types there are habitual behaviors. Roles are habitual and after the passage of a few years, they are rarely questioned in a marriage. Role patterns can be changed only by changing your behavior. Paying attention to your habitual behaviors and staying aware of your desire to change these behaviors is the first important step toward changing your role patterns.

Triangles and Anxiety

A triangle involves the inclusion of another person into a relationship that is already struggling with more anxiety than the relationship can handle. Any two-person relationship, be it a marriage or a parent-child relationship, may add a third person who then creates a relationship that one of the original pair can turn to for closeness. This lowers the anxiety factor for one of the partners, usually the one who is the distancer. Unstable, anxiety-ridden dyads are made "stable" by the addition of a third person.

For example, if you are feeling suffocated by your partner, and overwhelmed by your need for emotional closeness, you may be tempted to divert your attention toward a child, a friend, or an object (e.g., television). The example below may help to clarify this concept.

John and Julie

John and Julie had spent every day of the past week with each other. John had loved it. He wanted to share all his thoughts and dreams about their future life together. Julie, however, was feeling quite uncomfortable. She knew she cared deeply for John and she loved spending time with him. But she was beginning to resent how she was never allowed by John to be silent with him.

He talked to her continually and asked her so many questions. These questions were always followed by statements of how much he loved her. She was beginning to feel suffocated. But she could not bring herself to tell him how she was feeling and what changes she needed.

Julie wanted to unwind and get rid of the anxiety that had been building when she was with John. So she called an old friend, Helen, to get together for a visit. When Helen arrived to pick up Julie she was greeted by a very quiet, sulking John and a bubbly Julie. John asked Julie about where they were going, when she would return, and what they would be doing. He became terse with Julie, which only increased her desire to distance herself from him. Each partner responded from his/her family-of-origin map of behavior patterns when they experienced anxiety. Neither spoke of the real issue of their tension.

The fact is that John and Julie have not learned to deal with the anxiety in their relationship. Julie needs to learn to speak about her need for more space for herself within her marriage. John needs to learn to deal with his anxieties and fears if Julie takes more space for herself. Instead of dealing with the issues they need to, these deficits help them to divert the anxiety in their relationship to a third party, Helen, who is blamed by John and seen as a rescuer by Julie. The result, however, is a lessening of intimacy.

Triangles are a fact of life. Even when we strive to live emotionally healthy lives, triangles frequently occur as an outgrowth of our internal relational map from our family of origin's ways of handling anxiety. If you think about the many possibilities for relationship triangles in your life, then you know how difficult it is to stay out of them. You may form triangles with coworkers against a supervisor. A husband can form a triangle by becoming too involved with one of his friends. A wife can create a triangle by having an affair. Either can create a triangle in their relationship as a parent with one of their children. All of these triangles are, in the end, ways to handle anxiety.

Multigenerational Transmission of Anxiety

As you think back on the generations before you, it is easy to recognize the family members who were the "worriers," the ones who were constantly anxious. Among other things, they tended to be the family members who were always pursuing emotional closeness. They were often the relatives with whom you had conflicts, or the ones who you constantly "pushed away" emotionally. The result of this type of reaction for worriers is actually a passing on or transmission of anxiety. To "push away" a worrier is to react to that family member. Reacting means that one is defined by the anxiety passed on by the worrier, rather than by defining yourself by not reacting.

The transmission of anxiety from one generation to another can have a negative impact on a child's development. The child's emotional maturation can be delayed by such a pattern. A parent's anxiety can make it difficult for a child to break away and establish an independent sense of self, let alone find healthy ways to deal with anxiety. When a child is in an overly close relationship with one parent, that child's ability to sustain normal peer relationships can be adversely affected. In the same fashion, parents may be unable to work through their difficulties because of the overly close relationship one of them has with their child. The child may serve as an emotional friend to one parent, excluding the other parent from the normal involvement in parenting. Therefore, the normal growth processes for the child, the family, and the marriage are stunted indefinitely.

The hallmark of healthy family functioning is that all members, children and adults, are able to progress normally through the stages of their lives addressing the needed tasks and accomplishments. Children need to develop skills for relating with their peers and their siblings that will prepare them for adult life and the challenges of marriage (e.g., sharing and negotiating needs).

How Do You Handle Anxiety?

Think about the way anxiety was handled in your family. Who were the members who were most anxious? How did their anxiety affect you? What key triangles were you part of when growing up? Did either parent try to block you from being yourself? Take a few moments and summarize the ways in which anxiety was handled in your family. Think also about how you handle anxiety in your present relationship. Do you pursue, distance, overfunction, or avoid conflict?

_____

_____

_____

_____

_____

Automatic vs. Intentional Responses

Unless you are aware of the baggage you have brought from your family of origin, you may be acting on automatic, instead of intentionally choosing your responses. We bring many beliefs with us from our family of origin, including those about what makes a good marriage, about intimacy, about conflict, and certainly about gender roles. Furthermore we learned about intimacy and distance from watching family members. We learned a particular role in our families that we might still be playing in our current relationship. Finally, when we are anxious, we are even more likely to fall back on the models we learned from our families of origin.

Building awareness and understanding of these generational patterns can be helpful. As you begin to understand the relational map you brought into your marriage with you, you can begin to shift from automatic anxious functioning to more thoughtful, intentional functioning. You will be able to begin building a new, more relevant relationship map for your marriage.

Toxic Family Issues and Family Secrets

You must also learn to be alert to emotionally toxic issues. All families have issues that they would rather not talk about. These issues become family secrets, matters that are not to be discussed. Every family has them. When these issues involve unsettled emotional memories from your childhood years, they can be toxic.

Every painful aspect of a family's life, such as alcoholism, domestic violence, sexual abuse, or extramarital affairs, can turn into toxic issues, especially if the family rule is not to talk about them. As the result of not talking, these issues become even more toxic. Think about some of the toxic issues in your family of origin and how your family members handled them. Try to summarize what those issues were in the space below:

_____

_____

_____

_____

Sexual Abuse

Nowhere in any family history is there a more toxic issue than sexual abuse. These issues are rarely talked about or dealt with by family members. As a result they leave emotional scars in the children, which then make the children's marriages even more difficult when they grow up. Mary and Fred's story illustrates this problem.

Mary and Fred

Mary had recently been having nightmares caused by her memories of abuse during her childhood. She spoke to Fred about them. At first, Fred wanted to be supportive and he listened patiently with true caring. He understood how her childhood trauma was affecting her. He even understood that she could no longer be comfortable in her sexual relations with him. What he had the most difficulty with was that, although there had been no physical or sexual abuse in his own family, there had also been no example of how a husband can support his wife when she is dealing with highly emotional issues. His father had always been at work, leaving his mother to fend for herself when she had needed support.

Fred found himself not knowing how to support his wife emotionally, while his own needs for physical and emotional comfort were going unmet. He also felt guilty that he still wanted Mary to be attentive to his needs. He was tempted to stay later at work, just as his father had done. And like his father, he didn't know how to tell Mary what he needed from her, given the terrible troubles she was enduring. He felt trapped.

Mary, too, did not know how to deal with the flood of emotions and confusion she felt, as she tried to make sense of the abuse she had endured as a child. She was constantly anxious, and in her anxiety she pursued Fred for emotional support. At the same time, she felt guilty for not being able to be the wife to Fred that she truly wanted to be.

You can see how the complex issues of abuse in the family of origin can haunt a marriage's daily health. Fred and Mary each have very toxic issues and needs that are colliding. They need to work out how to share and understand each other's struggles. They also need to be aware of how their interactive pattern of pursuit-distance plays out as a result of Mary's history of abuse. It is very likely that they need the help of a trained marital therapist to sort out these complex issues.

Addiction

A family history of addiction (i.e., drugs, alcohol, sex, gambling) has a serious impact on how parents nurture and care for their children. Addiction brings chaos to a family, forcing at least one member of the family to overfunction so that the family can survive. Rarely are the needs of children adequately met in these families. Furthermore, the impact of these addictions can be passed on for many generations.

Too often the children of parents with addictions are thrust into the role of overfunctioners. They may have cultivated a detached view of life, as a way of surviving, and such defenses did help them to survive growing up. But their emotional needs have seldom been met, and, consequently, they find it difficult to be emotionally open and trusting in their marriages. The defenses that helped them to survive as children may be causing difficulties in their marriages. As adults, these individuals may struggle with old roles and ways of being.

What Are Your Wounds?

What are the secrets or toxic issues in your family? Was there addiction, abuse (physical or sexual), domestic violence, or mental illness? How were these issues handled? How did the toxic issues in your family affect you? The answers are not always obvious. If, for example, there was violence in your family, you may become conflict/avoidant in your marriage. If there was abandonment in your family, you may anxiously pursue your partner out of fear of another abandonment. If there was addiction in your family, you may have learned to overfunction to make up for an parent who was a substance abuser or an alcoholic. In general, it is important to know how the problems of your family have wounded you, and how those wounds influence your interaction style and belief systems. Those wounds may even influence what you expect from your partner.

Putting It Together

Before moving on, you may find it helpful to reread this chapter. Many of the belief systems described in chapters 4 and 5 took root in your family of origin. The matters discussed in this chapter about your family-of-origin influences may be unique to your family, but certainly they are also matters you may have thought about previously. It is important to recognize how you are a part of a much larger system of beliefs and relationship practices than you might have realized. You came into marriage with an internal relationship map. So, be sure to think about the following points when thinking about the state of your marriage:

- Each one of us carries a legacy of family values and experiences and beliefs that colors how we approach marriage and how we think a couple relationship should work.

- Each one of us has a conscious or subconscious sense of how much closeness or distance we prefer in a relationship that grows out of our experiences in our family of origin. This preference directly controls whether we pursue or create distance from our partner whenever we feel anxiety over an issue with him/her.

- If you have left home (emotionally and physically) with low reactivity and anxiety (no unresolved conflicts with your parents), then any future effort at a couple relationship has a greater potential to succeed.

- True separateness involves connection with others. We cannot be truly separate and experience low or no anxiety if we avoid contact with our parent(s) or our family of origin.

- Beware of family secrets and the way they can follow you and have an impact on your marriage.

- Finally, remember that in order to have your responses become more intentional and less reactive, you will need to understand your unique relationship map, and eventually compare it with the relational map of your spouse. These are the first steps in drawing a new map.

CHAPTER SEVEN

Putting the Pieces Together

This chapter's focus is on understanding how every issue in a marriage can be made into a serious problem by the interactional pattern that forms while you try to resolve that issue. Furthermore, those interactional patterns are fueled by belief systems that originated in your childhood experiences. This chapter will "put the pieces together" and introduce a grid that will help you to change.

After working your way through the previous chapters, you may be beginning to see by now the part you play in the problems in your relationship. We hope that you are beginning to understand how you contribute to difficulties in your relationship without intending to do so and without realizing what you are doing. First, we talked about how couples create communication patterns that take on a life of their own. These interactional patterns often become the problem. Understanding how *you* fuel a communication pattern that has become the problem in and of itself, and what *your steps* are in that interaction, is a key step to change.

We also described how the problematic communication patterns are fueled by powerful belief systems and that these belief systems reinforce each other. Finally, we looked at how belief systems often are rooted in family-of-origin issues, and how these powerful family-of-origin influences form a powerful relational map that greatly influences our behavior in our marital patterns. So, now that you understand the basics, let's get down to the real issue. How can you change all the ways in which you sabotage yourself and your marriage?

Creating Change

Change begins when we ask ourselves what we are contributing to the problems in our relationship. As we have stated repeatedly throughout this book, *the only person you can change is yourself.* When we clearly understand how we contribute to our marital communication patterns, what our core belief systems are, and how we often misinterpret facts and situations by viewing them through the filters of our belief systems, then we are ready to change the way we function relationally.

To summarize this process of change in terms of a problem-solving grid it would look like this:

The Problem-Solving Grid

Problem
(You have a problem.)

Communication pattern arises around the problem.
This patterned interaction becomes the problem making the original issue more difficult to resolve.

Belief systems

Your core belief systems fuel the interaction and reinforce those of your partner.

Family-of-origin issues arise.

Change Has Multiple Levels

The process of beginning to change your role in your marriage begins by understanding that most problems have multiple levels. In other words, for every marital problem, be it sex, money, in-laws, parenting, or career issues, there are several levels to the problem. If you dissect a serious problem carefully, almost always you will find that it exists in multiple layers.

First, you will always find a predictable and often counterproductive interaction around the issue itself. This means that, no matter what the issue is, a patterned sequence of communication develops around the problem. This can either cause the problem to become better or to worsen. Frequently, the pattern of communication becomes an intrinsic part of the problem and makes the problem impossible to solve.

Second, the interaction around the problem is fueled by belief systems related to the issue. These beliefs can be about the problem itself; be gender-related; be beliefs about your partner; or all of these. For example, Max believes that money should be saved carefully. He also believes that his wife, like all women, wants only to spend money, and does not understand the value of savings. This, of course, leads Max to take a controlling style, which only creates more conflict with his wife. His belief system fueled his role in the interaction with his wife over money. His controlling style was the result of his belief systems both about money and about his wife.

Third, these beliefs are often grounded in strong family-of-origin messages. In Max's case, his parents and grandparents had suffered and survived the Great Depression of the 1930s, and so they always stressed saving money and being ready for any future emergency. They knew firsthand about financial disaster.

Change involves the ability to step back and look at any problem through multiple lenses and multiple levels, always asking yourself, "What I am contributing to this problem." As you examine the multiple levels of problems in your relationship, the focus must stay on you. To do this, you will need to learn to be nonreactive and nonanxious in difficult situations, and also learn to step back and look at the problem from a distance. Getting some emotional distance from any relationship problem, and then trying to understand the issue from many levels, is almost always helpful.

Let's look further at Max and his problems around money, and examine the issue through several lenses, using the grid that we just outlined.

The Problem

The problem is simple: It is a disagreement over the use of money. Max thinks that, as a couple, they should save a large part of their income to have enough for any future emergency: His wife believes that they should have fun and enjoy the income they earn. This leads to many arguments. Should they put their money into long-term savings—or take an expensive vacation? Should they buy a new car, or start a savings account for their unborn children's college education? Each money-related issue creates a new argument.

The Patterned Interaction

As they try to solve their disagreement over money, Max grows very anxious. He becomes afraid that they are not saving enough, and begins to lecture his wife, Mary, about the value of savings and then he segues into shouting a list of all of her shortcomings in regard to managing money. Naturally, this angers Mary and she yells back that she is not about to be controlled by him, and that she does not need a father. The more anxious he becomes about money and possible future disasters, the more he lectures and rants. The more he lectures, the angrier or the more distant Mary becomes. Either way the money problem does not get resolved. Their counterproductive patterned interaction is now the true problem: Money is only the issue to fuel the interaction.

The Belief Systems

Max and Mary's difficulties with money, and difficult patterned interactions around money, are further fueled by powerful beliefs.

Max's Beliefs

1. Money should be saved for emergencies and never spent on anything "frivolous."

2. One must always be ready for an emergency.

3. Women love to shop and spend money, and if they are not stopped from doing so, will spend far too much.

4. Mary knows what I value, but she chooses not to cooperate with me.

Mary's Beliefs

1. Life is short. Let's enjoy the money we have and live comfortably.

2. Max is a very controlling person, and this is just one more way he wants to control me.

3. Max doesn't want me to have fun, and acts as if he is my father.

Obviously their arguments over money confirm both of their belief systems. That is, the more they argue and go around and around in their patterned interaction, the more their beliefs about each other are reinforced. Max will continue to believe that Mary will never save, and that he should try to "control" her spending. Mary will continue to believe that Max is trying to be her father and to control her, and she will continue to find ways not to be controlled by him. This may result in her going on an extravagant shopping spree to prove that she will not be controlled.

Their beliefs are rooted deep in their early experiences in their families of origin. Most of our powerful beliefs are learned directly or indirectly during our childhoods in the families in which we were raised. Attitudes about money, for example, often have a multigenerational legacy and a long-term pattern.

The Family of Origin

Max's family was hypervigilent about money after having lost most of what they had in the Great Depression. They had had a major family business failure and were bankrupted. His grandparents lost everything, including their house, and they ended their lives in poverty. This family legacy left a large imprint on Max's psyche and had been internalized as part of his belief system far more than he realized.

Mary's parents, on the other hand, had been able to save diligently. And, as a result, they had accumulated a large sum of money and looked forward to years of traveling in their retirement. Unfortunately, her father died during his first year of retirement. He was never able to enjoy the money he had accumulated. Given that family history, Mary's response was to form the belief that it is better to enjoy the present moment, and to spend money as fast as you can earn it, because the future is not guaranteed. Mary had vowed that she would enjoy her life in the present and not postpone pleasure waiting for a future that might never arrive.

Obviously Max and Mary's belief systems, grounded in their family histories, dovetailed and reinforced each other. The result is that they inadvertently continue to reinforce each other's beliefs, growing more and more frustrated in the process. The harder they work at trying to change each other, the more they both adhere to their beliefs, which are now becoming even more rigid.

Starting the Change Process

The problem-solving grid above provides a way to better understand the multiple levels of any problem, and what makes the problem so difficult to resolve. It allows you to step back from your emotional reactivity and gain some distance from the problem. However, the grid is simply a starting point for change. Just going through the grid and using it to better understand the multiple levels of your problem will not in itself produce change. If, for example, Max used it to better understand his role with the problem of money within his relationship, that would be a good starting point for using the grid to begin changing himself.

If Max wanted to change his marriage, he could begin by changing himself. His starting point could be to step back from his internal dialogues about money, and use the chart to look at the problem from several other angles. He could then zoom in *on his part* of the problem.

He needs to focus on how he increases the tension with his wife by his *particular communication style.* And he needs to recognize the critical parental tone that he often uses in his arguments with his wife. He needs to learn that this communication style actually guarantees that he will not be heard nor understood. Furthermore, he needs to understand that his current "solution" to the issue of his anxiety about money causes him to become overly controlling and parental, and that this style has become a large part of the problem about money.

Next, he needs to begin to look more carefully at his belief systems both about money and about his wife's attitude toward money, and begin to challenge those beliefs so they will not have so much impact on the way he communicates with his wife. Finally, he needs to begin to explore the family-of-origin aspects of the problem and look more carefully at the family legacy he inherited about money. Understanding the impact of his particular family legacy might be a first step toward reducing the conflict with his wife. Understanding his powerful multigenerational anxiety about money, and the way he has internalized those family messages, is an important part of understanding his role in the maintenance of this problem.

The dilemma for Max—and for you—is how to take in all of this theoretical information and use it to begin creating change. There are a number of steps that will help with this process. Now, think about the issues in your relationship that cause you to struggle with your spouse and never seem to get resolved.. Then follow the steps below to change your thinking.

Step 1 for Creating Change: Using the Grid

Will insight alone produce change? Does simply understanding the problem and your contribution to the problem create change? Not very likely. Insight is simply a start. It is a decision to look nonreactively at the problem through several different lenses. Most people get caught up in their reactivity to a problem in such a way that they respond automatically. That is, their response is not thought through but, rather, is an automatic emotional reaction. As a result, their response often causes the problem to worsen. As discussed in chapter 6, the more anxious we are, the more we respond automatically and reactively. This response always makes things worse. For Max, money was a toxic issue that activated increased anxiety. The more anxious he became, the more reactive he would be. His reactivity always made the problem worse. Using this grid will enable you to step back from your emotional reaction and to become more thoughtful and less reactive. *Using the grid means thinking about your feelings first, before allowing those feelings to determine your response.* It will allow you to better choose your response, instead of responding automatically. Using the grid allows you to make a thoughtful response, instead of an emotionally reactive one.

To see and understand your role in any given problem, create such a grid or chart on paper. Set it up like this:

Your Problem

(Describe an issue in your relationship that causes problems as concretely as possible.)

↓

Your Patterned Interaction Around Your Problem

(Describe in as much detail as you can the interaction that forms around the issue of your problem. Describe how this communication pattern becomes a problem in itself. Then try to describe your particular role in that communication pattern.)

Your Beliefs About Your Problem

(First describe your beliefs about the problem.)

1. _____

2. _____

3. _____

(Next, describe your belief about your partner in relationship to the problem. For example, Max believed Mary loves to spend money.)

1. _____

2. _____

3. _____

(Next, try and describe your partner's beliefs about the problem and your partner's beliefs about you.)

1. _____

2. _____

3. _____

4. _____

5. _____

Contributions of Family of Origin

(Finally, try to describe how your beliefs were formed by your family of origin, and also the long-term patterns in your family around that issue. Try also to describe how your spouse's family-of-origin issues contribute to his/her belief systems.)

The first step toward change begins when we step back from a problem, when we become less reactive, and *choose* different responses. This chart can help us to do this. It allows us to step back from the problem, as well as from our counterproductive communication patterns around the problem, and to use it as a flow chart to look at the problem through a number of lenses and see the interconnection of all the levels.

For Max it would mean stepping back and diagramming his communication patterns around the problem, his belief systems that support the interactions, the way those beliefs reinforce each other, and his family-of-origin contributions to the problem.

Remember that as you work through this process, you must focus on yourself. Your goal is to understand as fully as possible what you are contributing to the problem on a number of levels. It may be tempting to study your partner's contribution to the problem, but that would only make the problem worse.

Step 2 for Creating Change: Learning to Be Nonreactive

After you understand your role in the many levels of the problem, step 2 is to learn how to hold back your reactivity and do something different. This is a difficult concept both in theory and in practice. How often have you said to yourself, "This time it will be different. I will not get defensive, and I'll simply try to be more understanding"? Then, as the discussion or argument gets started you find yourself saying the same things that you always say and becoming just as reactive. Your great intentions evaporate just as soon as you once again become emotionally reactive. This represents a failure to control your reactivity.

To hold back your reactions and do something different, you must develop the ability to predict where the interaction is going, anticipate your response and then the response of your partner. For example, Max knows all too well what he says about money when he gets anxious, and how his wife will respond. He knows, if he stops to think about it, what she will say, how he will respond, and how the discussion will escalate. Since he has the ability to predict this, Max can try to hold himself back and not say what he always says.

In reality, we are all much like Max and frequently we know where our communication patterns are heading. Most of the time these patterns are predictable. The better you become at predicting, the more likely you are to put your typical reactive response on hold and to say or do something different.

How do you slow down your reactivity and do something different? First, as just described, cultivate your ability to predict where the interaction is heading. Next, listen to your body. Your body will let you know when you are becoming emotionally hooked. When you are about to become more emotionally reactive, where do you feel the tension? Does your chest become tight? Do you get a headache? Does the tension in the back of your neck become painful? Let these physiological symptoms function as your "anxiety meter" (Bowen and Kerr 1988). Try to literally picture a meter that displays the level of your increasing anxiety when you are talking about a difficult topic. When you feel your body responding with increased anxiety, visualize the anxiety meter moving toward the reactive "red" zone. This red zone can become your warning light. It should signal you that you are in danger of slipping into your reactive mode.

When you feel your anxiety increasing, acknowledge to yourself that you are in danger of becoming reactive and overly emotional. Then, try to slow down your breathing. Breathe slowly and allow your body to relax. Then think about your response.

One good way to not become emotionally reactive is to ask questions rather than make reactive statements. In other words, ask clarifying questions of your partner. Ask for more details of his or her views of the problem. Spend as much time as possible trying to better understand your partner's position. Review the skills in chapter 3 that address changing your communication patterns, and be ready to use them as a way of not allowing yourself to become emotionally reactive. Keep the discussion on track, but do not react the way you always have reacted. Note that this is the most difficult step in the process of changing yourself. You may have to do this step over and over before you master it, but if you keep practicing, you will master it.

Step 2 is about cultivating an observing self. That is, building the capacity to observe yourself as you engage in a habitual pattern, as a way of keeping yourself from becoming emotionally reactive. Watch yourself as if you were watching a videotape, and observe both your response and where the conversation is heading. Be alert to the need to keep the discussion from becoming either counterproductive or emotionally reactive.

Step 3 for Creating Change: Moving Toward Empathy

The third step for creating change involves *moving toward increased understanding of and empathy with your partner*. Increased anxiety always reduces our capacity for empathy or understanding our partner. The greater your anxiety, the more you will want to "convert" or change your partner to your way of thinking. As your anxiety increases, so do your unhealthy communication styles.

When we are anxious, we try to control, we use "parental" voice tones, we shout and accuse, and engage in a variety of equally combative responses. The result is not only that we do not succeed in better understanding our partners, but they end up feeling increasingly alienated, hurt, and angry.

This third step is difficult. In Max's case, if he can begin to better understand his wife's attitude toward money, he would become less anxious. But first, he needs to stop trying to control her. To do that, he needs to change their communication patterns. As discussed in chapter 3, he needs to practice constructive confusion. For Max it means not lecturing, or controlling, but asking his wife, Mary, many more questions about her feelings about money. The third step means moving from "preaching" to her about his views of money toward asking her more questions about how she thinks about money—about the attitudes in her family, her family history, and so forth. It also means that Max must allow himself to become more vulnerable to Mary about his anxieties about money, so that Mary can see him not as someone trying to control her but as someone who is anxious about money, because he grew up in a family where there had been a tragic loss of money.

Imagine Mary's surprise if Max came to her after pouring a cup of coffee one morning, and said to her, "Mary, I realize that I really don't understand how you look at our financial situation. I know that we argue a lot, and that I can be a real pain in the ass sometimes, especially when I get anxious. Tell me how you think we should manage our money together. What do you think the solution to this problem should be?"

If Mary does not have a heart attack on the spot, this might be the beginning of a healthy dialogue about money. This would be a dialogue that they have never had before. In this sense, they are like many other couples: Their arguments and counterproductive communication patterns have become so powerful that they never really understand each other.

The initial goal in creating change is not to solve the problem, but to create better understanding. *Too many couples become increasingly stuck attempting to solve the problem without realizing that their process is the problem.* The way out of the problem is not only to change the communication pattern, but to work toward increased understanding and empathy. This, obviously, is easier said than done. For Max, it means trying to better understand the origin of Mary's views about money, as well as why she came to see him as a domineering, controlling person. For Mary, it means trying to understand the anxiety that Max experiences when money is involved. Empathy and understanding always slow down escalating interactions between people. Often, when people feel genuinely understood, they will soften the ways in which they relate to each other.

What most people crave more than anything else is the experience of being understood and feeling empathy. *Real change follows understanding and empathy.* Max and Mary will never solve their financial problems simply through a problem-solving approach, or through a compromise. This is the problem with too many of the therapeutic approaches to improving marriage. Too often the focus is on skills at the expense of understanding and empathy. Only when couples begin to understand each other better will they be on the road to true change.

To summarize, real change can come about in the following ways: First you try to understand your problem using the multilayered diagram provided, and paying special attention to your role in the problem. Second, change demands that you acquire the ability to not become emotionally reactive in an automatic fashion. You can do that by changing your habitual response to an entirely different mode of communication, such as asking further questions in a calm, sincere way. Finally, change means moving toward empathy. Empathy is not simply understanding the other person's perspective, but trying to see the world and the problem through the eyes of the other person. Change always follows empathy. If you do not eventually achieve some empathic understanding of your partner, change will not occur.

Step 4 for Creating Change: You Can Only Change Yourself

The next step in creating change is to accept another fundamental law of relationships. For many couples, this is a difficult step to truly accept. This law says that the only person you can change is yourself. Any attempt to change your partner is doomed from the start. As we have said previously, the harder you try to change your spouse, the more things will stay the same.

By recognizing that the only possible change is to change yourself, your focus can begin to shift. As a rule, there is very little focus on the self in the midst of intense couple arguments and interactions. The more you focus on your partner, and try to change her/him, the more things will stay the same.

The more self-focus is cultivated, the more change becomes a real possibility. This is not easy, it takes a lot of discipline. It means cultivating a way of seeing that focuses on what you contribute to your relationship problems. It means constantly looking for what you might be doing that frustrates or enrages your partner and makes all your arguments worse.

Again, you cannot change your partner, or convert him or her to your point of view. But changing yourself inevitably means changing the way in which you interact with your partner.

Step 5 for Creating Change: Accept Your Partner

The final step in creating change is no less difficult than the previous steps. It means moving toward *acceptance of your partner*. Does this mean that you will like everything your partner does, or that you will never again be frustrated by your partner's acts? Not at all. It does mean, however, that you accept that you cannot change your partner and can only change yourself. Part of changing yourself involves working toward acceptance of your partner. Of course, that is easier said than done.

Although your focus is on changing yourself and understanding your role in your relationship, this should also help you to understand your partner. When you begin to understand your partner's belief system and family-of-origin issues, you may learn to see them somewhat differently. The reality is that people do not change all that much. What can change is the interaction between people.

You can change *your* responses, but you will have little luck changing your partner. In light of that *fact*, use your increased understanding to better accept your partner. Try to visualize your partner as a child in his/her family of origin playing out a child's role in family interactions. Try to see your partner as vulnerable and doing the best s/he can do. By accepting your partner for who s/he really is, you will have much more luck in changing your role and thus in changing your marriage.

Acceptance is the greatest gift you can give to your partner. Change can follow acceptance. In moving toward an attitude of acceptance, you are setting the stage for future change while simultaneously beginning to change your interactions in the present.

Putting It Together

How do these steps come together to produce change? Think back to Max's dilemma. To create change around the toxic issue of money he could first step back and try to look at the problem nonreactively, using the grid to see the different dimensions of the problem. For Max, this would mean understanding more about how he and his wife interact around money and identifying his role in their discussions and arguments about money.

Next he would try to examine his own belief systems and those of his wife. This would lead to improved understanding and allow him to see why the subject of money has become so toxic in their marriage. He would then have greater insight into how both he and his wife were influenced by their families of origin in their attitudes toward money.

By taking the time to think through the problem from several perspectives with the help of the grid, Max can step back from the problem. Rather than continue the argument with Mary, where the argument becomes the problem, he can step back and spend some time looking at the problem from several different perspectives.

His next step would be to honestly try to figure out what he was contributing to the problem. By pretending to watch their arguments on videotape, Max would see his lecturing and controlling style, and the powerful impact that has on his wife. Further, he would be able to own his "own baggage" about money. He could better understand some of his powerful, emotionally charged beliefs about money, and see the way his beliefs were shaped by his family's history. He might realize that his family history provided way too much emotional fuel, and was also the force behind much of his anxiety. He might realize that he is the recipient of several generations' anxiety about money.

After using the grid, he might begin not only to understand the source of his anxiety but also to see where Mary's beliefs about money originated. Although Max might still disagree with Mary's spending habits, he would be able to understand her better. This would be an important shift in his attitude toward his wife. Rather than see her as intentionally sabotaging his financial plans, he might be able to understand and why she holds the views she does.

The *next level of change* would be more difficult. Although Max would have lowered his reactivity and increased his understanding, the problem would not have been solved. They would still disagree about money. However, what we are suggesting is that if the argument around the problem changes, and the powerful beliefs that fuel the arguments are better understood, then there is a greater probability that solutions to the problem will be reached.

However, using *a one-person guide to creating change*, will put some pressure on Max. He must find a way to hold off on his emotional reactions, and then take a clear position without being overwhelmed by anxiety about his financial future. That is, he must then find a new way to talk more with Mary about money, using the information he would have developed from using the grid, while not getting caught in the old patterned arguments about money.

To do this, Max might do well to try to predict where the discussion about money will get stuck or become emotionally heated. If he can predict where the discussion will likely break down, where he might become overly defensive or where Mary might begin to feel controlled, then he can plan strategies to keep the discussion from going in that counterproductive direction. Using the strategies introduced in chapter 3, such as 1. constructive confusion, 2. asking questions, 3. taking time-outs when necessary, and 4. setting ground rules, would all be helpful.

The question that often is asked at this point is, "Isn't this a lot of work?" Or, "Doesn't it seem too 'mechanical' to plan so much for a conversation?" On the surface, this may seem like a lot of work. However, consider the alternative. For Max and Mary to continue having the same argument about money in the same counterproductive manner will keep things from ever moving toward a solution, and, in the end, will cause more pain and marital distance. These arguments can only produce increased tension and distance between them.

To be sure, this is a highly disciplined approach. It takes practice to learn how to hold off with your reactions and define and hold a nonreactive position. To use this approach, Max must learn to hold his defensiveness in check, and not become emotionally reactive when Mary brings up what she wants to purchase next.

Change Does Not Mean Giving In

Following this approach does not mean that Max should simply give up or give in or take on the entire responsibility for making his marriage work. To cave in and allow his wife to spend whatever she wants would be emotionally reactive in the other direction. It would mean becoming conflict/avoidant to keep the peace. In the end, however, it would cause just as many problems as their counterproductive arguments. When people cave in to their partners' requests, they either become martyred, depressed, resentful, or all three. Giving in is not a solution to the problem. It will make the problem worse.

The problem of caving in is just as serious as becoming defensive and emotionally reactive. Change requires the ability to stay nonreactive and not get caught in the old patterned interaction, nor to simply give in. Rather change means to find a way to communicate differently, a way in which your spouse will feel understood. This style of communication tries to find a win–win solution. Obviously, this is a process that does not take place instantly. If Max can communicate to Mary that he really understands how he has been overly domineering in his tone, and apologize for the impact of his controlling, parental style on her, he will shift their interactional pattern.

If Max can then talk to Mary about what she believes about money, and about his style of communication and her control issues, he will be headed in a positive and productive direction. From that good start he might consider taking a "one-down" position. A *one-down position* tries to diffuse the perception of control by coming at things differently. A one-down position tries to de-escalate a situation by not communicating as an authority or expert, which always appears to be controlling. Rather, this position gives power away by trying to learn from the two partners' "expertise."

For example, if, after talking for a while, Max said, "Mary, I know that I have been a real pain about this. You must get exasperated with me! Please try to understand that I'm trying to change my style. But, as you know, I do get very anxious when we talk about money. So if I sound controlling, please tell me right away. I need your help and reminders to make this change. And, if you have any suggestions about how we could work better together on the issue of money, I'd be all ears. I really need your help and suggestions."

Would this solve their problems with money? No, but it would be a starting point toward creative problem solving, and a potential win-win solution. Remember, the "problem" is their counterproductive patterned argument—not money. Money for Max and Mary is simply one issue that became a problem because of the style and pattern of their interactions.

Experimenting with Change in Your Marriage

Take some time to think about this model of change as you experiment with making changes in your relationship. Try experimenting with the grid and working on a problem in your relationship.

Step 1: Using the Grid

The first step toward creating change is to use the grid and begin to fill it in with the details of your issue.

My problem:

_____

_____

My interactions around the problem:

_____

_____

My beliefs that fuel the interaction:

_____

_____

My family-of-origin contributions:

_____

_____

By going through this process, you should begin to get a better understanding of the different dimensions of your problem. Remember, spend most of your time looking at *your* contributions to the problem and look for creative ways to introduce change.

Once you have diagrammed your problem and developed some insights, move toward using new skills to shift your role in the way the problem is maintained. Remember to try to use the gentle art of "constructive confusion." Your goal is to confuse your predictable, patterned interactions so that they move in different directions. Using questions, listening skills, paraphrasing, and remaining nondefensive will certainly help. You should also try to confuse any beliefs that your partner has about you.

For example, if you are seen as controlling or parental, be careful to not sound parental. Watch your tone and your body posture carefully to avoid being controlling. If you are seen as irresponsible, try to act responsibly. If you are seen as an overfunctioner, experiment with doing less. Try to shift your role from the predictable patterns described in chapter 3.

Step 2: Hold onto Yourself

Step 2 is to hold onto yourself. Don't allow your old communication patterns to emerge. Keep your discussions on track. Don't generalize or become too intense. At the same time, make sure that you do not simply cave in to keep the peace. In addition to listening, do not hesitate to state what you need from your partner.

Step 3: Accept Your Partner

Work toward feeling empathy with and acceptance of your partner. Help your spouse see that you really understand where his or her position and why it is held. The more your partner believes that you truly understand his or her position, the more probable it is that your problem can be resolved. When people feel genuinely understood, they are more likely to move toward win-win solutions.

Partners crave empathy, understanding, and acceptance from each other. If your partner feels that you are offering empathy, understanding, and acceptance, it is likely that the two of you will be able to solve your problems.

In chapter 8, we will explore the concept of reining in your reactivity and defining your own position, in greater detail. For most people, this is a difficult process, at best.

CHAPTER EIGHT

Can I Really Change This by Myself?

This chapter focuses on using the insights gained by reading the previous chapters to "define yourself." Defining yourself will allow you not only to understand your role in the problems of your marriage, but even more importantly it will provide you with tools that will allow you, even when you are anxious, to change your role and take a new position in your patterned interactions with your partner.

This Is So Much Work

Donna sighed deeply, sat back, and began her counseling session by sadly saying, "Why do I have to be the one doing all the changing? It isn't fair. I feel like I'm doing all the work trying to change so much of what I do in this marriage. Do you really think it's worth it? Can I really change this marriage by myself? Why can't John take some of the responsibility for changing this marriage? It's just so unfair that I have to do all of this work."

At this point, you might be identifying with Donna's frustration. It can seem unfair to carry the responsibility for changing only yourself for the well-being of your marriage. Donna needed to remember that although she was working hard to change herself, that is not the same as taking responsibility for changing her marriage. All she can be responsible for is changing herself. If she is successful in changing her roles within her marriage, her marriage will change one way or another. And, though it is certainly a lot of pressure to maintain self-focus, the reality is that without changing yourself, there is little else that will change for the long term in your marriage.

In previous chapters, we described a method for staying nonreactive in your marital arguments, interactions, and patterns, and focusing on changing yourself. We provided a grid you can use as a way to achieve some emotional distance from your habitual patterns and problems (see chapter 7), and we suggested that there is a great need to learn to "hold onto yourself" in a variety of ways.

The late family therapist Murray Bowen called this "differentiation of self"(Bowen and Kerr 1988). Edwin Friedman, in *Generation to Generation* (1985), called it "nonanxious presence." David Schnarch (1991; 1997) in his detailed description of differentiation in marriage referred to it as "holding onto yourself." No matter what it is called, we are discussing the ability to be who you are, no matter where you are, and no matter whom you are with. It is the ability to be yourself nonreactively and not defiantly. This is not about autonomy, rather it is a way of staying connected intimately without losing yourself either by being reactive or avoidant.

Those who become emotionally reactive allow their anxiety to push them back into their old roles like pursuing, overfunctioning, rapidly escalating, or becoming very defensive. Those who are avoidant put all their energy into avoiding conflict and keeping the peace, usually at the expense of defining themselves clearly.

Central to our model of change is the capacity to stand apart from your relationship: to be able to observe it from a distance and to recognize your predictable patterns in conflicts, as well as to understand your particular role in those patterns. This change model demands that you do some serious and thorough self-investigation to better understand your own belief systems, interpretations, and family-of-origin influences. Finally, it demands that you nonreactively change your role in the relationship, while remaining connected with your partner.

Like Donna, many people think that this sounds like a lot of work. It certainly demands a high level of maturity. Wouldn't it be easier if your spouse would just change, and take some of the pressure off you? Yes, it would be easier, but it isn't likely to happen. Yes, making these kinds of changes is certainly a lot of work, but what is your alternative? As we have said repeatedly, any attempt to change your partner is doomed to failure. Changing yourself is the surest road to changing your marriage.

Long-Term vs. Short-Term Solutions

We believe there are no simple answers that will produce marital change despite our cultural preoccupation with gimmicks and quick fixes. We are always looking for something that works quickly and with minimal effort. Yet we all know that fad diets never work, and, certainly, simple solutions to complicated marital problems have the same probability of success as the latest fad diet. The approach suggested in this book is not a short-term model for change. The road to self-focus and to differentiation is a long-term, disciplined path. It is clearly "the road less traveled," but, in the end, it is the only long-term way we know that will create beneficial change in marriage and, over time, it can help to produce greater intimacy in marriage.

What Is Differentiation?

Differentiation demands that you be yourself without giving into the pressure to become the self that your partner or family want you to be. This is not easy. Being yourself is not that simple. Watch adolescents try to define themselves. They struggle to fit in with a peer group and often become the self required by the norms of that group. Their anxiety and depression grow quickly if they believe that they are not fitting in. To stand apart from the pressures of a peer group and define your own self and your own values takes great strength and courage; most adolescents cannot do it.

Defining yourself as an adult is just as difficult. For starters, it means that you know who you are, what you believe and stand for, and what your needs are. Then it requires you to hold onto your reactivity in the midst of pressure from your spouse to be something else. Angie, for example, was an extrovert. She loved to hang out with her friends and thrived on group gatherings with friends and coworkers. Harold, her husband, was uncomfortable in social settings. Not only did these gatherings make him anxious, he became even more anxious when Angie went out with her friends without him. He handled his anxiety by trying to control Angie, and trying to persuade her not to go out with her friends. If Angie is to define herself, she must be able to not lose sight of who she is, what she enjoys and needs, and then be strong enough to not allow Harold to change her. As you can see, there is a lot involved in defining yourself.

Think about all the things that could go wrong in the example above. First, if Angie is not clear about who she is or what she needs, she will begin to feel very frustrated in her marriage. Second, if she cannot be strong enough to hold onto what she needs, she will begin to feel dominated, and may even feel that she is losing parts of herself. In the long term, these feelings will cause her to become depressed and angry.

As matters between them escalate the tension, Harold may deal with his anxiety by trying harder to control Angie and he will want her to "fuse," or grow closer to him. As Angie becomes anxious, she may not be able to continue to assert her needs. Or, at the other extreme, she may begin to attack Harold and to distance herself from him, reactively doing whatever she wants to do, as a way of proving that she will not be controlled.

Self-definition and differentiation are not easy for any of us. Like Angie, we struggle with how to achieve them without being reactive. The main difficulty of differentiation lies in being able to be clear about who you are and what you need, to hold onto that definition in the midst of anxiety (both yours and your partner's), and still stay connected to your partner without falling back to your old patterned, reactive responses. Admittedly, this is very hard.

When we become anxious or angry, we fall back on older, less mature reactions. Remember the types of couple patterns described in chapter 3? Often when people become anxious they fall back on those patterned reactions. For example, some people when they get anxious, pursue, and push hard for greater closeness, often blocking their partner's growth. This is the case with Harold.

Others handle anxiety simply by becoming conflict-avoidant. If Angie backs down, and becomes the person Harold wants her to be, then she avoids the conflict, but at the expense of being herself. She would then give up parts of herself for the sake of peace in her marriage. In extreme versions of this behavior, people become almost invisible to their partners and share little of themselves. Others attack their partners and rapidly escalate their quarrels to near warfare. Still others, when they become anxious, become overfunctioners.

If Angie becomes reactive she might attack Harold, accusing him of being just like a domineering father, or worse. Or she might just do what she wants to do and progressively distance herself from him. If Angie chose to respond as an overfunctioner, she would take too much responsibility for Harold's anxiety and his feelings and spend much of her energy making sure that he feels okay. She might even give up some of what she wants and needs for the sake of helping Harold to feel better.

Issues in Differentiation

Part of working on differentiation issues is learning to be aware of which responses to anxiety you are most likely to use. When you are anxious, do you pursue or create distance? Do you attack, overfunction, become defensive, or just become emotionally reactive in a generalized way? All of these responses work against self-definition and differentiation. To define yourself requires you to know who you are and to be strong enough to hold onto that definition of yourself, despite your partner' anxiety. It is difficult to do this and still stay emotionally connected to your partner.

Differentiation also requires the ability to separate your feelings from your thoughts. The capacity to separate feeling and thinking is a central aspect of this model of change.

In times of intense anxiety and conflict it is easy to assume that what you feel is reality and to act or react accordingly. Separating feeling from thoughts becomes more difficult in times of anxiety. Harold, for example, would panic when Angie went out with her friends. He felt frightened and anxious and deep down in his psyche he was afraid that she was really going out to meet another man. Unfortunately he acted on those frightened feelings and became reactively angry and controlling. He was unable to slow down and think about his feelings, so, of course, he could not talk about how he felt more calmly with Angie. The more you act on the basis of your feelings, the more emotionally reactive you will become, and the more difficult it will be to move toward differentiation.

To examine how well-differentiated you are within your marriage answer the following questions:

Do I routinely get caught in emotionally reactive arguments?   Yes _____ No _____

Do I often find myself getting emotionally hooked by my partner's statements, and then become too reactive?   Yes _____ No _____

Do I often find myself playing the same role within the same pattern in our arguments? Yes _____ No _____

Can I nonreactively ask for what I want from my partner without getting angry or overly defensive?   Yes _____ No _____

When I try to change my role in arguments (as discussed in chapter 3), I am usually successful. Yes _____ No _____

When my partner gets moody or irritable because of my needs, do I cave in and try to make him/her feel better?   Yes _____ No _____

Can I recognize when arguments begin to escalate and can I keep myself calm and nonreactive? Yes _____ No _____ (See chapter 9 on conflict.)

When I visit my family of origin, do I slowly but surely find myself in the same role that I played growing up?   Yes _____ No _____

Do I have a hard time being myself with my spouse?   Yes _____ No _____

Am I different when I am with my friends than when I am with my spouse?   Yes _____ No _____

Do I feel pressured to become the person my spouse thinks I should be?   Yes _____ No _____

What do your answers tell you about your own level of differentiation? The more your answers indicate some degree of emotional reactivity, difficulty detaching from reactive arguments, or too easily falling back into old roles, the less differentiated you are. Most people have some work to do on differentiation. It is a lifelong process. It is not an easy task to be yourself and still be intimate with your partner.

Differentiation Is Not About Just Saying No

Too often people believe that to be differentiated only means that they simply become nonreactive instead of understanding that this is just the first step. Sam, for example, explained with great pride his plan for dealing with his marital arguments nonreactively. When talking about his wife, Linda, he claimed with some enthusiasm, "When she gets angry and emotional, I call a time-out and go for a walk." Sam, however, is unclear as to why his wife does not see this as a great breakthrough on his part.

His problem is that he has taken only one small step in the complex task of achieving differentiation: He has learned to take a time-out. Unfortunately, he has not taken the next step, and perhaps he does not even realize that there is a next step. After taking a time-out he does not try to reengage his wife in their discussion after things have calmed down. Differentiation is not simply about staying nonreactive. It is about staying nonreactive, and it is about *staying emotionally connected*. Staying emotionally connected can be even more difficult than staying nonreactive.

In Sam's case it means not just calling a time-out and going for a walk. That is just a good first step. His next step should be to come back to his wife and say, "Things were getting too intense and I was afraid that I would say something I might regret. But now I really want to understand what you were saying. Help me understand what I wasn't getting. I will try to listen without getting so defensive." If Sam were to do this, he would be staying nonreactive, moving out of their counterproductive patterned marital interaction, and moving toward emotional connection and understanding with his wife.

If he could do this, he would be demonstrating the capacity to listen without emotionally reacting. Next, he would be able to share his own thoughts without antagonizing his wife, because his thoughts would not be based on emotionally reactivity. He would keep moving toward deeper levels of connectedness with his wife. *That is true differentiation.* Staying nonreactive, breaking predictable cycles, and then emotionally reconnecting are all essential aspects of moving to deeper levels of differentiation.

As you struggled to "put the pieces together" in the last chapter, you may have realized how difficult it is to become differentiated and to stay out of patterned arguments (without withdrawing), and then to move on to a deeper level of connectedness. Our model is based on developing progressively deeper levels of differentiation that will allow you to stand apart from your relationship and observe its patterns and sequences, as well as your particular role within it. Going further, it demands the ability to better understand your own belief systems and family-of-origin issues because they might be making it difficult for you to stay nonreactive. Our model of differentiation also demands the capacity to change your beliefs and your roles in your marital arguments and patterned interactions. Finally it suggests not just changing your role, but moving toward a deeper understanding of your spouse. Only then can you successfully blend together the tensions of togetherness and separateness. Our model is built on moving toward deeper levels of differentiation. That is, eventually, you will be able to be yourself nonreactively, while moving toward deeper levels of empathy and intimacy. This is ongoing work for all of us.

What Does Marital Satisfaction Have to Do with Differentiation?

In our opinion, successful marriage requires both partners to achieve increased levels of differentiation. The increased level of self-definition will allow you to step back from your marital arguments, to observe your role in those arguments and your patterned responses, and then begin to change your role. When you do this, you will begin to see some positive changes in both your marital arguments and your predictable patterns. As you change your role in the arguments, and then as you stay nonreactive, the interaction itself will begin to change. Over time as these patterned interactions shift, the marriage itself will begin to change.

Being differentiated also means being able to examine your key belief systems about your partner, about marriage, about yourself, and any number of other issues. Understanding your belief systems, and, more importantly, understanding how they act as the filter through which you interpret your spouse's actions is essential. Only when you are fully differentiated can you stand back and observe your beliefs and your interpretations about your partner, and then begin to change both the beliefs and at least some of the interpretations.

Doing all of this requires you to develop and nurture your *capacity for self-reflection, introspection, and the ability to stay nonreactive enough to move from intense feeling to thinking about those intense feelings, and then to reflect on your beliefs behind your feelings.*

Furthermore, being differentiated means being able to understand the impact of your family of origin upon your emotional makeup. This involves understanding the role (or roles) you played in your family of origin, and the way that role affects much of your adult life. It means understanding the messages you received from your family about conflict, intimacy, sexuality, parenting, and money.

Being differentiated also involves understanding your family-of-origin rules about being yourself. In some types of families, developing different interests and values from the family is considered disloyal or even rebellious. If this was true in your family, this makes your differentiation process even more difficult. Finally becoming differentiated implies understanding how your family dealt with times of great anxiety, and how you deal with times of great anxiety, as well.

Many people mistakenly believe that differentiation is simply an intellectual exercise, involving the ability to think about our belief systems and family-of-origin issues in a detached manner. They assume that if they understand their belief systems and family-of-origin issues, they are differentiated. But understanding is only a small part of the process.

For example, differentiation means not only the ability to understand your family-of-origin issues, but also the ability to return to your family of origin and not become emotionally reactive with your parents, or be caught in your old roles. It is the ability to be yourself nonreactively while maintaining a one-to-one relationship with each person in your family. In other words, differentiation is not just the ability to be reflective and understand your role within patterns, it is also the ability to be yourself nonreactively in difficult family situations. If you can stay calm, and remain totally engaged in an emotionally charged situation with your parents (one that would have caused you to react with rage or tears in the past), then you will know that you have achieved a high degree of differentiation.

Bryce's Story

Bryce understood that his role had been the overfunctioning, high achiever in his high-pressure family. He understood this intellectually. However, whenever he returned home to visit his parents, he noticed he got progressively more tense and would find himself falling back into his old competitive role within the family. He would describe his achievements at great length, like an adolescent trying to win his parents' approval. He never mentioned the more personal parts of his life nor was he able to connect in any way with his parents emotionally. Not surprisingly, his wife had frequently complained about his Type-A driven personality, and his inability to connect emotionally with her. He was able to talk to her only about his work-related achievements.

Bryce needed to learn that differentiation is not simply about understanding his family issues. It is also about learning how to be himself more genuinely, and how not to get caught in old roles and interactions. He needed to learn how to build emotional connections with his parents, just as he needed to build an emotional connection with his wife.

The Key to Successful Marriage

This is the key for successful marriage: *It is the ability to stay nonreactive while at the same time being emotionally connected to your spouse.* This is obviously far more difficult than it seems. This is especially true when anxiety increases. All marriages struggle with the tension between separateness and togetherness; it involves a delicate balance. In times of increased anxiety, when patterned and predictable arguments heat up we tend either to move toward greater closeness and, at times, fusion, or toward greater distance and, at times, detachment as a way of dealing with the increased anxiety.

As discussed in chapter 3, there are a number of patterns that couples fall into when there is anxiety in their lives. These include the pursuer/distancer pattern, the conflict/avoidant pattern, the rapid-escalation pattern, and the over/and underfunctioning pattern. All of these patterns make it more difficult to be differentiated and nonreactive as well as to stay emotionally connected.

The Role of Anxiety

When you are ready to move from understanding the concept of differentiation to making changes in your life, you will find that there are predictable blocks that will interfere with your progress. As you work on your own level of differentiation within your marriage, what can begin to go wrong? As a rule, the central problem is anxiety. As we have been saying throughout this book, anxiety is an important part of life. It is certainly part of marriage and family life. The many life cycle crises that we have referred to create anxiety. Life crises and challenges and changes also can create crises. These types of anxieties are often easy to recognize. The more hidden types of anxiety that are triggered by the fear that our partner is either creating distance between us or getting too close is far more difficult to recognize. Many types of anxiety are difficult to recognize consciously. Much of the time we recognize them only after they have caused us to become quite reactive.

How Anxiety Works

When you become anxious often you will notice physical changes such as tension in your neck, headaches, tightness in your chest, and so forth. What is less obvious is that you become less differentiated and tend to fall back into old roles and old patterns automatically. It is frightening how quickly this occurs. Our clients often tell us that when they return home to visit their families over the holidays, after a few days, they feel as if they were fifteen years old again. They become "hooked" into acting out their old patterned behaviors and roles.

In the same way, when your are trying hard to change your role within your marriage, as matters become more anxious you will often find yourself falling back into your old patterns and roles. If, typically, you overfunction in your relationships, in times of anxiety you will drift back into your overfunctioning pattern. If you tend to be emotionally reactive, when your anxiety level rises, you automatically become reactive and defensive once again. If you work at avoiding conflict, then the greater your anxiety, the harder you will work at avoiding conflict. As previously said, in times of increased anxiety we fall back to old patterns, whether pursuer/distancer, conflict/avoidant, rapid-escalators, over/or underfunctioning. These patterns can trap us into patterned interactions which make differentiation much more difficult.

The following examples demonstrate how quickly and easily this reversion to old behavior can occur. Remember, anxiety accelerates old responses, roles, and patterns. In the examples below, pay particular attention to the role of anxiety.

Charlene the Overfunctioner

Charlene was very frustrated with her role in her marriage to Rob. She overfunctioned in many ways that left her tired, frustrated, and angry. In addition to working hard at her job as an executive secretary, she had the bulk of the responsibility for raising their three children, did most of the housework and cooking, and had little or no time for herself. Most of the hobbies she had once enjoyed had long since been let go. Earlier in her marriage she had tried to nag and cajole Rob into taking some time from his engineering job to be more involved with his family. But Rob had always had an excuse like a project deadline, and, in the end, he ignored her pleas and resented the pressure that she had put on him.

Over time, and after much frustration, Charlene began to recognize her role in this pattern, and she was determined to change it. She realized that her nagging got her nowhere, and left her more and more frustrated and, at times, depressed. She decided to stop nagging and seek help from a family therapist.

Initially, using the insight she gained from therapy, she succeeded in changing her role. She was able to stop pursuing and nagging. But this left her doing all of the work in the house without any help. As a result, she became even more resentful. She understood that in her own family of origin she had been the overfunctioning eldest child, responsible for her three younger siblings. She knew how hard it was for her to ask for her needs to be met. She also knew that at times, she did not even know what her needs were. However, this knowledge did not diminish her anger. She knew she needed to make some additional changes. She decided to calmly tell Rob that she was exasperated, and then she would begin to make some changes within herself. She thought through what she was going to say so that it would not come across as emotionally reactive.

One morning, over coffee, she informed Rob, "I can no longer do it all in this house by myself. It is just not fair. I know that you are stressed but so am I. I refuse to nag or be your mother. So the only thing I can do is to stop doing everything. You can either help me, or certain things will just not get done."

Rob got noticeably agitated. He knew she was right. But he could not help being defensive. Nonetheless, he vowed to change and help out. Charlene felt some initial relief and, for a while, her anxiety decreased.

But then the really difficult part started. Charlene decided to stop doing everything, beginning with the laundry. She thought that her husband and teenage kids could take responsibility for their own laundry chores. As the dirty clothing piled up next to the washing machine, the anxiety in the whole family slowly increased and Rob and the kids complained. She responded to their complaints calmly and said that she was sure they could figure out how to use the washing machine, or find their way to the dry cleaning shop.

Other tasks were delegated and things began to change. But then Rob had another major project at work and began coming home later and later, complaining about how stressed out he was. The kids began to complain that that they were behind on their school projects, and, after all, how could they be expected to do school homework and keep up with their chores? The anxiety in the household increased dramatically.

As the level of anxiety increased in the entire household, Charlene's anxiety also increased and she was tempted to fall back into her old role of overfunctioner. This was the first serious challenge to the changes that she was trying so hard to put into effect. She found herself thinking, "I can pick up the slack for a while. Is this really fair to everyone?" Yet as strong as the temptation was, she knew that if she caved in now all the progress she had made would vanish. She was feeling guilty and more and more anxious. She felt terrible for the pressure that her husband and kids were under and was sorely tempted to relieve their stress. Despite her increasing anxiety, however, she knew she needed to hold onto to her position and not shift into overfunctioning again.

This is the most difficult part of becoming differentiated: holding on to your position nonreactively when your anxiety increases. It is difficult because after you have made an initial change, your partner will try to persuade you to change back to your old position.

In Charlene's household, matters got worse and worse and Rob became angrier than ever at her. At one point, he even accused her of sabotaging his career. Although it was extremely difficult she held onto her new position nonreactively. She avoided the temptation to cave in and take care of everything, as well as the temptation to fight back and counterattack. She continued to work with her therapist at staying both firm and nonreactive.

Eventually, she and Rob began to problem-solve. Rob offered to pay for a housekeeper to come in and clean every two weeks, and said that he would continue to do his own laundry. In time, he helped her to organize a chart so that the kids could take increased responsibility for doing chores around the house. Over time, the result of all this work was that Charlene was able to slowly leave her role as the overfunctioner of the family and she began to achieve more balance in her marriage. Obviously, this took a lot of work and discipline. Her increased differentiation resulted in an increase in marital intimacy. If she had given in to her increased anxiety and fallen back into either reactivity or her old overfunctioning role, she would have been left with ever-rising levels of frustration, resentment, and marital distance.

Charlene's Steps to Defining Herself

When you examine the process that Charlene went through to achieve change in her marriage, you will notice that she took a number of important steps:

1. *She identified the problem.* She did not try to pretend that the problem did not exist. Rather, she acknowledged that her stress and resentment about getting so little help with balancing household responsibilities was a real problem. She took steps to solve it by complaining to her husband about what she was feeling and requesting help. She was not passive, but tried to solve the problem.

2. *She was able to step back and see her overfunctioning role in her marriage.* She noticed two things about this pattern. When she overfunctioned by doing everything, her husband and kids continued to underfunction and did less and less. As we said in chapter 3, this pattern balances and reinforces itself. Next, she noticed that when she complained and constantly asked for change, her husband became even more distant and detached. She realized that if she continued to pursue her goals this way that it would have the same negative effect on her husband. In this second change step, she was able to observe both the patterns and her role in those patterns as she tried to raise the issue of her needs. As a result, she stopped nagging her husband. She stopped asking for help and complaining about how her needs never got met. She realized that continuing to complain and asking for help would be futile.

3. Going deeper, her third step involved better understanding her belief systems and seeing how they contributed to the problem. She realized that she truly disliked tension and conflict and that she believed the family would function better if she could just swallow her resentments and do everything. Further, she realized that earlier in her marriage, she had bought into the gender-based idea that a women's role in marriage should be the caretaker for all of the family's needs. She also remembered that earlier in her marriage, when she first bought into the gender-based role that had become so confining, she had not held down a full-time job. Further, she realized that her beliefs were grounded in the

role she had played in her family of origin. She had been the overfunctioning eldest and had believed she needed to overfunction to keep family tensions low. When she was growing up, if family tension increased, she had been the peacemaker, as a way to calm things down.

4. Her fourth step, however, was the most difficult. Achieving all of the insights listed above did not change her situation one bit. To create true change, she had to challenge her beliefs, as well as her family-of-origin role. This work of challenging old beliefs and roles leads, in turn, to an additional step. *She knew that she needed to stop talking and take action. So, she began by defining what she needed, took her position, and then "held on."* Specifically, rather than try to change everybody else in the family, she changed herself. After warning her husband that a change was coming, she simply stopped doing many chores that she had been doing. She stopped overfunctioning. But, by then, she was fully prepared for the increased number of complaints and the increased anxiety that caused in her family. That was her final change step, and it is often the most difficult part to accomplish. The increase of tension and conflict in her family was a severe test of her resolve to change her role. After all, when we make changes, the normal reaction is a family or spousal response that goes: "Please change back, I liked you better the way you were!" That was certainly the case for Charlene. Her husband and children were less than enthusiastic about the changes she was making. She survived the first round of complaints but the second round was much more intense. That time her husband really did have greater than normal job pressures, and the kids did seem genuinely stressed. The entire family's anxiety level rose dramatically. That was her real test. Holding on to the changes she made nonreactively until a satisfactory resolution could be reached. By reviewing these steps you can see how she put into place the steps outlined in chapter 7, as well as how she held onto her position nonreactively but firmly. To have caved in, would have left her feeling an enormous emotional distance from her husband as well as much resentment.

Exposing Yourself to Anxiety

To define a self and work on change means to expose oneself to greater levels of anxiety. Unfortunately, facing anxiety is a necessary part of change. Self-definition is forged in the fires of anxiety. That was certainly the case for Charlene and it will certainly be the case for you if you try to apply these principles in your own marriage. Your anxiety will increase and you will be tempted to revert to your old style. This was certainly the case for Ramon and Maria.

Ramon the Anxious Avoider

Initially, Ramon was attracted to Maria's charm and high energy. She was the life of the party and he came to life in her presence. He loved her spontaneity, charisma, charm, and emotionality. That was also the problem. When she was "up," she was wonderful. But when she got angry, Ramon aptly described her as "hell on wheels." Over the years, Ramon came to fear her temper and screaming episodes. He dreaded the times when she would lose control and keep him up until the three in the morning with her tirades. He felt anxious, trapped, and paralyzed. He sometimes prayed that somehow she would fall asleep or at least let him sleep. But Ramon had no such luck. If Maria suspected he was falling asleep, she would attack him with even more energy and accuse him of ignoring her feelings. Over time, Ramon grew emotionally distant and detached. He spent more time at work and dreaded coming home. He would feel chest pains when he pulled into the driveway of his home, not knowing what was in store for him.

Ramon was convinced that Maria was the problem. He described her to his friends as "bitchy," "out of control," and "hysterical." Of course he painted a picture of himself as a calm, rational husband simply doing the best he could manage to do. His solution to the problem was to become intensely conflict-avoidant. He tried everything he knew to ignore arguments, and over time to ignore Maria. Of course Maria just became angrier, and she described Ramon to her friends as "uncaring," "insensitive," and "unloving." And, of course, she did not add a description of how she responded to him.

Over time, as Ramon decided to work harder on his marriage, he discovered that his solution to the problem had become part of the problem. His conflict-avoidant style was only making the problem worse. The more anxious he became and the more he tried to ignore conflict (and his wife) the more emotional Maria became. His first step was to try to understand his conflict-avoidant style. But he knew he had to try something else. He knew that he would have to change his role. That was quite clear. But then what? If he stopped avoiding conflict, what could he do? Just the thought of dealing more directly with Maria gave him chest pains and increased his tension. Yet something had to change.

As Ramon explored his own beliefs about conflict (his second step), he discovered that he held several powerful beliefs that he did not like to admit were part of his belief system. He realized that his fundamental belief about conflict was this: When there is conflict, someone always gets hurt. Furthermore, he acknowledged that, in his mind, there was little point to engage in conflict with a woman "because they are all hysterical." He cringed when he found himself saying that, because he realized it was a sexist generalization. Nonetheless it represented his beliefs about conflict and women. He believed that Maria was out of control, and that it would be futile to talk to her when she was upset. He was convinced that talking to her could only make things worse.

Not surprisingly, exploring his family of origin revealed that Ramon's mother was an alcoholic who was prone to screaming whenever she drank. He described his father as a wimp who "had no balls," and never challenged his mother. Ramon's pattern while growing up was just to stay clear—and keep his mouth shut. He stayed away from his home as much as possible. While he was describing this he cringed, because he recognized that he was acting just like his father, not to mention he was still staying away from his home, just as he had done as an adolescent.

Ramon's Story

As with Charlene, gaining these first insights was just the beginning of change. Ramon admitted that he liked to "think about his problems." Facing them head on was another story. As much as the insight he gained about his family of origin was helpful, although somewhat unsettling, he liked that part of the change process. He said it was "like putting the pieces of a jigsaw puzzle together." While he was "thinking about his problems," Maria was complaining as much as she ever had that he was distant and remote. All of his insights had no effect on his conflict-avoidant style

Finally, Ramon realized that the time had come to begin "defining himself" differently in his marriage and it was time to make some changes. At the same time just thinking about change created increased anxiety. He realized that he was going to have to "take Maria on." He decided to tell her more about his beliefs about conflict, and how much his current family life reminded him of what it was like when he was growing up; he also decided that he was going to try to change. When he told this to Maria, initially she became defensive and angry and asked if Ramon was saying that she was just like his alcoholic mother. He assured her that that was not the point of what he was saying. He went on to say he knew that he had been emotionally distant from her, and he knew he needed to change that. So far so good. The first round went well.

The test of the progress he was making came a week later. Maria was angry and began one of her emotional tirades about Ramon's lack of affection. She accused him of having someone else in his life since he obviously had no interest in her. She began to rapidly escalate into more and more emotionality while Ramon just stood there feeling anxious and emotionally frozen. This time, however, despite his chest pains, Ramon decided to not back down. He said firmly, "I love you and I really want to hear what you have to say, but I am not going to review our whole history, and review all of my faults."

Maria persisted with even more emotion. She accused Ramon of being an "unfeeling bastard" who never wanted to listen to her. Ramon did not back down. Despite his growing anxiety, he said, "I'm not going to listen to you insult me. I'm going for a walk to get my head together, and when I come back, I'll try to talk to you again." Maria continued yelling while Ramon left the house. He felt good about his decision to not allow the argument to escalate, but he dreaded coming home. He wished he could just run away. But he returned home an hour later. He went to their bedroom where Maria was lying on the bed, crying softly. He calmly said to her, "I love you and I really want to understand your frustrations. I just do not think it will help if we keep having the same old argument. We need a better way to talk." Maria didn't respond. Ramon said he could understand that she had valid frustrations, and he could see that he had not been emotionally connected to her. He told her he knew he had to do a lot of work on that issue. At the same time he made it clear that he could not continue in the same old pattern.

To his surprise, Maria softened. She even said that she appreciated him talking to her. Finally, she suggested they go to sleep and talk some more the next day. Ramon felt great relief. By staying present, defining himself, and trying to understand the essence of what Maria had to say, while refusing to escalate the argument, their discussion did not explode out of control. The next day Maria was considerably more affectionate.

Was this a magic solution? Of course not. It was simply the *first step* Ramon took while learning to define himself differently and not be so conflict/avoidant. He made a beginning move toward understanding Maria's emotions while setting some clear boundaries about what he would tolerate and what he would not. This made a huge difference, and he recognized that. At the same time, he was all too aware that whenever things got anxious, and Maria got angry, he would be tempted to retreat and become conflict/avoidant again. But he now realized that his habit of running away had the effect of accelerating Maria's anger.

Ramon also had to deal with the power of anxiety as things became even more tense in their marriage. He began to see that when he became anxious he fell back on his less mature ways of relating—or not relating. As he learned to step back and watch himself in their painful interactions, he was able to see his conflict-avoidant style more clearly and to recognize the impact it had on Maria. At the same time, he became clearer about the core belief systems he had formed about conflict while he was growing up in his alcoholic family, and about the family-of-origin patterns around conflict that had been modeled for him.

But as for Charlene, insight alone did not produce change. Although Ramon certainly better understood the impact of his beliefs and family-of-origin issues on his conflict-avoidant pattern, he was still left with the problem of working through the anxiety which struck him whenever he sensed that Maria was becoming "emotional." His tendency was still to shut down. His biggest challenge was to stay nonreactive and present when Maria became angry and not shut down or back down. As an alternative to shutting down, he learned to take brief time-outs as the way to pull himself together so that he could respond differently and more proactively.

The most difficult part of all this for Ramon was learning how to observe his growing anxiety, and then use it to move toward changing his role, as opposed to allowing the anxiety to shut him down. Anxiety, as with Charlene, was a significant issue for him. Like Charlene he needed to understand how to observe his anxiety and then how to not allow it to shut him down.

Defining the Self as the Key to Change

As we have been saying throughout this workbook, the only person you can change is yourself. The chapters have outlined several steps in changing yourself. Chapter 2 asked you to examine and challenge the myths you hold about marriage. Chapter 3 helped you to understand your role in patterned and counterproductive arguments and interactions, with suggestions for changing your role in those arguments. Chapters 4 and 5 helped you to identify and challenge your belief systems and the ways in which they can lead to misinterpretations of your partner. Chapter 6 looked at the baggage you bring from your family of origin and the impact that baggage has on your marriage. Chapter 7 helped you to put the different chapters together by offering you a theoretical grid for use in integrating your knowledge about yourself. Finally, we have suggested that all of these steps should lead toward defining yourself, taking a defined position, and then nonreactively holding on to that position. This is a necessary but difficult final step of change.

Defined Positions

What does it mean to take a defined position? Both Charlene and Ramon provide two good examples. Too often, the positions we take in marriage are reactive, as opposed to being defined and proactive. These reactive positions are the product of emotional reactions, unexamined belief systems, family-of-origin issues, or the result of patterned marital interactions. They are certainly not based on thought-through or reflective positions.

Creating a defined position is quite different. It involves stepping out of your patterned arguments or roles and observing yourself from a distance. It means studying your role and the way the interaction is going and how your behavior in your role adds to the problem. Finally, creating a defined position means being able to do something different: to choose and define a new position and to hold it nonreactively.

That is easier said than done, as both Charlene and Ramon demonstrated. What does a defined position look like? It looks like going through the processes that Charlene and Ramon went through. It means examining your role, choosing a new role and way of being, and holding onto that new role, or position, as your anxiety increases, and as the anxiety of your family members increases. For Charlene, it meant holding on to her position of not overfunctioning even when the family and marital anxiety increased dramatically. For Ramon, it meant choosing not to avoid conflict, and setting boundaries. It meant not putting up with emotionally and verbally abusive behavior from his wife, and, at the same, time trying to stay connected to her. Choosing your new position or defining yourself in a new way is not that difficult. But holding on to that position nonreactively as the anxiety and conflict increase all around you is another story.

Anxiety Helps Self-Definition

Real self-definition takes place only by exposing yourself to greater levels of anxiety and learning to hold onto your position nonreactively. This means not reactively attacking those around you. For Charlene, it meant not attacking her husband for being a "self-absorbed, entitled, male chauvinist who thought he was living on the set of *Leave It to Beaver*. Obviously, this would not have helped matters at all. For Ramon, reactively counterattacking and calling his wife colorful names would also not have helped. Note that caving in, or reverting to your old behavior, is equally unhelpful.

Most people are uncomfortable with the notion that growth in self-definition takes place only by exposing yourself to greater levels of anxiety. In martial arts training, students carefully study and practice a variety of offensive and defensive moves. However, they improve only as their anxiety increases. Sooner or later they must face their anxiety and spar and test their moves in the midst of the anxiety generated by an opponent coming at them. Only then can they learn and become adept at the martial art they are studying.

Self-definition is much like that. It develops only during anxious times. This workbook can help you learn a variety of skills. It can help you to learn to stand apart from your relationship and to observe your patterns and belief systems, and your role in problems. We will make suggestions for how to change yourself. But in the end, you will have to take a position and hold onto it nonreactively. That is where your self-definition will grow, and better self-definition is a necessary step toward greater marital closeness. Defining yourself anew means overcoming your natural tendency to fall back into your old patterned responses whatever they might be. Self-definition means defining a new position for yourself in the midst of the anxiety of the moment and holding on to it without caving in.

Part II

CHAPTER NINE

Staying in the Ring: Resolving Conflict in Your Relationship

Next time you are having a boring night, and can't find anything on TV that is worth watching, watch a few rounds of the World Wrestling Federation (WWF). Obviously, it is violent, ridiculous, and fake. It is choreographed like a gaudy, bloody soap opera with many different subplots, each more ridiculous than the next. But, by analogy, the contestants can show us much about marital conflict. Theoretically, there is a ring in which the contestants must stay. There are rules that are supposed to be obeyed (no eye gouging, no biting, no low blows, etc.). In addition, there is a referee who has the responsibility of making sure the contestants abide by the rules. Finally, there are timed rounds, meaning there is only a certain amount of time in which the fight can last.

So far so good. It sounds almost civilized. However, if you have watched WWF wrestling, you know what happens next. The contest quickly goes out of control. Rules are broken. Chairs come into the arena. Friends of the wrestlers jump into the ring. Some contestants jump out of the ring. And, of course, the referee "misses" most of the "dirty fighting." In the end none of the rules hold, the fight moves outside the ring, and the referee is often incompetent. All in the interests of bizarre entertainment. In the end, very little real wrestling takes place.

Compare this to the "real" sport of wrestling. The rules are observed, as is the length of time for each round. The referee makes sure that "dirty fighting" wins no points, and there is respect between the contestants. In this case, there is real sport, requiring good conditioning, and a minimum of injuries. Athletes can enter the "ring" or mat with confidence that the conflict will be tightly controlled.

Conflict Is Part of Marriage

Now what does this have to do with changing your marriage? Obviously, our goal is not to turn you into wrestling fans or to endorse any type of violence, fake or otherwise. But the sad reality about marriage is that far too often marital conflict resembles the mayhem that takes place in the arenas of the WWF, complete with trash talk and no rules, as compared to the sport of "real" wrestling.

Conflict is an integral part of every marital relationship. Some conflict is obvious; some subtle. But no matter the form it takes, it cannot be avoided. To move toward marital intimacy, conflict must be faced and worked through. If it is avoided, anger and resentment go "underground," and become something like an insidious cancer, destroying the possibility of marital intimacy. Many people have a difficult time accepting that some conflict is usually necessary to arrive at intimacy. Most couples would prefer to avoid conflict. That may be because they view conflict as a type of World Wrestling Federation event. They imagine out-of-control emotionality, hurt feelings, problems that cannot be resolved, violence, and, finally, the end of the marriage. This type of conflict may result in emotional flooding (Gottman 1999), which, in turn, results in problems appearing to be too severe to resolve.

Let's face it. Who wants to fight? When things are going well, and life is smooth, who wants to get into a conflict. Most couples want to keep life as calm and as free of conflict as possible. They mistakenly think that this is the key to a good marriage. Often, they evaluate the success of their marriage on the basis of how few or many fights they have.

The reality is, however, that some conflict, if handled right, actually can improve the depth of intimacy in marriage. In this case, both partners understand that conflict is not dangerous and has some benefit. To get to this point means you must carefully examine the way conflict is handled in your marriage.

Steps to Creating Change

To shift the way you deal with conflict in your relationship, there are several steps you must take. As our model suggested in previous chapters, the first step is to look at the types of interactional patterns that emerge in your relationship around conflict. There are a number of steps in that process, but a basic understanding of the patterns of conflict in your relationship is essential. Another step is to look carefully at your beliefs about conflict. This means examining what you believe about anger, about your fears of what might happen if your conflict heated up, as well as your beliefs about your partner, and the beliefs you have about yourself.

Step 1: Understand Your Conflict Style

As we have said throughout this book, understanding the interactional patterns that emerge in your conflicts is the first step toward creating any type of real change. Change follows clear assessment and being able to visualize and describe what you are doing. As long as your pattern continues to manifest in the same old way, change is impossible. Understanding your typical patterns in regard to conflict, that usually emerge around issues that are difficult to talk about, is therefore, a necessary first step toward change. This means you must begin to understand the conflict patterns that develop around the issues that are the most difficult to talk about.

There are a number of predictable conflict patterns that emerge in most relationships. The best way to understand and assess your particular pattern is to pretend one of your fights has been videotaped and, as described in earlier chapters, then "watch" the way you fight. This is obviously a very difficult process. It is always difficult to see yourself and your role in a fight, especially after it is over. If you are brave, you might try audio-taping one of your arguments to better analyze your role in the pattern.

Now, read about the different styles of conflict below, and see whether any of these styles describe the kinds of fights you and your partner have.

The Rapid Escalators

Rapid escalators engage in a dangerous style of conflict. No matter how the conflict starts, "rapid escalators" intensify the conflict quickly. Couples who are rapid escalators have the type of conflict that often look like the WWF wrestling matches. Other issues are added on to the subject of the conflict, voices are raised, emotions become very heated, and, of course, no one stays on the subject.

If this style of conflict were recorded, it would show that the fight began with a simple disagreement, but became more and more intense as it continued. It would look as if there had been a small fire, and then gasoline was poured on it. Obviously, the more gasoline, the bigger the fire.

Rapid escalators do not stay on the subject, old history is brought up to be rehashed and used as artillery, emotional intensities increase, and the conflict veers out of control very quickly. The original subject of the conflict is lost and, often, the couples cannot even remember what they began arguing about. Old bitternesses and the many unsettled, unresolved conflicts of the past fuel the intensity between the rapid escalators.

This style of conflict can be a one-person style or a two-person style. In some marriages, both partners mutually escalate the conflict by continuing to introduce other issues as well as increasing the intensity of their emotions. In the one-person style one person predictably tries to increase the emotional intensity by upping the ante in a variety of ways.

The Peacemaker

The peacemaker, in vivid contrast to the rapid escalator, always wants to smooth over conflict. S/he cannot stand the anxiety that emerges as a conflict increases, and, as a result, tries to end the conflict quickly. Rather than intensify a quarrel, they minimize. They too quickly smooth over the conflict to create peace as fast as possible. They are not as interested in an equitable resolution as they are in calming things down. This style is *motivated by anxiety.* Their anxiety motivates these individuals to end conflict and restore peace as quickly as possible.

As a rule, this style is a one-person style for handling conflict. Although their partners may attempt to intensify the conflict, peacemakers wants to calm it down, and will frequently cave in and give up what they want to make peace.

The Conflict/Avoidant Couple

This couple wants their marriage to be as conflict-free as possible. They carefully avoid controversial subjects, as well any issues that might produce conflict between them. The good news is that these couples do not have a lot of conflict. The bad news is that because so much conflict is avoided, the relationship never grows into a deep, true intimacy. Their politeness produces emotional distance. To go back to the wrestling metaphor, this is the couple who will never actually step into the ring. If conflict does actually arise, one person is ready to jump right out of the ring.

The Dominant/Submissive Couple

With this couple, one person is dominant and the other submissive. The dominant person appears powerful, and loud. This person has no difficulty asserting his or her needs quite forcefully. The submissive person always ends up giving in. On the surface, this makes it appear that the conflict has ended. But, the reality is that, far from ending, the conflict has been forced to go underground. The submissive person, who always gives in, winds up feeling resentful or depressed, and always finds a way to get back at his or her partner. The submissive person will "lose" all interest in sex, become depressed, or emotionally withdraw from the dominant partner. In the final analysis, the submissive person creates as much conflict as the dominant partner by submerging his or her anger and resentment, pushing them underground, and by becoming increasingly distant and unavailable within the relationship.

The Seekers of Objective Reality

Seekers of objective reality set up an interesting and frustrating type of conflict. When an argument becomes heated, they begin to argue as to who said what, and what was meant by it. "You were the one who said...," which triggers the response, "But that's not what I said, I really said...," which triggers greater frustration and the response, "But I know you said.... You don't even listen to yourself...." Occasionally, this dialogue takes a different turn, to "But what I really meant was...," which draws the response, "But that's not what you said.... You're changing now to cover yourself."

This argument can go on for quite a while. The fallacy of this type of thinking is that there is an objective reality that can be proven. Couples who have been married for a while know that this is rarely the case. When the argument degenerates into trying to prove precisely who said what to whom, there cannot be a winner. There is as much chance of arriving at objective reality as of finding the Holy Grail. What is truly important is the ability to subjectively understand what the other person is experiencing. By focusing on "objective reality" people will never really feel understood.

Mr. (or Mrs.) Fix-it

When any problem is brought up, Mr. Fix-it tries to reach a solution as quickly as possible. (This is often but not exclusively a male response to conflict.) Mr. Fix-it anxiously wants to solve the problem and lower the anxiety as quickly as possible. He is a genius at creating solutions to problems. So what is the problem? The problem is that Mr. Fix-it's wife is often left frustrated and she says, "You are not listening to me" to him frequently.

One day Cheri came home after a long, difficult day from her job as an elementary school teacher. She was stressed, tired, and had a headache. Over dinner she said to her husband, Harold, a midlevel manager at a local company, "I have had the most frustrating day. All the kids were so off the wall, it must have been a full moon. Plus, on top of that, I had an argument with my assistant principal, which left me feeling misunderstood. I'm getting sick of this job." Harold (Mr. Fix-it) responded, "You really need to get stricter with those kids. Kids these days need more structure. Besides the assistant principal is an airhead. Don't take her seriously." To which Cheri predictably responded, "I don't remember asking for your advice. You're not even trying to listen to me. I just need to vent. I don't need you to tell me what to do." With that, she left the table and in great disgust, flopped down on the couch and watched the news.

Mr. (or Mrs.) Fix-it always leaves his/her partner feeling frustrated and often angry. His partner frequently asks, "Can't you ever just listen?" But Mr. Fix-it cannot be attentive to another's emotions, not even his spouse's. He just wants to fix a problem, and without any desire on his spouse's part to do so, he causes conflicts to worsen. As a conflict escalates, he is often heard to say, "But I was only trying to help!!"

These are some of the more common types of conflict styles. Obviously, there are many more variations that you may be recall. Which category does your type of conflict fit? The tricky part in making this assessment is that couples may have several different styles that they employ for different problems.

Step 2: Map the Steps of Your Conflict Pattern

Martial arts training teaches a sequence of moves and blocks used during sparring. They involve using moves and countermoves, which when done properly look like a dance. Although couple conflict is rarely as smooth a dance, like martial arts sparring, couple conflict uses a series of moves, countermoves, blocks, and attacks. As a rule, these moves are predictable. They involve a beginning stage, a middle stage, and an end. Being able to assess the progression of your conflict pattern is an important step in your movement toward change and growth.

Beginning the Conflict

To better understand your pattern of handling conflict, try to list the steps of your pattern from the beginning to the end. First, how does the conflict begin? Who usually initiates it? Does it begin with accusations, or a harsh tone, or a raised voice? Or does it begin softly and slowly? Obviously, if a discussion begins with a statement like, "You drive me nuts when you. . . ," matters will not go well. On the other hand, if a discussion begins with a sentence like, "Can I talk to you about something that has been bothering me?", it has a much better chance of going well. The beginning of the conflict often sets the stage for how the rest of the conflict will go.

This relates to what we have said previously about conflict styles. For example, the *conflict-avoiders* may stockpile their resentment for a long time. Then, when they finally blow up their partners do not know what hit them. When conflict-avoiders blow up, they will appear unduly agitated and extremely angry, and release all of the frustrations and issues they have been carrying for some time. *Rapid escalators* can begin anywhere but escalate immediately, right from the beginning. Understanding their beginning stage is important. *Peacemakers,* on the other hand, move very quickly to extinguish conflict, often at the cost of obtaining what they want.

The Middle Stage of Conflict

After noting how your conflicts begin, move to describing the next level of the conflict. What is the response to the opening statement? Is it defensive, angry, or tearful? For example, Dan, after a long tiring day, suggested to his wife, Diane, that he wished she spent more time housecleaning. She responded defensively, "Sure, with all my spare time! You are never satisfied with anything around here! You should clean the house! I can't help it that your mother was addicted to housecleaning. Why don't you go live with her." Her response provided fuel for even more conflict. Although Dan could have raised the issue differently, her defensive response threw gasoline on the fire. It also introduced several new topics. What happens next is predictable.

Now, think through the next level of conflict in your relationship. Try to predict where your conflict moves to next. What escalates it? Is it bringing up old history? Making accusations? Or do you resort to name-calling, or raised voices? What happens to the original problem in the escalation?

The End Stage of Conflict

Finally, how do your conflicts end? Do they end with angry passionate statements? Does someone leave the house for several hours? Or do they end with a compromise, or a commitment not to do "it" again? That is, do your quarrels end peacefully or with more anger? Do they fade out or crescendo to a huge blowup? When a quarrel has ended, is there any effort to make a "repair"? If so who initiates the first step toward a reconciliation? If no efforts at repair are made, why not?

For all quarrels it is extremely important to reach emotional closure, with each partner truly satisfied with the result. No one should be the "winner," and certainly no one should be the "loser."

Emotional Repair

As mentioned above, the concept of emotional repair is a very important issue in regard to conflict. This repair refers to the way in which couples come to review the conflict later in the day, or even the next day, and check in with each other. It can be as simple as, "How are you doing after our misunderstanding yesterday? Is there anything else we need to talk about?" Or it may mean taking even more responsibility by saying, "I know I hurt you yesterday. I tried to apologize last night, but I'm not sure where you are right now. Are you okay?"

These types of questions are efforts at making emotional repairs, and making sure that the relationship is okay again. Too often, we have watched couples engage in ferocious arguments, and then never come back to them, thereby not making the necessary emotional repairs and reconnection. Evaluate how well you and your partner deal with this important component of conflict.

Charlene and Dan

Charlene was fuming when she put the kids to bed, and she was mumbling to herself, "9:30 and I still haven't had a minute for myself. I do everything, while Dan watches *Monday Night Football*. It must be nice to be able to sit down and watch some TV. I've had it." She finished putting her six-year-old son to bed, after two extra drinks of water, an additional trip to the bathroom, and an extra story. She was furious. She went downstairs, walked into the family room, and blew. "It must be nice to have nothing to do but watch football. I'm sick of this. We both have had long days, but I'm responsible for everything. This is so incredibly unfair. I'm so angry right now that I don't know what to do."

Note *the beginning of her statement*. It was not a calm or soft beginning. It was not thought through. It was fueled by history, as well as by her exhaustion, and the obvious unfairness of the situation. It was delivered in an emotionally reactive way. It was a harsh, angry beginning, with no attempt to think through all of what she wanted to say.

Dan, of course, reacted totally defensively. "What is your problem? If you wanted help why didn't you ask? I can't just read your mind. Why do you have to be so angry all the time? Can't I ever watch football without feeling guilty? I never get to relax without feeling guilty." Note the *defensive reaction*. Dan made no attempt to hear what Charlene said to him. He countered her outburst with an immediate defensive response.

Charlene grew even angrier. "You relax? What a joke. You get to relax every night while I'm doing all the work. You are just like your father, and you expect me to react like your mother. Well, forget it! I don't ever want to be as miserable as that woman."

Dan of course upped the ante by angrily responding, "My father? Think about how you are just like *your* parents! You are just as hostile and bitchy as your mother. No wonder your father worked two jobs. He wanted to get away from your bitter mother."

Note how each intensified the interaction by moving further away from the original conflict. Neither was able to stay nonreactive. To stay nonreactive, and hold onto a more defined position would mean to be able to predict where their argument is heading. It would mean working to change the direction of their discussion by changing their styles.

For Dan it would mean slowing things down realizing that Charlene was having a bad night, and trying to stay nondefensive. It would mean trying to better understand her feelings and attempting to legitimize as many of her feelings as he could. For Charlene it would mean slowing down and realizing that her "harsh" introduction was part of the problem; and then it would mean trying to lower the intensity and bring the argument back to the main issue of role definition.

As their argument progressed, it became increasingly clear that the initial problem did not stand a chance of being addressed. When there is an angry beginning, followed by a discounting defensive reaction, matters are going to escalate very quickly.

Your Conflict Patterns

Now, take a few minutes and describe one of your conflict patterns. Describe how it begins, what the steps are, how it escalates, and how it ends. Look carefully at your part in the pattern. Try first to name the toxic topic, then watch how the conflict opens, how it progresses, how it ends, and what type of emotional repair takes place (or doesn't). Fill in your observations under the appropriate headings.

The opening statement might go like this:

_____

_____

The initial response might go like this:

_____

_____

The patterned escalation might go like this:

_____

_____

_____

_____

Fill in more detail on what you contribute to worsen the argument. Do you become defensive or do you attack? Do you bring up the past, become patronizing, or use too much humor? Try to describe your particular style of conflict. Be attentive to the specifics of your escalation patterns. Look especially at what you do that pours fuel on the fire.

_____

_____

_____

_____

Finally, after describing how the conflict escalates, describe how the conflict ends. Who ends it? Does it end with some sort of resolution, or without one? Is there a final blowup leading to one person leaving the house, or do you both go to sleep without speaking to each other? Does it end because you "wimp out" and surrender because you don't want the conflict to continue? How do you and your partner feel when the conflict is over? Are you depressed and distant from each other? Or are you angry because you gave in and, as a result, you are left feeling resentful and misunderstood and like a martyr. Or are you satisfied that you have successfully resolved a difficult conflict and have come to a new understanding?

How a conflict ends is very important. Often, the end to a conflict sets up the next conflict. For if it ends with one person feeling as if he or she surrendered without being heard or understood, then the resentment felt will be more than likely to add to future conflict or emotional distance.

Describe the ending of your typical conflict:

_____

_____

_____

_____

Finally, what type of emotional repair occurs after your conflicts are over? Do you check in with your partner to see how s/he is doing and to make sure that both of you have emotionally reconnected? Such repair is an extremely important part of conflict because it allows for emotional reconnection.

Describe the way you and your partner make emotional repairs:

_____

_____

_____

_____

Step 3: Change the Steps in Your Conflict Pattern

After finishing the exercises above, decide what you can do differently to work through your conflicts in a more beneficial and productive manner. Look specifically at the steps you can take to change your conflict patterns.

How conflict starts is very important. Focus on the _start_ of your conflict and the _first_ step of escalation. If you are the one who initiates the conflict, then it is important that you be sufficiently disciplined to begin the conflict "well." If you begin "well," then the conflict stands a much better chance of being resolved.

This probably sounds strange, but how a conflict starts has much to do with where it goes. Starting a conflict "well" means thinking the matter through before you initiate the discussion. *The best way to stay nonreactive is to not initiate conflict if you are overtired or too angry.* Step back and think through what you really want to say. Ask yourself, "When this conflict is over, what is the one thing that I want my partner to hear?" *Try to start the conflict slowly and calmly.* Take several deep breaths before starting. Begin with an "I message." For example, "I'm feeling very frustrated because of . . ." or "I am angry because of . . ." Do not begin with a "you" attack, for example, "You are such a self-centered, inconsiderate . . ." "You" attacks will not get matters off to a good start. Obviously, this is difficult and takes a lot of self-discipline. However, in the end it takes less work than trying to rebuild after a terrible argument.

After starting the conflict slowly and nonreactively, prepare yourself for your partner's defensiveness. This is inevitable. Only in your dreams will your partner ever respond, "Well thank you so much for sharing your frustration with me. I will do my best to not let this happen again, so you will not become so frustrated and angry again." More than likely, your partner will counterattack. "Who are you to be attacking me? What about all those times when you. . . ?" Or your partner might say, "That's not what I meant. You misunderstood where I was coming from on that."

In response to this inevitable defensiveness try to "hold onto yourself" and stay on track. Try to validate what your partner said, but bring the topic back to where you began. Do not let it escalate into a discussion of everything that has gone wrong in the last few years. By responding like this, "I can understand that you are frustrated with what I'm saying and this is probably taking you by surprise. But I'm not saying you are a bad husband/wife. Rather, I am concerned about this one issue. I care about our relationship, and I really want to work this out, so can we try and stay on this topic?"

Obviously, this is easier said than done. However, it suggests several principles of effective communication:

- First, start soft and nonreactively.

- Second, whoever begins must take the initiative in keeping the discussion on track and not allowing it to escalate.

- The third principle of successful conflict is that of changing the pattern. That is, you know where the conflict is heading from past experience. Because you know the pattern, do something different so it does not go where it always does. Do not allow it to escalate, or overly generalize, or resort to explosive name-calling, or mutual accusations. Rather keep it on track, and use the listening skills discussed in earlier chapters, particularly those discussed in chapter 5, where you were instructed to listen to your partner's underlying belief systems.

- Finally, when your partner "attacks" you, try not to counterattack. Rather than throw back another argument, ask for further clarification, or let your partner know you understand that s/he is hurt and/or angry. By encouraging your partner to "vent", it will be easier to move toward a good resolution. Visualize yourself catching all of your partner's anger in a large garbage bag that you can throw away. If you can listen while your partner vents, the conflict will often slow down. Periodically, ask your partner if s/he believes you really understand their anger. Again, this takes great discipline. It means holding reigning in your reactivity, and your inclination to counterattack, or to become defensive. It means slowing down, breathing deeply, and keeping the conflict from going where it always goes.

Step 4: Beware of Quicksand

Although this all sounds great in theory, it is terribly difficult to put into practice. Too often the best plans turn into disaster. Step 4 involves knowing where you may get into trouble while you try to make change. When you are trying to change the way you and your partner conduct your quarrels, it is important to know where the quicksand is. Know where the danger spots are and where you are vulnerable to sinking in too deep. There are two types of quicksand: the quicksand of belief systems, and the quicksand of family-of-origin issues.

Belief systems are rich in swampy marshes full of quicksand. There are several components to belief systems that are relevant to conflicts. First, you need to be aware of any myths about conflict to which you or your partner subscribe.

Remember, myths are popular beliefs you may hold without being fully aware that you believe in them, and which you may use to evaluate your marriage's health. Some dialogue with your partner about these myths can be enormously helpful (see chapters 2 and 4).

One reason conflict is so hard to work through relates to myths about conflict that we hold onto without ever realizing they are part of our belief systems. Think about those myths that apply to you and describe your relationship.

Myth No. 1: A Good Marriage Means No Conflict

This myth holds that as a marriage ages and couples get to know each other better, there should be little or no conflict between them. Any sign of conflict is evidence that the marriage is in trouble and is certainly not as intimate as it should be. What is missing from this myth is the understanding that marriage passes through predictable cycles, and that each of those cycles can bring conflict and anxiety. Furthermore, both people and situations change.

After we marry, most of us change considerably. If, for example, you married right after college and you are now in your forties with adolescent children, your life has changed dramatically. You know only too well about pressure, midlife issues, mortality, career issues, and aging parents. Such types of pressures can cause considerable stress and turmoil. These changes then necessitate significant adaptation, and conflict is often part of the adaptation process. This myth forgets that life changes constantly. Conflict is just one result of processing and adapting to change.

Myth No. 2: Who Needs Rules?

This myth holds that intelligent couples do not need to have rules about conflict. If there is love, then rules are not needed. The myth assumes intelligent people should be able to move through whatever conflicts emerge without negotiating ground rules. And, since most couples do not want to experience conflict at all, they certainly do not want to talk about setting ground rules for conflicts.

This would be fine if they were able to successfully negotiate conflicts easily and effortlessly. That, however, is rare indeed. Most conflicts are not easily resolved, and too often the patterned interaction that is created around conflict becomes a basic part of the problem. Obviously, most couples would feel much safer if they knew that their conflict would be contained by clear ground rules. But too often they never think of this as a possibility.

Myth No. 3: When It's Over, It's Over

Many couples assume or act as though they do not need closure after they have had a conflict. How often have you heard someone described like this: "He blows up, yells, gets it all off his chest, and then is happy the next day. He acts as if nothing happened." Conflict without repair, or without some form of closure, leaves deep wounds and emotional distance. Every conflict needs repair. Closure means making sure that the emotional effect of the conflict has been repaired, and that your partner is left feeling whole.

This seems like a no-brainer—one of those commonsense gems that "everybody knows." Yet it is rare that true emotional repair is ever attempted. As a result, couples go through arguments, watch the arguments escalate, and arrive at some type of conclusion. But after the conclusion, the argument is never mentioned again—until the next argument. Neither partner provides emotional reassurance, or asks, "How are you doing? Do you feel that we came to an okay resolution?" At the end of any argument some emotional repair is needed. The loop needs to be closed so that both partners feel understood and not blamed. The reality is, "When it is over, it is *not* over" until some emotional repair has taken place.

Myth No. 4: S/he Is Just Too Sensitive

When people buy into this myth, they do not have to take responsibility for their own actions. This myth is used by men *and* women. Not only men say their women are too sensitive. Often women say their men are overly sensitive. It is easier to call your partner oversensitive than to acknowledge a poor communication style or an unfair style of conflict. John Gottman's research (1999; 2000) suggests that couples who use a "soft start" to engage in conflict (not coming on too strong or too critically at the onset), have much better end results from their quarrels.

Accepting the myth that s/he is just too sensitive, absolves the partner of taking personal responsibility. S/he does not have to develop self-focus and look at how they present their argument. They do not look at their tone, or body language or hear the anger in their voices, or their insulting phrases, or even the way they go from neutral to 100 mph. No matter what their role in the conflict might be, it is always the fault of their oversensitive partner. Their partner just has to learn to deal with conflict better. So long as this myth is maintained, the conflict will worsen.

Myth No. 5: We Never Fight, Therefore We Have an Intimate Marriage

Many couples are proud of the fact that they never overtly fight. However, such couples often end up with polite, friendly, but distant marriages. In fact, we have worked with several couples who were on the verge of divorce after twenty-five years of marriage without ever having had a single fight. They could not understand how they had grown so far apart. For example, Helen and Fred did not understand why their marriage was falling apart. They explained to their couples therapist that they never fight, and are always polite to each other. Most of their friends admire their ability to get along. When their therapist asked them to describe their problem, they struggled to put it into words. Finally, Fred broke the ice. "It just feels dead between us. We have nothing to talk about. We never have sex anymore, and if we are not talking about how our kids are doing, we haven't got anything else to discuss."

Couples like Fred and Helen know something is badly wrong, but they have a hard time describing it. They know they are too polite, and not emotional intimates. All through their marriage they carefully avoided conflict and/or difficult conversations. As a result, they do not have overt disagreements. On the surface it appears that their marriage works well. But they know they are emotionally and sexually as far apart as they can be. They do not understand that this is the result of their lack of conflict.

Myth No. 6: If We Never Talk About It, Time Will Take Care of It

This myth is similar to the executive who decides not to got through his or her mail and lets it pile up on the assumption that it will all be obsolete in a month's time. Obviously, this will result in a long-term disaster. Important issues will never be addressed and this could result in crucial business problems.

The couple who avoid conflict by not talking about difficult subjects will have similar results. Their unresolved conflicts will grow. The old image of sweeping things under the carpet comes to mind. Sooner or later, the pile under the carpet gets too big, and people start tripping over it. The danger is they do not remember what they are tripping over. What happens to these couples is that they "sweep things under the rug" and then have blowouts over small issues. They cannot understand how and why matters got so intense so quickly. They do not realize that the conflicts they buried under the rug become the fuel for the smaller conflicts. That is why the smaller conflicts blow up into disasters.

Myth No. 7: Conflict Leads to Disaster

This myth says that conflict is inherently dangerous because its underlying assumption is that conflict always unleashes powerful anger that always leads either to violence or to the breakup of the relationship. Individuals who hold this belief are highly anxious about getting into conflict. Frequently, they grew up in violent or otherwise abusive families and witnessed what happens when conflict goes out of control. As a result, they try not to participate in any kind of conflict so as not to invite disaster.

This was especially true for Wally. He grew up in an abusive, alcoholic family and still hated his father for the violence he had wreaked upon his family. Wally vividly remembers hiding in the closet when his father was raging. He had vowed his marriage would be totally unlike his parents' marriage. The problem in his marriage, though, was that Wally never talked about anything unpleasant. His wife, Jen, complained that whenever she brought up a tense subject, he tried to fix it instantly, leaving her more and more frustrated.

In the long term, however, people like Wally create a different type of disaster than abusive parents do. They never state their positions clearly, or articulate their needs, to avoid possible conflicts. This results in their needs not being adequately met, and they begin to feel resentment, or like martyrs. Because they do not feel comfortable sharing these feelings, they often become depressed and withdrawn. In the end, their partners feel distanced and they complain about the lack of intimacy.

This is, of course, not a complete list of the many myths about conflict. Instead, it is an effort to open up discussions between couples about their beliefs about conflict.

Now, which myths best describe how you or your partner view conflict?

Try to answer the following questions with the first thoughts that come to mind.

Marital conflict means:

_____

_____

_____

Which myth do I believe is true?

_____

_____

Now, describe how the myths that you hold about anger influence your conflict style.

_____

_____

My partner believes that conflict always

_____

_____

_____

These questions are simply a starting point for understanding some commonly held myths about marital conflict. Clearly, conflict is a difficult subject for most couples. At the same time, having a way to process conflict is key to any type of emotional intimacy.

Beliefs About Your Partner

How do you believe your partner handles conflict? Your answer to that may govern the way you respond to him or her. If, for example, you believe that your partner will blow up and become enraged when any level of conflict is introduced, then you will be very hesitant about raising controversial issues. You will feel as if you are constantly walking on eggshells. If, on the other hand, you believe that your partner is conflict-avoidant, then you will never really know where you stand or what your partner really thinks about important issues. In either case, you will have difficulty processing conflict.

Marty, for example, described his wife as a "time bomb." "I never know when she is going to blow up. I come home cautiously to find out what type of mood she is in. The last thing I want to do is set her off." Marty's belief established a predictable pattern around conflict in his home. Marty carefully avoided conflict, did not express his needs, and was often heard to say sarcastically, "Whatever you say, dear." His kids thought he was a wimp. The result was he became withdrawn, resentful, and emotionally distant. This fueled his wife's belief that he really did not care about her. This, in turn, caused her to get upset, further cementing Marty's beliefs about her. The more he refused to respond to her emotionality, the more frustrated she became, until, finally, she did blow up. Ironically, Marty's beliefs helped to create the very problem he wanted to avoid. What you believe about your partner's conflict style greatly determines how you respond to your partner.

Now, take a few moments to describe the way you think your partner handles conflict, and how you respond to it.

_____

_____

_____

_____

How Anxiety Affects Conflict

In addition to looking at your beliefs about how your partner handles conflict, and how you respond to that, think about why you get anxious when conflict starts. Many people report that when a conflict begins, they get anxious. They feel tightness in their chest, get headaches, and begin to sweat. They experience all of these symptoms of anxiety because of their beliefs about conflict. Ask yourself, "What am I most afraid of? What do I believe this conflict will cause? Am I afraid that it will result in a final blow up, or violence? Or am I afraid of completely losing my self-control? Am I afraid this conflict will end our relationship?" Or, are you convinced that your partner's style is so intense that it is just not worth getting into a conflict? These are important fears to consider.

Now, take a few moments and describe what frightens you most about conflict.

_____

_____

_____

After describing these fears about conflict, take some time to talk about your fears with your partner. Your goal is not to attack or to change your partner, or even to criticize the way your partner engages in conflict. Your goal is to find a way to shift the manner in which *you* process conflict so that over time *your* anxiety level can be lowered. Telling your partner about your fears is an action that you can take to change yourself.

Family-of-Origin Beliefs

Too often, many of your fears and beliefs about anxiety are based in family-of-origin issues. Every family has its own way of handling conflict. How did your family handle conflict while you were growing up? In many families of origin, conflict was to be avoided at all costs. It always had to go underground, or be handled in triangles. It may have been easier to talk to a third person about your anger with another member of the family than to talk to that person directly.

For example, your mother might have said to you, "I am really angry with your sister. She hurt your father and me deeply with what she said on the phone. I am so angry with her." This type of family dynamic lowers anxiety, allows the conflict to be buried out of sight and then leaked to a third party. It is one of the inevitable results of a conflict-avoidant style. In these families, the peace is kept at all costs. On the surface everything looks fine, but when you look closely, what you find is emotional distance, resentment, often many symptoms of physical illness, and lots of triangles.

At the other extreme are families of origin where there was a lot of yelling and screaming. When addictions or violence were added to this mix, a traumatic combination resulted. What does a child do in this type of family? There are several possibilities. One is to hide. We have heard many adults describe how they hid under beds, or in closets, when the conflict in their childhood homes got out of control. Another possibility is to be the peacemaker. Children who were the peacemakers in their families did everything they could to keep conflict from exploding out of control. They believed that if they could keep their parents happy, then there might be less conflict. They paid a huge price for whatever peace they gained in terms of their own development.

A variation on the peacemaker is the child who tries to be his or her parent's counselor. This child, as a way of minimizing conflict, functions as a go-between or courier, carrying messages back and forth between warring parents. Still other children act out, become violent themselves, or use alcohol or drugs to deal with the pain of violence.

When these children become adults, they have internalized their childhood experiences into belief systems about conflict. Although they may seem to be mature, competent adults, they are terrified by any kind of conflict. Often they avoid conflict at all costs. Sometimes, to their own disgust and horror, they find themselves repeating the conflict patterns they grew up with.

Step 5: Changing Your Pattern

Changing the pattern of conflict in a relationship is not easy. The first step, as we have discussed, is to use our theoretical "grid" to diagram how the patterns of anger work in your relationship.

The Issue

Now, take the time to fill in your answers about conflict.
The issues that create conflict are these. Describe some issues that you often fight about:

_____

_____

_____

The Conflict Pattern

Describe the type of interaction that forms around the issue:

_____

_____

_____

Belief Systems

Describe your beliefs about conflict as well as the specific conflict at issue:

_____

_____

_____

Family of Origin

Describe the role of conflict in your family of origin and how it shaped your belief systems:

_____

_____

_____

_____

Filling in your answers to these questions is a good start to changing your patterned interactions around conflict. While this is important work to do on your own, when you have completed it, you may find it helpful to share it with your partner and engage your partner in a discussion about what you have written.

This final, most difficult step, is to change your specific role in the midst of conflict. As we have said this means learning how to reign in your reactivity, how to stay nonreactive, and how to change your pattern by developing new tools for handling conflict. This step means breaking free of family-of-origin patterns, as well as current relationship patterns. It means being able to stay outside of the conflict emotionally speaking, and learning how to hold onto yourself, and constructively confuse your spouse. It does not mean caving in or avoiding conflict. That would be just as damaging as explosive blowups. Your goal is to develop a new patterned interaction that will serve you better in processing conflict. Conflict is a fact of life. Resolving conflict in constructive ways can lead to greater trust and intimacy within your relationship.

CHAPTER TEN

Moving Toward Intimacy

This chapter explores the nature of intimacy and the common problems couples encounter in their efforts to achieve it. We explore predictable blocks to intimacy, including interactional patterns, belief systems and myths, and family-of-origin contributions. Finally, the role of self-definition in establishing intimacy is explained.

Barbara marveled at the delicate shape of the leaves on her houseplant as she watered it. She could see the benefits of her nurturing. Her plant was growing with vitality, vigorously and beautifully. At the same time, she was aware of feeling sadness, because her marriage, despite all of her efforts at nurturing, was not doing well and often felt ugly.

Her husband, Dan, believed that he was a dedicated family man, providing all the financial support the family needed, yet he rarely took part in the daily activities of the family. Barbara believed that he was not present in their marriage, choosing instead to immerse himself in reading, or spending too much time online exploring Web sites. She hardly knew anything about his inner life. What excited him? What did he cherish about their relationship? What did he dream about? She had not a clue. She believed that she could tell more about the leaves on her houseplant to anyone who cared to ask than what she knew about Dan . . . even after twelve years of marriage!

It wasn't that Dan didn't care about Barbara. He listened to her *dutifully* whenever she wanted to talk to him about her work, their children, or even her sense of emptiness in their marriage. He was always polite, never rude. But he never responded from his heart! She felt empty and unfulfilled as his partner. What could she do differently? She had pleaded with him until she was sick of trying. He didn't seem to understand what she wanted from him. How in the world did she ever pair up with him? She wondered. He was responsible, considerate, all the characteristics she had longed for in her life, but the two of them were not emotionally connected.

Barbara is hardly unique in this world. We have listened to many couples over the years describe how empty their marriage feels. Pressed for specifics, we often discover that one partner, usually the husband, states that he cares deeply for his wife, and that he has come with her to marital counseling because she is unhappy in their marriage. He doesn't say that he is unhappy or dissatisfied with the relationship. His wife will say with genuine anguish that although he says he loves her, and although he shows his love in many practical ways, he shares nothing of his inner life with her. A marriage like this is like having a relationship with a nurturing butler!

So, what is missing? In a word, intimacy. "Intimacy" is one of the most frequently used, most ill-defined words in a couple's discussions about their problems. Men are often characterized as equating intimacy with physical closeness, either through sexual encounters or affectionate touch, or both. Women are characterized as equating intimacy with verbal sharing with their partner, usually about feelings and opinions. But it is rare for troubled couples to converse using the same definition of the term "intimacy." They choose instead to assert that their partner doesn't understand why intimacy is important.

Intimacy: What Is It?

Part of Barbara and Dan's problem is that they do not have a shared definition of the term intimacy. An even larger problem is that they do not realize that they do not have a shared definition. They both believe that they are working toward the same goal. This is an important issue for many couples, since if they do not have the same goals for intimacy, obviously they are not going to get there. It is as if the two people are looking forward to a wonderful vacation together that they hope will be relaxing and romantic. Unfortunately, each has a different vacation destination in mind, and intends to take a different type of transportation to get there. Under those circumstances, the vacation, if it ever takes place, is going to be a disaster.

The first step in moving toward intimacy is to define the term. Ask a variety of people what intimacy means, and you will get a large variety of answers. Many will define it as deep emotional sharing and deep, satisfying conversation. Others automatically equate intimacy with good sex. Unfortunately, these two types of respondents are frequently married to each other. The result is predictable. An interaction develops that is guaranteed to frustrate and will prevent the problem from ever being solved. One partner will say, "We would have better sex if we were more intimate," while the other responds "We would be more intimate if we had better sex." Obviously this discussion can go nowhere. It will be like the couple looking forward to their ideal romantic and relaxing vacation, but who failed to tell each other where they wanted to go or how they would get there.

Rather than engaging in creative dialogue about shared definitions of intimacy, these couples practice the types of destructive interactional patterns we have described in previous chapters. Each partner tries to convert the other to his or her definition of intimacy. The result is that neither receives the kind of intimacy in marriage that they both desired.

There is no one definition of intimacy. There are many. Too many couples fall into a type of thinking that says, "We are either intimate or we are not intimate," instead of trying to figure out those categories in which they are intimate, and those where they need to do more work. Frequently couples will define intimacy as either sex or emotional closeness, forgetting there are a variety of other types of intimacy.

Types of Intimacy

So, what are some of the types of intimacy? There are several types worthy of discussion. The following list is by no means exhaustive, but it offers a simple way to begin to think differently about the different aspects of intimacy. The seminal work of Howard and Charlotte Clinebell (1970) provides a foundation for some of our thinking here.

1. Parenting intimacy

2. Spiritual intimacy

3. Recreational intimacy that develops through shared interests

4. Esthetic intimacy

5. Crisis intimacy

6. Emotional intimacy

7. Sexual intimacy

Intimacy Through Parenting

Consider first the type of intimacy that develops through parenting. For many, the notion that intimacy and parenting go hand in hand seems to be an obvious fact. Given that numerous arguments and conflicts inevitably occur during the years of parenting together, achieving intimacy as parents is far from easy. But, for many parents, the toils and tribulations of learning how to be a good parenting team actually enriched their lives.

When we struggle to be good parents in a healthy and effective way, we do so for the sake of our children's growth. On this, it is likely there will be very little disagreement between you and your partner. But what happens is that your model for parenting may conflict with your partner's model, both of which may be grounded in beliefs about parenting and the influences of our family-of-origin experiences (including daily editorializing by your own parent if s/he lives nearby).

To work through all the myths, beliefs, and family-of-origin influences as to how parents should operate takes a great deal of emotional work. Many marriages dissolve under this specific duress, especially second or third marriages. But to be able to manage these pressures and be rewarded not only with healthy, decent, growing children but also with greater emotional closeness with your parenting partner is truly experiencing a form of intimacy. Tessa and Fred exemplify this.

Tessa and Fred

Tessa and Fred value their marriage. Although they might acknowledge that some other forms of intimacy either are absent or quite thin in their relationship, Fred and Tessa easily refer to their sense of deep closeness and understanding that was developed over the years of raising three children into adulthood. There were many challenges they faced with their second son, Mark, in his early years. Mark had had a yearning to live on the wild side when he was in high school. For two years, he maintained a reputation with his peers as the Party King. His parents, however, were determined to guide Mark's (and the family's) growth in a way that permitted him to be an individual, yet still required him to become more responsible.

Tessa and Fred attended parenting classes together during Mark's high school years to get some additional perspective and learn some new skills. Each was determined to become a better and more adaptive as a parent than ever before. They pledged to each other to walk the parenting pilgrimage alongside of each other. Over time and many frustrated efforts, Tessa and Fred accomplished their goals with Mark. Mark found his own responsible path in the family without having to sacrifice his individuality. To this day, Tessa and Fred have a special feeling for each other that time cannot lessen. When they became grandparents, the same intimacy that developed from coparenting their children continued into their new roles as grandparents. They continue to feel deeply intimate in their marriage.

Spiritual Intimacy

What about *spiritual intimacy*? Spiritual intimacy might be defined as the deep feeling of sharing of religious beliefs and the practice of those beliefs between two partners. This form of intimacy is imbued with the mutual sharing of transcendent meaning. This gives the two partners a connection both verbal and nonverbal. As with parenting intimacy, the partners share a strong conviction and a deep commitment to their belief system that is spiritually rewarding to each one.

Ralph and Esther

Ralph and Esther were both raised in the Roman Catholic tradition. Ralph had been an altar boy through his school years, while Esther had been very active in the church youth group in her town. While attending churches hundreds of miles apart, Esther and Ralph each developed a deep love for the Church, its faith, and a commitment to community service via their faith community. They met in college and married soon thereafter. They resumed their spiritual life in a faith community nearby.

Each found joy in the practice of their faith together. Unlike their own families of origin, Esther and Ralph often found discussing Scripture and the teachings of the Church enriching and very gratifying. They routinely hosted small gatherings in their home over the years, adding to their spiritual joy and connection with others in their church community. Ralph and Esther firmly believe that they have developed an intimate relationship, especially because of their shared faith and spiritual experiences together.

Recreational Intimacy

Recreational intimacy is a unique form of closeness, often found in dual-career marriages. The demands on time and energy of managing two careers and family sometimes require partners to work almost as a tag team with home responsibilities. This is very common in our society today. But in the midst of juggling tasks and dealing with exhaustion, some couples find a way to share a hobby or another form of recreation together on a regular basis.

Athletic activities, photography clubs, antique auto clubs, hiking clubs, genealogical studies, and political action groups are just a few examples of the recreational activities or social causes that we have seen couples engage in over time together. Hobbies, causes, or mutual sports can provide an opportunity for self-expression and shared satisfaction. If you share a recreational connection with your partner, it is likely to be a way of connecting with him/her, as well as a means of self-development for yourself. When this combination exists over time for a couple, a deep form of intimacy may develop. Elise and Bill found this to be the case, even after their two children were born.

Elise and Bill

Ever since their college days Elise and Bill had enjoyed playing golf. Elise was on the college team, while Bill avidly took to the sport as recreation with some of his buddies. Following their marriage, they thought they would take the chance that golfing together would be enjoyable and not competitive. They had heard of a few couples who had damaged their relationships by sharing sports, because they had become too intensely competitive, or tried to coach each other. But Bill and Elise were tuned into the possible risks. In the end, their shared passion for golf became a wonderful form of recreational intimacy that they enjoyed immensely. They were able to make golf a priority so they would have adequate time to play together.

Golfing became a regular part of their relationship, requiring them to plan their time together and arrange child care in advance. Golf was always a "must" and, clearly, it was a part of the intimacy they felt with each other.

Esthetic Intimacy

There are different forms of intimacy. Married couples can share several forms of intimacy simultaneously. The number of forms it takes is less important than the depth of the shared time together. This is true when partners share a deep *appreciation of art and nature*. Partners who develop an appreciation of art can bring to their relationship a passion and depth of experience that they can share with no one else in the same way. This is a unique form of intimacy, as it often requires each partner to verbalize what is experienced with his/her senses for the partner. Putting into words the experience of hearing a symphony, seeing a ballet, or visiting an art gallery can be a daunting task. Similarly, a deep engagement with nature through the experiences of, e. g., outdoor photography, hiking, or bird-watching challenges each partner to find clear ways to express the depth of experience to the other partner.

Gil and Jackie

Gil and Jackie first met at an outdoor shelter in the Adirondack Mountains in upstate New York. Each had been hiking with a small company of friends and happened upon a lean-to shelter during a surprise snow squall near the peak of McBride Mountain. As they all journeyed down the mountain together, Jackie and Gil took to each other and their mutual interest in the outdoors. Both were struck by the beauty of nature around them, more than their companions who were mainly interested in the challenge of hiking as a sport. By the time they reached the end of the trail, Gil had asked Jackie for her telephone number, and she eagerly gave it to him.

It took only a few months of serious dating for Gil and Jackie to realize that they had found a "nature soul mate" in the other. Their courtship time was filled with hikes, activism in the local environmental lobby, and a developing interest they both had in watercolor painting. Now, after ten years of marriage, Gil and Jackie speak with conviction about their relationship intimacy, especially in regard to their annual trek north to the mountains to camp and paint watercolors outdoors.

Crisis Intimacy

Intimacy developed because of a crisis is never something you plan for with your partner. However, a crisis, health or otherwise, occurring in a marriage or in the extended family sometimes leads to deeper intimacy between marital partners. Although severe crises in a family can contribute to marital stress and breakups, they can also be used by couples to develop a unique form of intimacy.

Crises like a child's severe illness, a natural disaster that destroys the couple's home, a lengthy illness of one partner's parent or sibling, or a sudden loss of employment sending the couple into financial hardship can all strengthen that couple's relationship. The demands of these types of crises may elicit deep caring and sensitivity in each partner which far exceeds the intimacy that may have been experienced previously.

Jean and Tom

Jean and Tom had been married for seven years when Jean was diagnosed with breast cancer. Theirs was a second marriage for both of them, with children from their former marriages living in their home. Their children, aged ten through sixteen, visited their noncustodial parents regularly, with no chronic problems between any of the biological parents.

Until the crisis of Jean's diagnosis, Tom and Jean openly shared with each other that they wanted their marriage to provide a family environment for raising their children. Each partner had no desire to have more children from their relationship. They both loved each other, but there was relatively little intimacy between them. Tom was emotionally devastated when he learned of Jean's diagnosis. His mother had died from breast cancer.

As Jean consulted closely with her physicians regarding the suggested treatments and coping strategies, Tom began to modify his way of relating to Jean. Previously a quiet, contributing partner at home, he began to verbalize his feelings of fear, concern, and anger to Jean about her cancer. He connected with her daily, supporting and providing for her in whatever ways she requested. In turn, Jean also became more verbal about her own fears and anger about her cancer. They realized that they had a common foe that had to be overcome for the sake of her health and their marriage. Before the crisis, neither Tom nor Jean had ever considered what they wanted to create in their marriage, beyond providing family stability for their kids. Each had been badly hurt and disappointed in their first marriages, which had left them apprehensive about ever finding intimacy and closeness with a partner. This crisis turned all that upside down.

Jean not only survived her cancer, she and Tom developed a deep level of sharing and affection for each other that neither had thought possible when they married. They developed a form of intimacy that was both emotional and physical, and, most importantly, was forged out of their need to cope with a life-threatening crisis beyond their control.

You may find it useful to consider how you may have dealt with a similar crisis that had a heavy impact on your marriage, as well as the crises of other people you know. Was the crisis the death knell for the marriage, or did the partners see it as a cause to come closer together?

Emotional Intimacy

Of all the forms intimacy can take, emotional intimacy is the most difficult to describe. Many of the forms discussed previously were built on a common experience or focus that initially connects the partners in a common concern. With emotional intimacy, the depth of the sharing *of the self* is the connection, rather than the sharing of an event, object, or person. Many marriages are strong with multiple forms of intimacy; others may have only one or two forms. Partners who share emotional intimacy with each other may have very little in the way of shared interests, and they may not have weathered crises together, yet they find a special passion connecting with one another about each other's daily experiences.

Molly and Wayne

Molly and Wayne are just such a couple. This is the first and only marriage for both of them. They have been together now for twenty-five years. They have two children, both of whom are in college. Molly is employed as a secondary school principal, and Wayne is a self-employed financial planner. They both love their work and spend long hours at their jobs.

When they are together, they are each other's primary support person, even though neither partner has very much knowledge about the other's line of work.

Molly and Wayne listen to each other. From the early days of their courtship they spent hours talking with each other about everything and anything. They have never doubted that their marriage is a place of emotional sanctuary for both of them. Even when raising the children, and through their differences on parenting, Molly and Wayne held above all else the need to maintain their special time to listen and be with each other.

It has been the intangibles that provide the almost mystical connection these two partners feel for each other, instead of the obvious issues or challenges that might have helped them unite. If you ask either one about the other, you might get the same response . . . a smile, a facial glow, and praise for the other's great presence in the relationship.

Sexual Intimacy

Now, just because Molly and Wayne have a special emotional intimacy that they prize, do you also expect that they would have great *sexual intimacy*? Not necessarily. Although some couples speak of each other as their emotional soul mates and report that they are great sexual lovers too, those two forms of intimacy are not always found together. In fact, we have known several couples who had excellent sexual intimacy, the kind of intimacy that involves sensitivity to the physical chemistry and complementarity of lovemaking (not just having sex), but they also experience a total void when it comes to the ability to verbally relate and define themselves to each other. It is almost as if words are an encumbrance and barrier to their relationship intimacy.

Al and Justine

Al and Justine are like that. Over the nineteen years they have been together, they always have had exhilarating and wonderful sex. In fact, both partners can joke about how they can go from a heated argument to falling into each other's arms as physical soul mates. They have entirely separate hobbies and interests and work at very different jobs. If asked, Justine and Al would strongly assert that they have a true intimacy that no one else they know has. Their work schedules are very demanding and irregular. Their children have similarly complex schedules. And yet, Justine and Al "never miss a time we can be together, alone."

Intimacy Comes in Different Shades

After looking at the definitions and descriptions of the different kinds of intimacy, some assessment is in order. As we have suggested, too often we practice black-or-white thinking based on one definition of intimacy. So if good sex is defined as intimacy, a black-or white-determination is made about how intimate a marriage is on the basis of the quality or frequency of the sex. What is often missing from such a determination is that the couple may be quite intimate in their parenting activities or in shared recreational pursuits. All-or-nothing categories block this realization.

Moving toward intimacy begins by first asking yourself how you define intimacy, and whether you are practicing black-or-white thinking as a result of your definition. Second, it means beginning a dialogue with your partner about creating shared definitions of intimacy, so that your destination is agreed-upon and clear. Remember you must speak for yourself about what you like and want and what you would like to give. Your partner must speak for himself or herself equally. Make it a regular practice to talk about yourselves in this regard, so that there are fewer assumptions and black-or-white generalizations made by the two of you about the kind of intimacy you hope to achieve within your relationship.

Once you have done that work, the journey toward intimacy is made more complicated by a number of other factors. As we have said many times, every issue or problem gets caught up in you and your partner's interactional patterns or arguments, that are fueled by belief systems and errors in thinking, as well as by powerful family-of-origin messages. Even when you are clear about yourself with your partner, there can still be interactive obstacles present between the two of you. They may have to do with your ability (or your partner's) to listen and speak clearly. Or they may have to do with less-than-obvious aspects of family-or-origin issues. To understand what the blocks to intimacy may be means that you must fully understand the nature of your interactional patterns.

Problematic Interactional Patterns

As you read the list of the various forms of intimacy, you may have wondered how each type develops. It isn't that any form of intimacy "just happens." Unfortunately, it's not that simple. Intimacy is complicated because, in all of its forms, it requires a dedicated focus on yourself, your anxiety levels, and your desires for the relationship, as well as a dedicated focus on the well-being of your partner.

Intimacy and Anxiety

When you and your partner focus on an issue, like a parenting problem, each of you may be aware of mounting anxiety. It can be a great deal of anxiety or just a hint of it, but the likelihood is great that some anxiety will be present.

Each of you has your own preferred style for coping with mounting anxiety. We have referred earlier to the primary styles of pursuit (physical and/or verbal engagement) and distancing (physical and/or the use of silence) (see chapter 6). This style is activated when you identify an issue to discuss. That's because when you and your partner try to solve a problem, you are moving toward potentially greater intimacy through closeness and self-definition. Stating how you feel and what your thoughts are about a specific issue can bring each of you closer to an understanding and possible agreement. Even if you decide to disagree, you may settle your difference without inflicting any damage to the other's self-image or to the relationship. This will allow greater intimacy to develop.

But as anxiety increases, achieving intimacy is made difficult by these patterned interactions. As noted in chapter 7, each patterned couple response is fueled by your belief systems about an issue requiring intimacy (e.g., parenting). In addition, any possible errors in thinking you or your partner may have (e.g., all-or-nothing decision making) or influences from your family-of-origin may fuel these predictable patterns. Some people actively pursue while their partners distance. Others try to control as a way of dealing with their anxiety. Still others simply give in to avoid conflict. Any of these behavior patterns can generate predictable and counterproductive interactions.

Max and Mary Revisited

In chapter 7, Max and Mary demonstrated how patterned interactions can emerge, blocking intimacy. As you may recall, Mary and Max have an intimacy struggle around money management in their marriage. Their ongoing battle makes intimacy difficult for them to attain. Max manages his anxiety by pursuing Mary and lecturing her about the value of saving money and by accusing her of irresponsibility in money matters. Max could demonstrate his anxiety by distancing, but in this relationship, Max is more often the pursuer. He pursues through criticism and his efforts to exercise power over Mary through knowledge. When Max dominates the conflict, his anxiety about closeness and conflict diminishes.

In this marriage, Mary is the distancer, especially when the heat is on and she is made to feel defensive in the face of Max's pursuit. She becomes defiant, or else she distances herself from him through silence. Sometimes she weeps after Max's onslaught of criticism, which makes her angry at herself and frustrates Max even further. When her distancing behavior takes place, her anxiety diminishes, but the intimacy she experiences with Max does not improve. Rather, she and Max are left feeling even more negative about each other. Money management remains a toxic area in their marriage, but their interactive pattern and argument about money is really the problem and it continues to make intimacy difficult if not impossible to achieve.

How can they change this interaction? It really depends on how their beliefs and perceptions might change. For instance, Max could change his part by going to Mary and saying something like this: "Mary, I'm really worried about our finances and how we manage them. I know that we don't see eye to eye when it comes to money. But I need your help, I can't do this by myself. Maybe we can make some sort of compromise where together we have a plan we both support and where we can feel secure. Can we look at some alternatives that feel safer to me and not too restrictive to you?"

If Max tried an approach like that, Mary may, or may not, respond in kind. She might still feel defensive and try to distance from making plans about finances with Max. Or she might choose to take him up on his invitation and say, "Okay, but let's set some ground rules for how we talk together. I need to feel respected. I don't want to become emotionally overwhelmed by your way of talking to me. Would you agree to setting some ground rules? They don't need to be rigid, they just need to give us both some safety from attacks, and to provide ways we can cool off if we get worked up. I do want us to agree. The money issue to me is less important than how we treat each other."

The way Max and Mary handle their anxious responses to each other about money will have great implications for how intimated they become.

Patterned Interactions and Intimacy

The problem with all of the categories of intimacy we described in the previous section, is that any one of them can fuel a patterned interaction or debate which could make intimacy impossible. Couples can have patterned interactions or arguments about sex, parenting, recreation, or any number of other areas. This could block intimacy from developing in that area.

For example, if Elise tried to coach Bill on his golf swing, and pursued him to play and practice more, or if she constantly critiqued his game, Bill would progressively distance himself from playing with Elise. Their interaction would have prevented their intimacy through golf from ever developing.

Now, take a moment to reflect on the interactional patterns that you often find yourself engaging in with your partner around any of the types of intimacy we've described. Think about your role in the interaction. Do you pursue or do you create distance when you feel anxious in a discussion? How do you act out your role? What happens if you try to adjust it? Do you feel any different? What does your partner do in response? In the space below describe your role in the interactions around intimacy with your partner. Think about a typical scenario, how you feel, and what you do. In the space below describe how you engage in a patterned interaction in such a way that intimacy becomes even more difficult.

_____

_____

_____

_____

_____

Beliefs

There are many different beliefs that automatically affect our behavior when we move toward intimacy in our relationships. For instance, what are your beliefs about gender roles in marriage? If, for example, you believe that women should defer to men in marital decisions, then discussions about home management decisions, parenting, sexual relating, or social activities are likely to be infrequent. Similarly, if you believe that women should be the primary decision maker in all marital and family matters, there might be few conflicts, yet how much intimacy is present in your relationship would be questionable. These gender-based beliefs will of course have a significant impact on intimacy.

Other beliefs include your beliefs about your partner. For example, do you believe that your partner genuinely wants to be close to you? Or do you think that your partner wants to be distant and detached. Your answers to these questions will affect all of your interactions with your partner.

What do you think would happen if you were more intimate with your partner? Are you afraid that you might feel suffocated or overly controlled? If you believe this, then of course you will be reluctant to get too close to your partner. Your beliefs about your partner or your partner's motivations will often guide your interactional patterns. In addition to your beliefs about your partner, you also have beliefs about intimacy itself. What should it feel like? How does one know when it has been achieved?

Often, your beliefs relate to the different types of intimacy that we discussed earlier in this chapter. Your beliefs about what form intimacy should take and what it should feel like also will have a large impact on your interactional patterns.

Karen and Hal

Karen is in her second marriage. She married Hal four years ago. They have three children living with them, all from her first marriage. This marriage is Hal's first. Karen had been married to her first husband, Tony, for ten years before she filed for divorce. She had discovered Tony in an affair for the third time, prompting her to immediately pursue a divorce.

Going into marriage with Hal, Karen had been determined that she would never be put at his emotional mercy, as she had been with her first husband. She also believed that she would have to be far more assertive about her needs and rights than she ever had been with Tony. She believed that intimacy of any kind was nice, but it could never be something that she could fully trust. When she married for the second time, she made a vow to herself to never again feel vulnerable or financially insecure with a man. Therefore, she often took the initiative with Hal on domestic management issues, their social life, parenting, and finances.

Hal had been single for many years, managing his own life quite well with no help or need of consultation from friends or family. He had developed good financial habits and had firm beliefs about how money should be managed. His marriage with Karen has been stormy, especially in regard to finances as Karen doesn't dare trust her husband's money management skills or his fidelity to her. For his part, Hal refuses to defer to a woman's lead in their mutually shared finances, especially given his own success in this area previously. Both of them have a lot of pride and apprehension in this area. Their discussions and interactions are predictable, yet neither knows how to talk about it. They pursue through criticism, and they distance through silence. Obviously their beliefs block the development of their intimacy.

Family-of-Origin Issues

The impact and influence of your family of origin on your understanding of marital intimacy is huge. This is most true in matters regarding intimacy. Your parents' marriage, your friends' unions, and perhaps even your siblings' marriages have all had a profound effect on your understanding of what intimacy within marriage means.

Think about what you heard and saw as a child and what you were taught to believe about men and women in marriages, especially in regard to intimacy. Issues of fidelity, justice, gender equality (or inequality), work, and play are all involved. What you saw and heard about these issues when you were a child became potent influences in how you shape your choices and interactional patterns today, especially in regard to the struggle for intimacy. How intimate was your parents' marriage, and how did they define intimacy? In the space below, try to describe your parents' marriage in terms of their intimacy level:

_____

_____

_____

_____

_____

_____

Gender and Intimacy

What is the role of gender in understanding intimacy? In many families, women function as the emotional thermostats. They are unofficially responsible for the degree and depth of intimacy experienced by other family members. Unpacking your multigenerational, family-of-origin messages and understanding how they affect you is an essential first step toward change. Understanding how you internalized those messages is key.

From there, with your partner, you can begin to explore how you want your marital intimacy to be like or different from that of your parents. From there, you can begin to claim nonreactively what you want from your marriage. We call this process learning how to hold back your reactivity, and learning how to define yourself. Such learning begins with exploration and self-definition.

Family-of-Origin Messages

Unless some of your family-of-origin messages are understood and sorted out, they can result in devastating errors in thinking at highly anxious times in your struggle for intimacy with your partner. By errors in thinking we mean that your ability to think creatively about possibilities and new solutions to old patterns is adversely affected by unexamined and misunderstood family-of-origin issues and beliefs.

As a rule, such beliefs are summed up by all-inclusive phrases like these: All women are flirts. All men must be manipulated when it comes to home management issues, and so on. Beliefs like these are often rooted in family-of-origin assumptions that result in all-or-nothing thinking that can create obstacles certain to block intimacy. Never underestimate the impact of family-of-origin messages in regard to intimacy and the way these messages lead to powerful beliefs that can cause powerful frictions.

Now, try to examine some of your family-of-origin messages about intimacy. List as many messages as you can, and explore the types of belief systems that resulted from those messages. Use the sentences below to help you get started in your exploration. Spell out your beliefs about intimacy and its possibilities, and your family-of-origin messages.

My interactions around intimacy are.....................

My beliefs about intimacy are.....................

My family-of-origin messages about intimacy are.....................

_____

_____

_____

_____

_____

_____

Being a Self in a Relationship

Understanding your interactional patterns, belief systems, and family-of-origin messages is an important start. However, intimacy is contingent on more than changing your patterns, examining your beliefs, expanding your definitions of intimacy, or examining your family-of-origin messages. These are very important steps and will help you take further steps toward a more satisfying level of intimacy, but in themselves these steps do not go far enough.

Intimacy is utterly dependent on there being two separate psychological selves in the relationship. For deep intimacy to take place, there must be two separate people. Too often, couples subscribe to the biblical notion that "the two shall become as one." In the misguided attempt to "become as one" some couples forget to continue to define themselves. When people are not self-defined, they tend to become overly reactive and easily influenced by the people around them. They either lose their sense of self and become the self who their partner wants, or reactively they become the opposite of what their partner desires.

Self-Definition

What does it mean to be self-defined? The late family therapist Murray Bowen referred to it as "differentiation of self" as discussed in chapter 8. To be differentiated, according to Bowen

(1988), is to be able to be who you are nonreactively, no matter where you are, and no matter whom you are with. It means being nonreactive, and nonanxious in your relationships. This implies two things:

1. Not defining yourself in opposition to someone else, and

2. Not becoming the self someone else wants you to be.

For example, an adolescent male may become a die-hard Republican in opposition to his liberal, Democratic father, not because he is taking a well-thought-out political position, but simply to take the other side, reactively, in opposition to his father. The other extreme would be for that same adolescent to become a liberal Democrat to gain his father's acceptance. Neither is an example of differentiation because both are reactive positions. They are not the positions of a differentiated, or self-defined, person.

A differentiated person can take a nonreactive "I position" on any given topic, and not become overanxious or defensive if his or her significant other disagrees. Self-defined people "hold onto themselves" and do not lose themselves in relationship. This can be very difficult work. In fact, as Bowen taught, it is a lifelong process. Part of an intimate marriage requires each partner to continue working on self-definition, since the capacity to define oneself is key in the growth of intimacy.

Ann and George

Ann would often become very anxious when her husband George expressed strong opinions about his religious views. She felt that he was trying to convert or change her to accept his beliefs. As a result, she would become silent and listen to him expound his vehement opinions, often feeling resentful and distant but never responding. At times, she went to his church with him, but she never liked it. In fact, the church's very conservative theology made her feel uncomfortable. She grew more and more distant from George, and although she took a deep interest in spiritual matters, she never shared it with him. She felt that he would never understand. Needless to say, they did not have any shared spiritual intimacy.

The reality, however, was not that this was a "spiritual problem" or even a difference of opinion. The problem was her inability to nonreactively hold onto her own position and to express her opinions calmly. Not surprisingly she had grown up with a domineering father who made it very difficult for any family member to express any opinion other than his. Whenever anyone disagreed with his positions, he had erupted in rages. Ann had learned early in life that her best response was to remain quiet, not rock the boat, and everything would stay calm.

As a result, Ann's marriage was calm, but not intimate. She had learned very effectively how to keep the peace. The price she paid was the absence of intimacy. Secretly, she feared that, if she ever spoke her mind, her husband would react just as her father had. This belief became the grid through which she viewed her husband. Because she was too anxious to ever take an "I position" or define herself, her belief remained unchallenged. Her husband, however, often complained about the growing distance between them. Intimacy is built on the capacity of both partners to hold back their reactivity and define themselves. The inability to do this creates problems in several ways.

First, it can result in marital distance, or its opposite, high reactivity. Ann created distance by not being clear about her own beliefs. However, if she had become reactive and attacked her husband's beliefs, intimacy would still not have resulted. Ann needs to learn how to "hold onto herself" and how to nonreactively say to George: "I know that your church means a lot to you. I certainly don't want you to change churches. But you need to understand that I cannot work on my own spiritual life in your church. I need to find my own path, and that may look different from yours."

Ann also needs to learn how to respond if George were to become defensive, or try to convert her to his way of thinking. If she can learn to hold onto herself and not react, in the long term she will grow closer to George, and they will have a greater chance of achieving intimacy in their marriage.

The second problem is that if she cannot hold onto herself, she will not be able to feel empathy for George. When people do not hold onto themselves, they become too anxious to listen with empathy. Ann cannot listen to George if his opinions cause her to feel anxiety. Only when she can hold onto herself, and lower her anxiety level, will she be able to listen effectively. Lowering her anxiety requires her to accept her own thoughts and feelings, having no need to defend or justify them, and no intent to change George's views.

The Meaning of Differentiation

To summarize, differentiation, or holding onto your self, means having the ability to hold onto your own opinions, beliefs, and interests nonreactively. It means not being defined by your partner, or reactively becoming a self in opposition to your partner. Differentiation involves staying in touch with your own interests, friends, dreams, and feelings.

For many couples this is a lot of work. Too often, they buy into the marital myth described in chapter 2 that holds couples should do everything together. As a result, they lose interest in developing their own individual selves. This is a central tension in many marriages: being an individual self and being part of a couple. It is a fine balance. It is easy to put too much emphasis on individuality, in which case a parallel-track, polite but distant, marriage results. On the other hand, doing everything together as a couple results in a type of marital fusion, which makes it difficult for either partner to grow and develop. Finding the balance is not easy.

Finally, being differentiated and self-aware means being aware of some of the baggage you bring with you into marriage. We have talked a lot about knowing about the belief systems and family-of-origin issues that you carry with you into marriage. This is important work and, hopefully, it will become an important part of your dialogue as a couple. Going deeper with these concepts, however, means not just knowing about your beliefs, patterns, roles, and rules from your family of origin. It also means knowing about the types of old hurts or wounds that you bring into marriage.

Ann, for example, harbored a deep resentment of her father. Her inability to express her opinions on religion was just a symptom of a far deeper issue. For her, any attempt at differentiation or individuation while she was growing up had been interpreted as rebellion or disloyalty to her father. Consequently, she carried within herself a deep hurt. Down deep she believed that she could earn her parents' approval only if she adopted all of their ways and rules. To have truly been herself would have resulted in significant rejection.

Not surprisingly, that wound followed her into her marriage. She doubted whether her husband, George, would love and respect her if she pursued her own interests or if she expressed some of her own values, especially when they differed from his. Of course, she never explained this to George.

George, on the other hand, longed for an intimate partner with whom he could share deep, intimate dialogue. He had grown up in a very emotionally distant family where he had often felt invisible. No matter what he had done as a youngster, he rarely received any attention or validation. He had secretly hoped that marriage would provide a relationship where he would feel genuinely seen. But he, too, never attempted to put that longing into words. As a result, when Ann would politely shut down during their religious discussions, he felt very alone, and he did not know why.

Both Ann and George need to talk to each other about their beliefs and family rules and roles, and about the deep hurts they received in their families while they were children. For this couple, the key to the development of deeper intimacy in their marriage is to work on differentiation or self-definition. Only by increasing their capacity to nonreactively take "I positions," and increasing their capacity to hold onto themselves will their marital intimacy grow. Getting close is dangerous if you fear that you will lose yourself in the process. The more Ann and George define themselves and gain confidence in their capacity to manage their anxieties, the more they work through their family-of-origin issues, and hold onto themselves, the more intimate they will become. If they can talk to each other about how they were hurt and wounded in their families of origin, and see how those hurts are replicated in their marriage, their capacity for healing and intimacy can grow even deeper.

From Self-Definition to Empathy and Healing

Ann worked on her self-definition and on her anxiety about defining herself. She finally reached the point where she was able to discuss some of her spiritual views with her husband. She explained to him how she felt about going to church with him. Naturally, George became defensive and somewhat argumentative, but he did not blow up the way Ann's father would have done.

When he grew defensive, Ann held onto herself and did not react. Neither did she cave in to him. She was able to tell George that she respected his opinion and was glad he had found a church that suited him, but it did not suit her. Over time, they were able to share their spiritual interests more deeply and honestly and actually found some intimacy in their discussions. Of course, the discussion of where they should attend church remains somewhat tense. For this couple, self-definition allowed them to grow in intimacy.

Their increased self-definition indirectly also allowed them to increase their empathy for each other. Before she defined herself better, Ann was not able to listen or feel any empathy for her husband's spiritual interests. He made her too anxious. She always felt that he was trying to mold and shape her. Mates who feel frustrated and anxious frequently do try to change their partners. Anxiety moves people either to try to change or convert their spouse, or, as in Ann's situation, to shut down and not define their position. Both positions block the development of intimacy. In addition, they block the development of empathy and understanding.

Empathy

Empathy can be offered only when we are nonanxious. Basically, we all crave empathy and understanding from our partners. We want them to "get it." To really see us, understand us, and accept us. We often hope that they will even make up for some of the pain of childhood. Ann, for example, longed to feel accepted for who she was even when her opinions differed from those of her husband. Empathy is the capacity to put yourself into the other's frame of reference and try to understand their reality. Really try to see the issue through their subjective viewpoint. For Ann, this meant a sincere attempt to understand how important George's religious views were to him, how they provided him with a sense of meaning, but without having to adopt those views as her own. Obviously, this is not easy.

Think back over the course of your own life. How many people were there who related to you with empathy? How many really listened to you in such a way that you knew that you had their undivided attention, and that they were truly understanding your point of view? Think back on your family members, friends, teachers, ministers, and so forth. Make a list of all the people who come to mind. If your list is longer than two or three people, you are very fortunate and very unusual.

Empathy Is Rare

Empathic listening is rare. It involves listening that hears not only the content of what we say, but also understands on a deep level the way in which we see the world. The experience leaves us feeling understood, emotionally connected, and emotionally safe. It is the experience of feeling held emotionally rather than physically.

To reach that goal demands increased self-definition. To really listen, whether to your partner's views on parenting, religion, family, recreation, money, or sex, demands the capacity to listen without being overwhelmed by your own anxiety. The greater the degree of differentiation, the more you can listen without becoming emotionally reactive. Creating empathy is a lifelong journey. Those couples who stay on that path will enjoy increased degrees of intimacy. Certainly they will have their share of conflict and misunderstandings. But through it all they will hold onto themselves and come to understand and respect their partners more deeply.

The best road to deep intimacy does not come through a series of clever techniques. It comes from staying on the long-term path of self-definition or differentiation. Only a self that is defined can provide genuine caring, empathy, and healing.

Remember, to build a more intimate relationship follow these steps:

1. Be careful how you define intimacy. Make sure you and your partner are using the same definition.

2. Be clear about how your interactional patterns block intimacy, and change your role in those patterns.

3. Stay aware of the power of your beliefs about intimacy, and how they may have been shaped in your family of origin. Continue to engage in dialogues with your partner about your beliefs.

4. Finally, remember, true differentiation develops the deepest level of intimacy.

CHAPTER ELEVEN

Improving Your Sexual Relationship, or, I Can't Get No Satisfaction

Of all the issues in marriage, sex can be the most complicated and the most frustrating. As the Rolling Stones put it, "I can't get no satisfaction. . . . But I try, and I try, and I try, I can't get no, no, no, I can't get no satisfaction." This is the complaint of many couples. Although sex is a major part of what powerfully brings couples together, it frequently becomes a source of tension within marriage. How can something that was so much fun before marriage become routine, boring, and a source of conflict?

We routinely hear comments and complaints that sound like the lyrics just quoted. Comments like, "He thinks we can go right from a fight into the bedroom and that will make everything better." "She never takes any initiative sexually." "Can't he ever be more creative?" "Having sex feels like my last job before I can go to sleep." " It's not very good for me, but I know how important it is for him (or her)." "I feel like she is planning the dinner menu while we are making love." "Why can't he ever be affectionate in nonsexual ways instead of only when he wants sex?" "Why can't she ever do anything to surprise me?" "I dress up in my sexiest lingerie and he falls asleep. Talk about feeling rejected." The list goes on and on. Although the complaints differ, the tension level reflected by these comments is similar.

Many people are secretly afraid that they are missing something sexually. They think there must be a secret formula to sexual success that they just haven't found yet. The next time you are waiting in line at a supermarket checkout, take a minute to review the lead articles in the popular news magazines in the racks next to you. You will see articles on "The top ten positions," "How to make your man (or woman) go wild," "How to make him/her beg for more," or from a recent fitness magazine, "How to keep going all night." Or, just to add a little more pressure, "How does your sex life measure up to our new survey?"

A trip to the local bookstore will add to the possibilities. Most of the self-help books and articles suggest that good sex is a simple matter of finding the right position, the right technique, or developing the right body, or even wearing the right sexy outfit. Some of the books suggest trying a new technique every week to surprise your spouse. In the popular press, the answer to the question, "How can I have a more exciting sex life?" is simply to find new, more creative, and better techniques.

Add to this the increased amount of sexuality on TV and in the movies. It all seems so effortless, and so simple. Couples meet each other, have a drink, talk briefly, and then fall passionately into bed to make wild sex. If life were only that easy. These shows suggest that there is no work, little communication, or understanding required for having good sex. It "just happens" based on the right chemistry.

Sexual Myths

If you were to conduct a brief survey of all the articles about sex in popular magazines, and on sex in TV shows, advertising, and movies, certain widespread notions about sex would become evident. These include some of the following myths. As you evaluate your own sex life, ask yourself with which of the following myths you identify.

Myth No. 1: Good Sex Depends on Knowing the Right Technique

People who buy into this myth sincerely believe that if they could just find the right technique, or the right manual, or the right article, then they would be okay. They are convinced they are missing some important sexual information. They anxiously read the latest issue of *Cosmopolitan*, or *Men's Fitness*, or whichever magazine has the most exciting lead article claiming to have found the secret to sexual success. This myth conforms to our cultural preoccupation that there are simple behavioral solutions or mechanical techniques to solve any problem—including the problem of how to have a satisfying sexual life.

Many sex manuals support this myth. Some support it directly by promoting 101 positions or other such technique-driven suggestions. Others are more subtle and indirect. They routinely suggest "sensate focus exercises," designed to help couples get better acquainted with each other's bodies, in nongenital and nonpressured ways. Although this is often a very helpful exercise it does support the myth that good sex is a matter of finding the right technique. In so doing, these writers separate sex from the context of the whole relationship.

Myth No. 2: Good Sex Is a Matter of Having the Right Body

In a culture that prizes eternal youth and perfect bodies, it is no wonder that this second myth, popularized by the growing number of fitness magazines, suggests that getting in shape by lifting weights, running, or whatever will result in better sex. Many people are so self-conscious and preoccupied with their lack of a perfect body that they hold back sexually. Obviously, overall physical fitness helps in many aspects of life, including sex. However, making good sex contingent on the perfect body doesn't work. This myth of course gives no recognition to the intimate sexuality enjoyed by senior citizens who have had long-term marriages, enjoy great intimacy in many ways, but whose aging bodies do not fit the ideals of our youth-oriented culture. Instead, this myth offers a very shallow understanding of sexuality.

Myth No. 3: Good Sex Depends on the Right Chemistry

This third myth, popularized by TV shows and movies, holds that people feel a sudden, intense attraction and, then, within a short period of time, they have an incredible sexual experience that involves little or no work or communication. It "just happens," or in the case of many TV shows or movies it just explodes. The implication is that such explosive sex is contingent on just the right chemistry with just the right person in just the right circumstance.

Myth No. 3 has a corollary. It holds that when sex is not so explosive, that means the chemistry was not there in the first place, or it has vanished. Yet, what in the world does "right chemistry" or sexual attraction really mean? Is it really a constant that never changes once you find it? Too many people think that when their initial sexual attraction for their partner fades, it must mean that the "chemistry" is gone. They adopt a passive approach waiting for it to return, rather than being more proactive. The danger of this myth is that it promotes passivity, as opposed to taking action. It is the opposite of the model proposed throughout this book, which is that you can bring change into your life by taking active steps.

Myth No. 4: Sex Should Be Easy

This myth, which follows the "good chemistry" myth, suggests that good sex should come naturally, and there is no need to work on it. Working on sex: Isn't that a contradiction? Shouldn't sex just happen easily between two people who really care about each other? Shouldn't it just be something that feels good, and requires little work or communication? The reality is that good sex requires good communication and feedback. It demands mature partners who take the time to get to know what each one wants, and who talk, specifically, about what turns them on and what doesn't.

Myth No. 5: The Myth of Mutual Orgasm

This myth, similar to the myth of the right chemistry, suggests that couples with a good sexual relationship will easily achieve explosive, mutual orgasm. Again, review the sexual articles in the popular news magazines. They all focus on orgasm in one way or another. Unfortunately, this focus narrows the concept of sexual activity. When mutual orgasm is made the goal of every sexual encounter, it creates intense pressure. The sad result of making mutual orgasm the goal for each sexual encounter is that it increases performance anxiety and focuses exclusively on genital sex, at the expense of a less pressured but more intimate sexual encounter.

Myth No. 6: The Myth of Recreational Sex

This myth suggests that casual sex, between partners who barely know each other, is a fine form of recreation and can be good, clean, healthy fun. This myth implies that sex can be split off from emotional intimacy and become simply physical. Although, obviously, sex can be recreational and simply physical, it is dangerous to separate it from other forms of intimacy. In the end, sex is simply one form of intimacy. It is a form of communication. This myth separates sex from the context of whole relationships, making physical sex the only goal.

Myth No. 7: Sex Should Be Great All of the Time

If you were to ask most couples who have been married for a long time whether sex is great all of the time, most would tell you that it varies considerably. Sometimes it's incredible, and sometimes it's boring. Sometimes is lasts for a long time and other times it's a "quickie." Sometimes you are burning with desire, and other times you're not in the mood. The expectation or myth, however, that sex should be great and spontaneous all of the time just adds intense sexual pressure to the relationship. This myth causes couples to evaluate each sexual experience on a "greatness scale." On this scale, if it wasn't great, then it was no good at all. Those couples who understand that this myth is a fallacy, and accept that their sexual relationship will vary considerably over time, have a much healthier attitude.

How Can Something So Simple Be So Complicated?

Do any of the myths outlined above sound familiar to you? If you adhere to any of them, they only add to any sexual problems you might have. They suggest sexual goals and norms that are not helpful, and they further complicate the sexual lives of many couples. These myths suggest that you must be missing something. Down deep you know that the answer to sexual happiness is not simply a matter of technique. Yet most couples do not know where to start to improve their sexual life together.

Bill and Alice

Bill and Alice are a good example of a couple struggling to keep their sexual life alive after eighteen years of marriage that has left them feeling bored with sex. They described how when they were dating, their sex life was very satisfying, and they joked about how they couldn't keep their hands off each other when they were young. Sex had been one of the highlights of their relationship. Now, eighteen years and two kids later, the sparks are rarely there. Sex had become boring, routine, and not very frequent. Neither partner knew what the problem was.

"Maybe this is just as good as it gets," Bill complained. "It's not that it's terrible or anything like that, there's just no passion." Alice agreed. But she added some more information. "I always felt that it was too important to Bill. Early in our marriage, I felt we put too much emphasis on sex, and I began to resent the sexual pressure I felt. It seemed to be the only thing that helped Bill to relax. Now we both seem too tired most of the time."

After a few more counseling sessions, it became clear that Bill had secretly resented Alice's passivity and lack of sexual creativity for a long time. However, in the interest of keeping things calm, neither had said much to the other about their dissatisfaction. As a result, they had a polite, friendly relationship. They functioned well together in parenting their children, and both have enjoyed some success in their career paths. But sex lost its "fireworks" for them long ago.

Bill and Alice represent one fairly common type of sexual problem. They are one of those couples who have a decent and mostly stable marriage, but who have lost the passion they once knew. Theirs is a solid but passionless marriage. They do not realize that each of them contributes to the problem.

Diane and Steve

Diane and Steve represent a different type of struggle. After Steve complained about how she never was in the mood for sex, Diane got agitated. She seemed afraid to be honest and started talking hesitantly. She slowly described how Steve thought sex was the only way to be intimate, and said that he spent most of his spare time hanging out with his friends. He rarely talked to her, and when he did, it was in reference to the kids' schedules.

At that point, Diane began to cry. "I feel like I'm having sex with someone I hardly know. The only time you try to get close to me is when you want sex. I resent that." When asked for more detail about the sexual aspect of their relationship, Diane became even more embarrassed, but she finally blurted out, "There's nothing in it for me. He's always in such a hurry and never thinks of anyone but himself. For him, sex is 'Boom Bim Bam, thank you, ma'am,' and it's over."

Steve and Diane's sexual difficulty represents another pattern. They have a distant marriage, where the male defines sex as the only vehicle for intimacy, thus creating more resentment and sexual distance in his partner. Furthermore, their marriage represents another difficulty. That is, the absence of any real communication about sex. They have never talked about sex.

Steve has never taken the trouble to really understand Diane's sexuality, let alone to find out what she needs to feel sexual gratified. To do that would require the kind of communication that is totally lacking in their marriage. Again, notice how Steve and Diane each individually add to the sexual problem between them by their lack of honest communication.

Dawn and John

Dawn and John represent still another type of sexual difficulty. John described their problem as Dawn's inability to have an orgasm. He claimed that all of his previous lovers had been able to reach orgasm with him, and he did not understand why Dawn had a problem. He is quite sure that Dawn has the problem, and that she is the one who needs to change.

Dawn did not understand what the problem might be, either. She acknowledged that John did everything right and that he tried to meet her sexual needs. At the same time, she felt pressured by his expectation that his efforts should result in orgasm. As they continued to talk, she acknowledged that this was not the only area in which she felt pressured in the marriage. She felt that John had high expectations of her in a number of areas. She also felt that she never quite measured up to his expectations and that sex was just one more area where she did not meet his expectations. No wonder she experienced difficulty reaching orgasm with John.

Sexual Expression Is Complex

What these three couples demonstrate is that sexual expression can be quite complex. Each of the three represents different types of sexual problems, but despite their differences, the three couples do not need more information or better techniques. For these couples, sexual problems are a part of larger marital difficulties. Sophisticated techniques will not solve their problems.

Types of Sexual Problems

As the stories above illustrate, sexual problems come in a variety of forms. The first problem discussed is *the good but passionless marriage*. This is usually related to a lack of desire. The problem may be a lack of desire for both parties, or it might be that one person actually experiences much less sexual desire than the other.

The second type of problem relates to issues about intimacy. The absence of a more generally defined intimacy often results in problems with sexual intimacy. In these relationships, the couples cannot reach joint definitions of intimacy, do not have much in common, and are unable to share feelings or relate emotionally with each other. One of the partners then defines sex as the main avenue for intimacy, while the other partner resents sex being used for that purpose. This type of sexual problem could be categorized as *the lack of shared definition of intimacy*.

A third type of problem occurs when there are *specific sexual problems*. These include the inability to achieve orgasm, erectile dysfunction, premature ejaculation, and problems related to pain during intercourse. These are very specific problems. Some require the assistance of a skilled sex therapist or a physician; others may be a metaphor for larger issues in the relationship.

A fourth type of sexual problem results from disagreements over frequency, creativity, and experimentation. In this situation one person wants more frequency or experimentation and creativity, while the other person is either not interested or does not want change for whatever reason. This can become a variation on the *pursuer/distancer* type of relationship pattern described in some detail in chapter 3.

A fifth and final sexual problem is related to communication problems. For those couples who are uncomfortable discussing sex, or their sexual desires or fantasies, sexual adjustment can be difficult. These could be referred to as *communication-based sexual problems.*

Sexual Difficulties Are Part of Larger Interactions

Sexual problems must be understood in context. What all of the couples discussed above demonstrate is that sexual problems are usually a part of a larger problem. What these stories indicate is that sexual issues are tied to larger issues within the relationship. Throughout this workbook, we have described the interactional patterns that couples first create and then become trapped by. For most couples, sex cannot be examined in isolation from the larger issues in their marriage. Sex is simply part of a larger marital pattern. It is just another type of communication. In regard to the three couples described, each had predictable interaction patterns. Their sexual difficulties were simply part of these larger patterns.

Bill and Alice

For example, Bill and Alice had a *conflict/avoidant pattern.* We talked about this pattern in our discussion of conflict, in chapter 3, but, obviously, the pattern also can contribute to sexual difficulties. They valued their cordial relationship, and did not want to "rock the boat." They both held onto resentments and had strong feelings about their sexual relationship, but neither wanted to discuss it for fear of the conflict that might arise. As a result, their conflict/avoidant pattern keeps the sexual aspect of their relationship stuck.

Diane and Steve

Diane and Steve represent another type of pattern. Their problem is allowing themselves to feel intimacy in general. The first step toward solving their sexual issues would call for a frank discussion about the nature of intimacy and its value in human life. Steve creates distance from any type of emotional intimacy with Diane. Diane does all the emotional pursuing in their relationship, and assumes responsibility for the emotional temperature of their household. In other words, she is responsible for the overall nurturing of the relationship. She is the one who knows when the emotional climate is chilly. She knows when they need to talk more, and when they need to get out more, as a couple. Steve distances himself from Diane's emotional pursuit and enjoys hanging out with his friends, but he and Diane do very little together. When he does pursue Diane, it is only in the sexual arena. Sex seems to be the only kind of intimacy he can tolerate. But Diane creates distance from him sexually, because she feels that having sex is the only time he wants to be close to her. She feels devalued by him.

As you can see, their sexual problems—as difficult as they are—are only a part of their larger issue around intimacy. Diane pursues Steve for emotional intimacy and Steve is the distancer. Steve then pursues Diane for sexual intimacy, and then Diane creates the distance. Either way their pattern does not change. It remains the pursuer/distancer pattern. And resulting from their larger problem is a second problem: *the pursuer/distancer sexual pattern.*

Dawn and John

Finally, Dawn and John demonstrate an even more complicated sexual interaction. Their pattern is a variation of the dominant/submissive type of relationship. John appears to be dominant in his efforts to change Dawn. Certainly, she perceives him (rightly or wrongly) as trying to mold and control her, even though he does it very "nicely." This feels like pressure to her and so, of course, the pressure she feels emerges in their sexual relationship, where Dawn is unable to become the self that John wants her to be. In this arena, Dawn retains her power indirectly. Sex is the one place she cannot be controlled, while appearing to be submissive.

With all three couples, their sexual problems are part of their larger relationship patterns. To think about their sexual problems as related to physical techniques is to miss the point. Their sexual interactions have taken on a life of their own. For the sexual aspect of their relationships to improve, their larger interactional patterns must be addressed.

So, What's Your Problem?

Before you read much further, stop for a while and think about the sexual aspect of your relationship. How do you evaluate that part of your marriage? When it comes to sex, where do you think your problem lies?

_____

_____

_____

_____

Patterned Relationships and Sexuality

Now, try to understand the problem you just wrote about in a larger context. When thinking about the different couple patterns, some are predictable. Again, as you continue to read, keep asking yourself, "Which relationship pattern best describes my marriage?"

The Pursuer/Distancer Pattern

The most obvious pattern is the *pursuer/distancer* type discussed in chapter 3, clearly it has a lot to do with sex. In this pattern one person deals with his/her anxiety by pursuing the other for more emotional intimacy. Predictably, the more one person pursues emotional intimacy, the more the other deals with the anxiety aroused by the pursuit by creating distance. Each partner reinforces the other's stance. The distancer says he or she must create distance to get away from pursuit, and vice versa.

Sexually, however, this pattern is usually reversed. The distancer becomes the sexual pursuer. That is, the distancer deals with his or her anxiety by pursuing sexual intimacy. The distancer believes that if he or she were to become sexually closer, intimacy will follow. But, this time, the person who has pursued emotional intimacy rejects the sexual advances of his/her partner and creates sexual distance. The pattern changes dramatically in the bedroom—it reverses itself.

The Dominant/Submissive Pattern

The *dominant/submissive* pattern follows the same reversal dynamic. The dominant partner appears to have the power. The submissive partner always looks as if he or she caves in to the dominant person's demands. But this relational pattern has both overt and covert dimensions. The overt dimension, visible to most people, makes it appear that the dominant person has all the power. However, in the covert dimension, the submissive person takes power elsewhere.

The most logical place to take power is in the bedroom. Sex becomes a way to take back power indirectly, without assuming the responsibility for taking power. Often the submissive person is "just too tired," has a "headache," or is too preoccupied to be interested in sex. Or if the submissive person is willing to "give in" to the other's sexual demands, he or she literally "gives in." That is, "submissive" types don't really become engaged in the activity. They go through the motions, but are not involved, either sexually or emotionally. In fact, those persons with the least interest in sex or with the less intense sexual drive in the partnership always has control of the sexual relationship. If they "give in," they still indirectly control the sexual relationship. Saying, "Yes, I'll have sex with you, but please come quickly," is not exactly a turn on, but it does allow the "submissive" person to take charge of the relationship.

The Conflict/Avoidant Pattern

Other couples adopt *a conflict/avoidant* pattern. They keep things comfortable and maintain the status quo by avoiding difficult topics. On the surface, these couples appear to have very solid relationships, and they are unfailingly polite to each other. A closer look, however, reveals emotionally distant relationships. This distance reveals itself most acutely in the bedroom. It is rather difficult to have "polite sex." This pattern helps produce a second pattern, *the good but passionless marriage* discussed earlier in this chapter. When sex does happen, it is "fine," meaning neither person will complain about it. However, neither person has the courage to talk about their differences, or likes and dislikes.

The Problem in Defining Intimacy Pattern

Then, there is always the problem of *how intimacy is defined in a relationship.* Frequently this pattern is predictable, and it is often, but not always, a gender issue. One person (often the woman) states, "If we were more intimate then I might feel more sexual desire." Her partner usually responds, "If we had more and better sex, I would feel more intimate." Obviously there can be no winner in this discussion. They go round and round arguing their positions with each partner claiming that if intimacy was defined according to his or her understanding, they would achieve greater intimacy. In the end no one feels much intimacy with the other and neither person gets what s/he wants.

The Paradoxical Bind Pattern

Finally, there are those who try to improve their sexual problems with the command "Be spontaneous." By asking their spouse to be spontaneous, they create a paradoxical bind. That is, no one can be spontaneous on command; it is an impossibility. The harder you try to be sexually spontaneous, the more you have to think about it, and the more tense the sexual encounter becomes. This can set off another pattern.

For example, Carl was unhappy that his sexual relationship with his wife Maggie was never exciting. The harder he tried, the worse it became, especially because he was convinced that Maggie was the problem. He left articles for her to read around the house. When they did have sex, he made suggestions about what she should do differently. He even went shopping for

Maggie at Victoria's Secret, where he made many purchases. Unfortunately, those purchases remained in a pile in Maggie's drawer. The harder he tried, and the more he complained, the more things stayed the same. Their sexual encounters were far from satisfying and never spontaneous.

Clearly, there are many more variations of sexual patterns between partners. What they all have in common, though, is the fact that their larger interactional patterns prevent the sex from improving. All the physical techniques, creative positions, articles and self-help books in the world cannot improve sexual functioning. In the end, sex is simply one type of communication within marriage. As such, it runs the risk of any other communication problem within marriage. It gets caught in powerful patterns which take on a life of their own that, in turn, cause the issue of sex to become even more complicated.

Now, how would you describe the *overall* patterns in your relationship and how much of an impact do they have on the sexual aspect of your relationship? Take a few minutes and summarize the patterns in your relationship below:

_____

_____

_____

_____

_____

Changing Your Sexual Pattern

Remember, the only person you can change is yourself. Throughout this workbook, we have said that the key to change is first to understand the larger patterns of your relationship. Second, you must understand *your role in the pattern*. And, finally, you must try to change your role in the pattern by doing something different. This is as true for the sexual part of your marriage as it is for any other aspect of your relationship. Try to think about your sexual interactions objectively, from a distance, as it were. What role do you play? Are you the sexual pursuer, or distancer? Do you nag for more or better sex, without trying to understand the impact of your nagging on your spouse? Do you define intimacy too narrowly and, as a result, do you put all the pressure on sex as the chief source of intimacy? Do you just "give in" to avoid conflict? Are you even aware of your spouse's sexual needs and desires?

An even more difficult question to answer is this, Do you turn off your spouse sexually? If so, what do you do to turn off your spouse and make sex less desirable? That is a difficult question to answer. Nagging, putting too much pressure on sex, or not being affectionate during nonsexual times can all contribute to an answer. Reading pornography and spending time on adult Web sites may also send a message to your spouse that will not do much to create desire. Wrestling with these questions is an important part of the change process. Answering them honestly can be the beginning.

Break Out of Your Pattern

Are you the pursuer of sexual intimacy? Then, begin to experiment by creating more open space for your partner by not trying to initiate sex quite as often. Become more creative by offering more nonsexual forms of affection without sex being the goal. Unexpectedly offer hugs, back rubs, and gentle, loving, nonsexual kisses.

If you are the sexual distancer, begin to change your pattern by taking more initiative sexually. Surprise your spouse with your desire. Initiate sex more creatively: in the car, in the kitchen rather than the bedroom. Choreograph a sexual evening. Do something that will really surprise your spouse like offering a full body rub with scented oil, or kidnapping your spouse from work to spend an afternoon in a hotel.

Whether you are the pursuer or distancer sexually, what is important is to assess your sexual pattern and take steps to change it. Only when you abandon your efforts to change your spouse and start to focus on changing your own sexual patterns will there be the possibility for change in your sexual relationship. Remember, any attempt to change your spouse is doomed to failure. This is especially true of the sexual aspect of marriage. In the end, the only person you can change is yourself.

Observing Yourself

When you try to observe your sexual pattern objectively, keep the following questions in mind. They will help you to focus.

- Who initiates sexual contact?

- What is the response to that initiation?

- What is the next level of your sexual interaction?

- If your partner says no, what do you do? Do you sulk? Do you take it as a personal rejection, or even as a sign that you are unattractive? The way you respond often determines what happens next. What is important now is to fully understand your role in the sexual interaction from start to finish.

1. Understand your pattern of initiation. How does sex get started?

2. What do you do and how do you communicate during sex. Are you clear about what you want, what you like and dislike? Are you clear about what your partner likes and dislikes?

3. Do you talk during sex? Does talking turn you on or off? What about your partner?
   Remember the sexual myths discussed earlier. Good sex does not simply come naturally, nor is it just a matter of good chemistry. Good sex requires clear communication and feedback between partners.

4. Finally, what happens after sex? Do you smoke the proverbial cigarette, roll over and go to sleep without any further communication, or do you tenderly enjoy the moments of closeness?

As you examine your role, remember there are three phases to any sexual interaction: the initiation, the act itself, the time right after sex. The process of change begins when you start to change your role in your pattern in all three of these phases. Only then will change begin.

Changing Your Pattern and the Problem of Beliefs

As you read the suggestions above about how to change your sexual patterns, if you were honest, you probably groaned: "Why should I be the one to back off and not pursue as much?" "Why should I be the one to initiate having sex?" "Why isn't there a way to change my partner?"

One of the greatest sources of difficulty in changing your patterns has to do with your belief systems and the types of interpretations you constantly make. Remember, your beliefs provide fuel for the larger pattern, and make it even more difficult to change your sexual pattern. Nowhere is that more powerful than in the area of your beliefs about your partner sexually.

Beliefs About Your Partner

As you communicate and relate to your partner, you are constantly making interpretations about what your partner is saying or doing and what it means. This is especially true in the sexual realm of your relationship. Nonverbal cues, assumptions, and specific beliefs all fuel interpretations about our partner. Beliefs like "All he ever wants is sex! He doesn't want to talk to me let alone act romantic. His idea of a romantic afternoon is having a beer and watching football! Then he thinks I should be in the mood for sex." Or, "She's always too tired. When she does say yes, I feel that she is reviewing her to-do list for the next day right in the middle of the act. I know she is not really into it." These are two examples of strong beliefs. Whether they are true or not, they become powerful grids through which your partner may be seen. These are simple stereotypic kinds of beliefs. Your beliefs about your partner may be far more complex, but they can be just as powerfully limiting.

Arne and Jean

Arne and Jean's relationship illustrates such a complex and powerful set of beliefs about each other. After twenty-one years of marriage, they see an empty nest in their future. Their last child will leave for college in a year and they will have the house to themselves. The problem is this: They are not comfortable being with alone together anymore. This is especially true of the sexual part of their relationship. The "spark" has long since gone out.

Jean holds onto a lot of resentment about Arne, especially about sex. But she has difficulty putting her resentments into words. At one time, Arne put a lot of sexual pressure on her, and she still resents that. She still resents his negative moodiness when she was too tired or not in the mood. She had often felt that, when she said "no" to him, she would be forced to pay and pay and pay for her refusal over the next several days, because Arne would become cold, distant, and supercritical of her every move.

In those years, she often wondered whether it wouldn't have been easier just to go through the motions than to deal with Arne's surly moodiness. When she had those thoughts, she also resented even having to think that way.

Today, she remembers how exhausted she was from taking care of the kids all day and having to deal with Arne's sexual pressures at night. She remembers how often she felt as though she were living between a rock and a hard place. She still wonders: Should she have given in to his sexual demands more often so he would have been in a better mood most of the time? She also remembers there were whole years when she felt she never got enough desperately needed sleep.

Today, she believes that sex was always just a pacifier for Arne; that it was the one thing that helped him to relax and stay pleasant. At the same time, she feels more and more resentment that he had not been able to regulate his moods without sex as his tranquilizer of choice.

She believes that Arne has never been interested in her as a person, but has always wanted her to be sexually available. She has rarely thought about her own sexual needs, let alone her sexual fantasies, since she has been so busy responding to Arne's demands.

These are some of the deep beliefs she holds about Arne: She sees him as sexually demanding and as thoroughly uninterested in her needs. Today, even though Arne is far more mellow and much less demanding than he had been as a young man, and even though he no longer goes into grim moods so easily, Jean's powerful beliefs about him have not changed.

Arne, on the other hand, now views sex as somewhat boring. He has grown tired of Jean always having an excuse or just going through the motions. She always seemed tense or distracted; seldom passionate, much less interested. He has never understood why she had so rarely been in the mood or wanted to initiate sex. He had longed for her to take some creative initiative in their sexual life, and had frequently felt a sharp disappointment that she hardly ever did. Over time it all became less important and Arne had increasingly decided not to set himself up for disappointment.

These are some of Arne's beliefs. He wished that they had had more passion in their marriage, but he believed that Jean resented him and he believed that she really wasn't interested in sex. He believed that she had continued to withhold herself from him and punished him as payback for her resentments early in their marriage. On the basis of these beliefs he rarely talked about sex, and, nowadays, he did not initiate frequently.

They were both aware of the growing distance between them, but neither knew how to bridge the gap. Not to mention that they were both too frightened to open up such a difficult and painful subject. Unfortunately, their beliefs about each other have become powerfully fixed, and each has had years of accumulated evidence to support their beliefs. They are the lenses through which they view each other, which makes it very difficult for them to be sexually intimate.

Their beliefs had fueled several different types of sexual interactions. Early in the marriage, the beliefs fueled a type of pursuer/distancer pattern. Arne had pursued constantly, and Jean had distanced sexually almost all of the time. Her distance had not always taken the form of saying "no." Sometimes, she had distanced by going through with the act, but staying very tense, just going through the motions, to keep Arne pacified. Now, as they anticipate the empty nest and being alone together, their sexual pattern has changed again. Their pattern has evolved into a type of conflict/avoidant style where to keep things polite, they never try to talk about difficult subjects, like sex.

What Arne and Jean should do is talk about their mutual beliefs. If their sex life is ever going to improve, there are a number of old issues that must be discussed. They need to talk more about their sexual history with each other and try to understand each other's old hurts.

To be able to talk that way would mean first being able to control their defensive reactions to try to understand each other. They also need to make a sincere effort to talk about the beliefs they have about each other in the present, so that, hopefully, over time their beliefs might change. Although this is a difficult process, and at times discouraging, it can bring about change. When couples talk honestly and allow themselves to be vulnerable to each other, there can be great healing. Feeling understood creates intimacy, which often increases sexual satisfaction.

But beliefs like theirs are not easy to change. A history of unhappy sexual relations for nearly twenty years provides fertile ground for negative beliefs about one's partner to grow and flourish. "He uses sex as a pacifier." "He gets male PMS if I say 'no,' and is in a foul mood over the next few days." "He really doesn't care about what I want or need." "She refuses to ever take initiative and be creative." "She just doesn't like sex." "She must be thinking of someone else because she sure isn't attracted to me." "He wishes I looked like one of his *Playboy* centerfolds, and he probably fantasizes about her while making love to me." These are a brief sampling of sexual beliefs about one's partner which we often hear from couples.

Now, take a few moments and write about some of your beliefs about your partner, and then try to summarize what you believe your partner believes about you sexually.

My Beliefs About My Partner Sexually: _____

_____

_____

_____

_____

My Partner's View of Me Sexually: _____

_____

_____

_____

_____

How Do My Belief's About My Partner Affect My Sexual Interaction with My Partner?
(Do they cause me to pursue, distance, avoid, or get angry?)

_____

_____

_____

_____

Now, use what you have thought about and written about your beliefs as a springboard to try to talk to your partner about your mutual beliefs about each other sexually. Remember, your goal is to first really understand your beliefs about your partner, and his/her beliefs about you, and then work to shift those beliefs. Recognizing and taking responsibility, and even talking with your partner about your beliefs, is an essential part of the change process.

Remember Your Internal Dialogues

Many couples forget that they can talk during sex, and can express what they like and dislike and what they want more of, or less of. This can be a difficult concept for many couples. Even more difficult is to remember that during sex you are frequently engaged in an internal dialogue. An "internal dialogue" is the conversation you have with yourself inside your mind that you do not often share with your partner. It is fueled by your interpretations of your partner and is your automatic internal response. "I'm really too tired, but he will be disappointed if I say no." "She is tense right now. She is probably irritated with me. Why can't she just let things go." An internal dialogue can become very complicated and, too often, it is never shared and further fuels the beliefs we have about each other. It can also add great pressure and tension to a sexual relationship.

Think back to Arne and Jean. Their *internal dialogues about sex* are extremely complicated. They begin long before they get to the bedroom. Think first about their *pre-sex* internal dialogues. Suppose early one evening Arne is more affectionate than usual. Jean will immediately think to herself, "He must be in the mood for sex. Why can't he ever just be affectionate? Now he will be disappointed if I say no, and then I'll pay for it over the weekend when he goes into one of his crabby moods." That internal dialogue would fuel intense resentment in Jean. It has the potential to call up old sexual hurts and frustrations when Arne did sulk for days, and was often quite critical of her.

If she does feel a lot of resentment, that will cause her to feel even less like having sex. Remember, these beliefs and internal dialogues are not necessarily accurate. They are simply interpretations of an event—Arne being more affectionate than usual. Jean interprets his Arne's affectionate gestures as evidence that he is in the mood for sex, but she never really checks out her interpretation. Nor does she trust that, if she says that she is not in the mood, Arne will accept her answer without going into a major sulk.

Suppose later that night, Arne did begin to think that he would like to make love to Jean. At the same time he would also think, "She is never in the mood, so I'll move slowly and gently." However, if he were to move to gently embrace Jean he would sense the tension in her body, and would think, "I figured she'd be uptight. Why is she never in the mood? Why can't I ever get close to her?" And with that he would give up, roll over, and go to sleep without saying a word, as he has done so many times before.

These devastating internal conversations take place frequently for both partners, and they always end up reinforcing both of their belief systems and interpretations about each other. As a result, they both feel even more distant from each other. Yet neither of them do any reality testing. If they talked to each other about their concerns, their sex life might have a chance of improving.

For example, Jean could say to Arne, "When I'm not in the mood, I'm going to say no. And if you could respect that and not get so grouchy, that would help considerably." Or Arne could say, "I know you think that when you say no to me, I mope around the house. I know I did that years ago. But give me a chance. Trust me that if you say no, I'll be fine." Or, when he senses Jean's tension in bed, he could slow down and talk to her about what she is feeling. If they can both move in these directions, their beliefs about each other and their internal dialogues would shift.

Sharing Internal Dialogues

For many couples, one important way to improve their sexual lives would be to become clear about their needs and take responsibility for sharing some of their internal dialogues about sex with their partners. When these internal dialogues are discussed, there is at least the possibility that your beliefs about your partner will change over time. When you keep your internal dialogues to yourself, that possibility is lessened.

Now, think about some of your own internal dialogue about your partner. What is really going through your mind before, during, and after sex? What would happen if you took the risk of sharing some of these thoughts with your spouse? Wouldn't such a discussion begin to open a better dialogue about sex? Remember, too, that some of your internal dialogues and beliefs about your partner are gender-based.

Gender-Based Beliefs

Too often some of your beliefs about your partner are rooted in stereotypes about gender. Clearly, there are significant sexual differences between men and women. Some are obvious. For most men, orgasm is reached fairly quickly and with minimal foreplay. The movement from arousal to orgasm can be quite quick and the refractory phase is equally dramatic. In other words, when it's over, it's over. Most men have difficulty building up sexual tension again for a second orgasm. Hence, the old roll over and go to sleep routine.

For most women, the road to orgasm is not so quick. Arousal is often slower. From there, the move to the plateau just before orgasm can also be slow. After orgasm, women are quite different from men. Many women can have unlimited orgasms. When men reach orgasm, they are done, they lose their erection and, feeling depleted, they often forget about their partner and want to go to sleep. This can result in much frustration. In this simple summary the obvious problem—timing—is clear. Unless these differences are discussed and understood, a lot of misunderstanding, frustration, and anger will result. If men think that moving quickly to intercourse will bring their partners to orgasm, they will have very frustrated partners. If couples do not talk more specifically about what is necessary and desirable for their arousal and satisfaction, then resolving the problem of timing will be difficult, if not impossible.

Many of the gender-based sexual problems begin with these simple biological differences. If these are not understood, and if various types of foreplay are not experimented with and discussed, anger and frustration will grow. If a woman believes that her partner does not understand her needs, or is insensitive to them, she obviously is not going to be particularly pleased having sex with him.

Sex Is Not a Cure-all

When we conduct couple workshops, women frequently complain that their husbands want to use sex to fix everything, and that men often separate sex from the rest of the relationship. But the women also say they need to feel emotionally intimate before they can be fully responsive as sexual partners.

Of course, these are generalizations. They may be true for you or not. What is important for you is to first explore what you think about gender issues and sex, and to talk to your spouse about your explorations. You may come up with your own list of gender-related issues.

Now, try completing some of the following statements:

Men believe good sex is:

_____

_____

_____

Women believe good sex is:

_____

_____

_____

Men need _____ to be in the mood for sex.

_____

Women need _____ to be in the mood for sex.

_____

General Beliefs About Sex

In addition to beliefs about one's partner and gender-based beliefs we all have beliefs about sex itself. Some of these beliefs originated in our religious upbringing. Those who grew up in certain religious traditions may have been taught that sex was "sinful," "dirty," or "only for the purpose of procreation." There are also beliefs about birth control, and whether it is okay to have sex just for recreational purposes. Some religious backgrounds can leave you with a lot of sexual baggage.

These beliefs are often difficult to work through, and can interfere with a healthy sexual adjustment. Furthermore, if you grew up within a strong religious tradition that had a negative view of sex, then, too often, you received very little sex education. This, in turn, can result in sexual problems, since without basic sexual information, making a healthy sexual adjustment can be even more difficult.

Again, part of changing and improving your sexual relationship is taking responsibility for your own baggage. This means understanding your own belief systems about sex, about your partner, as well as your gender-based beliefs, and using this knowledge to improve communications with your spouse. Improved self-esteem can be built on taking the risk of being more vulnerable with your spouse about your beliefs, and having the courage to talk more honestly about those beliefs. Such conversations, when they result in better understanding and empathy, can pave the way for far better sex.

Family-of-Origin Contributions

Finally, any discussion about sex must consider what we learned about sex in our families. All families communicate their attitudes and values about sex to the children. These can include an overall feeling that is often communicated indirectly. For example, whether sex is a valued part of marriage or merely something to be endured are attitudes frequently communicated by parents to children without ever being expressed verbally.

Often family attitudes about sex are gender-specific. For example, the old adage "boys will be boys" implies a double standard for sexual behavior. It suggests that boys should have as much sexual experience as possible, but that girls should not. This puts women who were brought up in families that adhered to that tradition in a double bind when they marry. They were expected not to be as sexually adventurous during their dating years as their husbands were, but then they are expected to be sexually adventurous in marriage. This is just one of the many cultural double standards communicated by families about sex. There are many others.

Now, take a few moments to jot down what your family taught you about sex. For many this will seem like a very short list because their families never talked about sex at all. However, remember much was taught to you indirectly. For example, if your family never talked about sex, then that in itself makes a powerful statement. Write more generally about the overall attitudes that your family communicated to you about sex. Also try to summarize what your partner learned from his/her family about sex.

My Family's Attitudes Toward Sex

_____

_____

_____

_____

Remember, when you complete this exercise, that family messages were both direct and indirect, and were communicated in a variety of ways. Sometimes the messages were communicated quite directly. For example, those "wonderful" parent–child talks about sex. More often than not, these were tense discussions and became something to laugh about later in life. Although some families were able to communicate healthy attitudes about sex to their children, more often what was communicated was quite negative. "Don't get pregnant." "Be careful, stay away from . . ." (fill in the blank from your own childhood).

Some of those messages might have been helpful, but they did not convey much real information about sex. They mostly reflect parents' fears about their children's involvement in sex. These messages become even more complicated if the parents themselves had unresolved issues sexually, especially dating from their own adolescence.

Even when parents do not conduct talks about "the birds and the bees," they do communicate a great deal of information sexually in an indirect way. This can come through in the form of parents' tension when they talk about sex, or their comments that indicate sex is "dirty" or "wrong," or that "boys will be boys" and women must make sure their husbands are satisfied, so they "won't wander," or comments to an adolescent girl about her "suggestive attire," suggesting that girls are the temptresses and are responsible for controlling sexual interactions. There are endless variations on that theme.

Your Family's Sexual Legacy

All families leave some type of legacy, positive or negative, but a legacy is always left. Family attitudes about sex are part of that legacy. Add to that the fact that sexual attitudes are conveyed from generation to generation. If there are secrets in the family history, like sexual abuse, abortions, or affairs, all of this contaminates the attitudes about sex that are communicated. If, for example, there were affairs in the preceding generations, then the attitudes communicated are that "People are untrustworthy" and "Sex is very dangerous."

If there has been a consistent pattern of infidelity, then often there are gender-based beliefs communicated, as well. These can include "Men always wander," "Men think with their dicks," and "Women can't ever be trusted." Such gender-based beliefs are often the result of generations of infidelity, or other shameful family secrets.

Childhood Sexual Abuse

Obviously, if sexual abuse was present, that is a major factor in the formation of sexual attitudes. Although this is far too complicated a topic to be covered adequately in this chapter, it adds great confusion and trauma to the sexual discussion. However, if someone has been victimized by sexual abuse within the family, she or he will bring extremely powerful attitudes about sex into a marriage.

Abuse victims often associate sex with trauma and intense anxiety, and with shame. Adults who were sexually abused as children often have great difficulties with their sexual adjustment within marriage. Sexual relations with their partner may trigger flashbacks, great anxiety, or even panic. For any type of healing to take place, survivors of sexual abuse must process the impact of the abuse they suffered as children with their partners, often with the help of a skilled therapist. Their partners need to understand how difficult sexual functioning may be for them because of the continuing impact of the abuse. These are very difficult conversations to have without the assistance of a skilled therapist.

In general, it is important to understand your family's sexual legacy. What sexual attitudes did you inherit from the generations that preceded you? They are all an important part of your sexual legacy.

Family Boundaries and Sexual Messages

Often family attitudes about sex are communicated through family structure. All families have some type of structure, healthy or unhealthy. Structure refers to the way families are organized. For example, are both parents in charge of their children, and do they function as a team? Or does one parent not trust the other, and so does most of the parenting by him or herself? There are several important issues here. The first is the issue of boundaries.

"Boundaries" refer to ways in which families structure themselves. They are the invisible limits that define the relationships between the parents and between the parents and their children. Healthy boundaries allow kids to feel safe, knowing that their parents are appropriately in charge and will take care of them. In healthy families, the boundaries are developmentally appropriate. They are not too tight, allowing no freedom. Neither are they so loose that it is not clear who is in charge. They are developmentally appropriate, meaning that as kids get older and more responsible, they earn more and more freedom.

Boundaries in unhealthy families are either too loose, with no one in charge, or so tight that kids cannot breathe and therefore cannot grow. It goes without saying that sexual abuse occurs in families without healthy boundaries. Without clear boundaries, kids are not safe being kids. When boundaries collapse, the most blatant outcome is sexual abuse.

A less obvious form of abuse occurs when a parent makes a child a sexual confidant. Here, the child is unwittingly being turned into a partner or substitute spouse by having to listen to the parent talk about her or his sex life. No matter what is said, the information does damage. Whether that parent describes sex as horrible and unfulfilling, or as a job to be done, or whether the parent brags about sexual exploits, great damage is done to the child. Attitudes and beliefs are formed that can have a strong effect on the child's entire life. Becoming your parent's sexual confidant when you are a child can affect all of your sexual attitudes as an adult very negatively.

Family Messages About Closeness

As discussed in chapter 10 on intimacy, families communicate messages, directly and indirectly, about how close and how intimate relationships should be. For example, in families where abuse and/or addictions are a problem, it is often hard for children to feel close to a nonfunctioning parent. This can create a long-term fear of closeness when these children grow to adulthood. They often have deeply ambivalent feelings about intimacy. The same is true of adult children whose parents were overly close to their children. Often these adult children fear getting close to anyone for fear of becoming suffocated and engulfed. The fear of engulfment and fear of abandonment can both become problems sexually.

Now, take the time to summarize how your family legacy, family boundaries, and messages about closeness impacted on your attitudes about sex.

_____

_____

_____

_____

There is some truth in the old adage that states: "There are six people in the bed: you and your partner, and both sets of parents." Too often, we bring more baggage to the bedroom than we ever realize. Sorting out the impact of this baggage on your sexual life is part of growing together sexually with your partner. Sharing your thoughts about your family's attitudes about sex with your partner, even though this may be painful, is an important step toward a healthier, happier sex life with your partner.

Improving Your Sex Life

The key to a more successful sex life is not improved techniques or new positions. The key is to begin to understand your role in the overall sexual pattern you and your partner have created. This means understanding your role in your sexual interactions, understanding your belief systems and where they originated, and, finally, knowing more about how these beliefs and attitudes formed in your family of origin.

Use the grid to map your role in the sexual aspect of your relationship.

Your Sexual Pattern

(Begin by reviewing your role and the steps in your sexual interactions.)

_____

_____

_____

Your Beliefs About Sex

(Describe your beliefs about your partner and about sex itself.)

_____

_____

_____

_____

Your Family-of-Origin Beliefs

(Summarize what you learned from your family of origin about sex.)

_____

_____

_____

_____

Your Interactional Pattern

(Finally, summarize how your beliefs and your family-of-origin beliefs have affected your sexual patterns.)

_____

_____

_____

_____

After you have gone through the grid, the next obvious and the most difficult step is to _change your role_ with these new insights and understandings about your patterns.

How Does Change Take Place?

Throughout this workbook, we have described specific steps toward change, steps that focus on changing yourself. For sexual matters, these changes can be summarized in a series of three steps.

1. Begin using the grid to understand how your sexual pattern works, what fuels it, and how it is a part of your larger marital interactions. This means being able to clearly define what happens in your sexual pattern and how it is a part of your larger marital pattern. Then, it is essential to understand your specific role in your sexual pattern. We have discussed a variety of those patterns earlier in this chapter. But the first step is to really understand what your specific role is in the pattern.

2. Next, begin the process of change. Change begins by looking at ways to _creatively change your part in your sexual relationship._ This is a difficult step. It involves changing the things you do that create sexual difficulties. This might mean not initiating as often to provide your partner with time to take the initiative. It might mean being careful about how you react when your partner is "not in the mood." This is especially true if you sulk, withdraw, or feel personally rejected by your partner's refusal. If you are a sexual distancer, it might mean that you must try to take more chances at initiating sex. Take some risks and try something new.

   This step also means understanding your belief systems and family-of-origin issues, and their impact on your sexual functioning. By understanding your beliefs and their origins, and by becoming more vulnerable and open to your spouse, you will increase your level of empathy and emotional intimacy with your partner.

   Above all, talk during sex! Talk about what you like and don't like, and what you might like more of. Provide feedback. Experiment and surprise your partner. Remember, your head is your most powerful organ. The more open, natural, and sharing you are, the more you can improve your sexual intimacy. The more you can even maintain eye contact during sex, the deeper the level of your sexual intimacy may grow.

3. Last, is the all-important step of being able to reign in your reactions. As we have said throughout this workbook, holding onto yourself is the ability to be clear about yourself and to stay nonreactive. It means being able to understand your role in your sexual patterns and what you contribute to your problems. It means understanding your belief systems and family-of-origin baggage and how these issues impact your sexual relationship. It means being able to talk to your partner more about _yourself,_ as opposed to trying to

change your partner. Furthermore, it means shifting your role in the sexual patterns as we have described.

All of this is obviously much easier said than done. It is, of course, much easier to become defensive, believe the problem is your partner, and try to get your partner to change. Much more difficult is to define yourself clearly and nonreactively, taking responsibility for yourself and trying to change only your own role in your sexual interactions. Holding back your anxiety when your partner gets angry or anxious about the changes you are making is certainly not easy. But in the end, this is the only road to change that lasts.

Sex and Intimacy

Finally, good sex is related to developing deeper levels of intimacy. There are many different types of intimacy. Good sex is related to deepening your intimacy with your partner in many of these areas. The more a couple gets to know each other deeply over the course of their marriage, the deeper the level their sexual intimacy becomes.

It is one thing to take off your clothes and jump into bed. It is quite another to take off your masks and defenses and over time to allow your partner to see you naked emotionally, to really understand you. This means taking more risks and being more vulnerable with your partner. It means, too, being as empathic as possible with your partner so he or she will have the courage to open up more deeply with you.

CHAPTER TWELVE

Being a Couple with Kids

Angie paced back and forth in the living room. "It's three in the morning and he had a midnight curfew. Where in the world is he?" Her husband, Dan, came sleepily down the stairs. "Are you still up?" "Obviously," replied Angie sarcastically. "How can you sleep when he still isn't home? I can't live like this anymore. This the third weekend in a row, and I'm becoming a nervous wreck." Trying to be helpful, Dan suggested, "Can't you try and get some sleep? You've got to learn to relax, all we ever talk about is Evan." Angie shot back, "Well maybe if you weren't so caught up in your career, you would be more tuned in to what your kids need. I feel like I'm doing all the work here. He needs your input." Now Dan became agitated, as well as anxious, about where their son Evan was. "Every time I ground him, you go easy on him and give him a break. You undo everything I do. Why should I bother?"

At this point, fueled by exhaustion and anxiety, their all too familiar argument was about to take off. Although they both wanted only the best for their son, their differences in parenting philosophy, as well as the difficulty of parenting an adolescent, were taking a toll on their marriage. It was becoming more and more difficult for both Angie and Dan to focus on their marriage. Even worse, their differences in parenting styles were putting a great strain on their marriage.

It is not easy to maintain an intimate marriage and at the same time to function well as parents. How can you focus on kids' needs, school schedules, homework, soccer and other after-school activities; deal with adolescents' mood swings; save for college; maintain careers; and still have time to nurture the intimacy in your marriage? Obviously, it is not easy. Many couples put their marriages on hold, and put all of their energy into parenting their kids. The tension of trying to maintain an intimate marriage and a parenting relationship is often too much to handle.

The fact is *nothing tests marriage more than parenting.* All the influences from your family of origin, all of your myths about how parenting should be, and all of your beliefs about how you should operate as a parent and a spouse have a strong impact on you routinely during the everyday realities of family life. As a result, your interactions with your partner may be intensified by your role as a parent. Trying to be both a good parent and a good spouse can seem overwhelming and, at times, even impossible.

We believe that the dual roles of parent and spouse require skills of empathy, clear communication, respect, patience, and nonjudgmental listening. In addition, being a good parent requires some basic understanding of child development, knowledge of effective, nonphysical discipline methods, and the basic ability to understand your child's rapidly changing world. Each role is demanding. Together, the dual role may seem like too much to handle even on a good day. How do you focus on your needs, the needs of your spouse, and the often complicated and changing needs of your children? Too often, it may feel like there is just not enough time left to strengthen your couple relationship. At the end of an ordinary day, vegging out in front of the TV and sleeping take precedence over your relationship and catching up with each other.

The Difficulties of Balancing Two Roles

The problem is fairly obvious. In your efforts to balance two complicated and demanding roles, great tensions are generated. How do you work on ensuring the good health of both simultaneously? It is one thing to say that the best gift we can give to our children is the gift of being raised inside the boundaries of a safe and loving marriage. It is quite another to maintain that marriage with the constant pressure of raising kids.

In this chapter we explore the dynamics of balancing these two roles. (See chapter 13 for the specific nuances and dynamics of remarried couples and mixed families.) It is important for you to examine carefully these issues in your own unique family. The more alert you can be about how you are affected by these variables, the more you will be able to change your interactions with your partner when necessary.

Keeping a marriage healthy can be difficult in itself. When you add the responsibility of raising healthy, balanced children, it often seems that something has to give. Usually, it is the marriage. How is it possible to work on increasing marital intimacy and to parent demanding children?

Interactions, Arguments, and Roles

In the effort to parent together and still maintain an intimate marriage, some predictable patterns will emerge. When Angie and Dan anxiously waited for their son to come home with the car, they got into one of their predictable interactions. The familiar argument started up. It didn't take long for them to begin arguing about their different parenting styles. Angie argued that she felt responsible for the major share of parenting and said that she needed more help from Dan. Dan argued that whenever he tried to set boundaries and consequences for their son, Angie dismantled his efforts. Round and round they went with the argument going nowhere. All they needed to start their familiar argument was the anxiety of the situation. Dealing with kids can easily create predictable and counterproductive interactions that hurt both the parenting efforts and marital intimacy.

As you reflect on Angie and Dan's problem, think about your own interactions around the parenting of your children. As explained in chapter 3, there are two rules for couple interactions:

1. Your relationship has a predictable pattern, and

2. The patterned behaviors balance and reinforce each other.

These rules operate automatically once you have established a pattern for your interactions. This takes place regardless of the nature of the issue that you and your partner are addressing.

We believe that your style of communication, especially when you or your partner is feeling anxious or edgy about something, can be labeled as a type of interaction, as explained in chapter 3. Parenting issues easily create problematic interactions and arguments. To better understand your role in these problematic interactions, consider the following types of relational patterns. Do any of them fit you? Is there another type of relational pattern that would do a better job of describing how you interact with your spouse in anxious times, especially in regard to family life and children's needs? For starters, consider the following patterned styles and try to see which best describes your situation (see chapter 3 for more details of these styles).

The Conflict/Avoidant Couple

The *conflict/avoidant* couple sidesteps any potentially hot topic having to do with parenting. Each partner keeps his/her own anxiety about parenting at a manageable level by not bringing up any topic that might lead to a disagreement or an argument. When there are issues involving the children, usually one spouse hurriedly handles the problem to keep the other parent from becoming anxious. In the process, the parent handling the problem avoids consulting his or her partner in an effort to avoid any potential disagreement.

Partners in this type of relationship generally are threatened by the possible emotional needs of the other, many of which might surface during times of higher anxiety (e.g., parenting disagreements). Obviously, when important issues or problems with kids are ignored, matters always will worsen. Tension in the marriage may increase and the problems with the child might become even more serious.

The Pursuer/Distancer Couple

The *pursuer/distancer* couple goes round and round with no or limited closeness and a complete lack of consensus on parenting decisions. The partner who distances does so in reaction to the partner who is always pursuing in order to discuss parenting issues or to solve problems. For example, "Dan, we need to have a serious conversation about Evan. I'm really worried about what his teachers are saying. I think we should be doing more." Often the distancing partner will respond, "There is really nothing to worry about." The distancer then distances emotionally, leaving the pursuing partner even more anxious and frustrated than before. Obviously, the issue is not resolved and the distance and tension between the partners increase.

In a variation on this pattern, the pursuer, out of his/her anxiety and uncertainty, criticizes the distancer about a parenting decision. Usually, the distancing partner either has made a unilateral parenting decision or has completely passed the buck to the pursuing partner. This behavior can then trigger the pursuer to push the distancer even harder to deal with the problem.

The Rapid-Escalator Couple

The *rapid-escalator* couple consists of two partners who both seek to convince the other of the correctness of their opinion and intentions regarding a parenting issue. Neither partner tries to reach a consensus with the other. Instead, each partner tries to bring the other around to his/her way of thinking. There is seldom any thinking or reflection done by either person before the discussion. Each chooses to speak out of their own anxiety and reactivity, thereby causing the discussion to become even more volatile. The child's problem may be completely lost in the process because the conflict quickly veers out of control and no longer focuses on what the child needs.

When this type of couple tries to work on a problem regarding their child, they often get into an argument with each other. For example, instead of trying to resolve a school-related problem, they begin to attack and blame each other over who has caused the problem. Soon, they are so caught up in attacking and blaming each other that they become incapable of trying to find a creative solution to their child's problem.

The Passive/Aggressive Couple

Passive/aggressive couples engage in emotional guerilla warfare. Taking sides and creating a triangle (with the child as the third person) often takes place with these couples. The child becomes the leverage factor in an ongoing power struggle between the parents. Partners can develop this type of couple interaction because of a history of mistrust of one another and a fear of open conflict. Both partners passively refrain from revealing their thoughts on a parenting issue, choosing to act behind each other's back in their efforts to achieve their desired outcomes.

For example, if you want your child to attend a particular function, and you suspect your spouse would disagree, you might arrange for the child to attend without telling your spouse until it is too late for him or her to overturn your decision. In these kinds of interactions many kinds of triangles can occur. Triangles, as we have explained in our earlier chapter on family-of-origin issues, occur easily in families. They happen when parents do not agree and one parent pulls in a child as an ally (see chapter 6). For instance, saying something like, "Your father said you can't use the car this weekend, but since he is out of town, he will never know. This will be our secret," creates a triangular situation.

These types of triangles are very damaging for children and for parents. They result in more arguments, distancing, and pain for everyone in the family. Not only do these triangles hurt kids; they dramatically reduce the possibilities for marital intimacy between couples.

The Dominant/Submissive Couple

Dominant/submissive couples are easily identified by other people. One partner overtly makes all the decisions regarding large and small issues, while the submissive partner defers all decisions to the dominant one. However, when you look beneath the surface, you see that each partner is equally emotionally dependent upon the other.

Without a compliant partner, the dominant person would not be able to control someone, and, therefore, to feel better about his/her self-concept. (If no one is depending upon the dominant person, s/he may feel worthless and unlovable.) Without someone leading, the submissive partner also feels alone and unloved because s/he has no one's attention, and thus no one relying upon her/him.

In parenting issues, this couple runs into obvious problems. The dominant parent appears to be loud and controlling and seems to make all or most of the decisions. The "submissive" partner, however, often creates an unhealthy alliance with the children, and frequently undercuts the other partner's decision. Children in such families learn early to ignore the dominant parent and to turn to the "submissive" parent with their requests.

For example, Mike was a loud, powerful, domineering father. He barked orders at his kids, was very demanding, and held them to very high expectations. His wife, Megan, was softer and appeared to be much more submissive and easygoing. She never directly confronted Mike on his parenting style. However, she routinely ignored the strict curfews he imposed on their kids, and when Mike was away traveling on business she allowed them to do whatever they wanted. The kids always came to her when they needed money or permission to go somewhere. For all practical purposes, Mike had very little say about much of what his kids did, and he was rarely consulted by anyone in the family.

Because of this dynamic, dominant/submissive couples often create triangles, which, as stated earlier, become dangerous both for kids and for marital intimacy. Any kind of real balance or partnership is absent in this kind of dynamic.

The Over/Underfunctioning Couple

The *over/underfunctioning* type of couple also have very little balance in their roles. The overfunctioning partner assumes most of the responsibility for parenting. The underfunctioning parent is not nearly as involved in their children's everyday life. These roles are frequently cultural and/or gender-based. The more the overfunctioning parent does, the less the underfunctioning parent does. The underfunctioning partner may feel free to pursue business, hobbies, and/or friends and, over time, may become progressively less tuned in to what is happening in the family's life.

This type of pattern results in at least two problems. First, over time, the overfunctioning parent will start to feel resentment. As a result, marital intimacy will suffer, because the person feeling resentment can create progressively more emotional distance from his or her partner. Second, it hurts the kids. It becomes too easy for the overfunctioning parent to become overinvolved with the children, which, at times, can lead to too much investment in the children's lives, while the underfunctioning partner is largely absent from family life.

The Stable or Healthy Couple

The *stable* or *healthy* couple generally do not hesitate to discuss any issues regarding parenting or any other potentially hot-button issues. Each partner, although not relishing conflict, sees it as a sometimes necessary step in the process of making joint, sometimes complicated, parenting decisions. Each partner views their couple relationship as a strong asset in their parenting, providing strength, support, and diverse ideas.

This couple protects their time together throughout their child-rearing years, so they continue to know each other throughout all of the changes that parenting brings. They are able to tackle head on some the most difficult problems of parenting, and they work together well on issues like discipline and punishments. As a result, they balance the dual roles of parent and spouse.

What Kind of Parenting Pattern Do You Use?

After you have reviewed the parenting patterns described above, can you categorize which type of pattern you use? You may not be using just one but, rather, a combination of several styles. To shift your role and change your parenting style, it is essential to understand which of these styles best describes your pattern.

Now, take a few minutes and describe the types of patterned interactions you and your partner regularly use in your day-to-day parenting activities. Think about a typical week and the type(s) of interaction you and your partner create as you go about the daily activities of parenting. Describe it in the space below:

Our Parenting Patterns

_____

_____

_____

_____

After you have answered the question above, think about which type of couple interaction you and your partner drift into when you have to deal with a difficult problem in your parenting issues. Does this pattern differ greatly from your day-to-day patterns? If so, describe it briefly in the space below:

Our Couple Interaction Pattern for Problems in Parenting

_____

_____

_____

_____

_____

_____

As you zoomed in on your own responses, were you paying attention to your specific role in these interactions? In parenting interactions, especially when things are anxious, what role do you play? Do you overfunction, pursue, distance, avoid? Try to describe your contribution to the problem:

My Parenting Style

_____

_____

_____

_____

The Impact of Interactional Styles

All of the interactional styles described previously emerge in times of anxiety. When things are difficult, it is easy to drift into one of those patterns. At least three negative results are possible:

1. The problem you are trying to resolve with your child will not be resolved. Too much energy is used in the counterproductive interaction with your partner, and not enough will be left to solve the problem creatively with your child.

2. The tension caused by the argument that inevitably occurs as a result of the interaction will leave you feeling more distant from your partner. Consequently, the increased distance will make it even more difficult to feel close, let alone able to work creatively together on parenting issues. The greater the marital distance, the less effective you both will be as parents

3. When tension increases between you and your partner regarding parenting issues, it becomes easy to form triangles with your kids. Many types of triangles can be formed. For example, one parent may side with the child in an argument against the other parent. Or a parent may confide his/her marital problems to the child, thereby creating distance

between the child and the other parent. (This, of course, places a very stressful burden on that child.) An overfunctioning parent may seek inappropriate help from the oldest child when he or she gets too tired. A pursuing spouse may become so frustrated with his/her spouse that the pursuer may try to make the child into a friend. The possibilities are endless. In the end, such triangles and faulty interactions hurt both children and the intimacy between the marital partners.

Belief Systems About Parenting

Belief systems about parenting itself are part of what fuels these counterproductive interaction patterns between partners. Too often, basic beliefs about parenting are not openly discussed by the partners. Many hidden assumptions are never brought to light, and, as a result, it may be difficult to form a parenting partnership.

As a marital partner you may have chosen your husband or wife to be your companion, your lover, your friend, or your "business" (family finances) partner. Before marriage you might have discussed having children. Perhaps you were in agreement about your desire for children. You may even have discussed how many children to have. But it is unlikely that you chose each other exclusively to produce and raise kids. The key point here, though, is that you probably did not think about the tension that might occur between filling the dual roles of parent and spouse.

Subsystems

In any family there are *subsystems* operating when spouses and children interact with each other. A *subsystem* is a subgroup within a larger group. For example, in an intact family with two children, there are three subsystems. There is the marital subsystem, the parenting subsystem, and the sibling subsystem. Each one of these subsystems has particular needs to be met and roles to play.

The marital subsystem needs time for itself. The couple needs to go out on dates, time to talk, and time to nurture their marriage. The parenting subsystem needs to deal with the ongoing and changing developmental needs of their children. The sibling system needs to focus simply on the siblings' need to form their own sibling relationships.

Each of these subsystems has its own boundaries, or invisible divisions, that keep it separate from the other subsystems. The membership (e.g., marriage) or activity (e.g., all those who love fishing, go fishing together) defines where the boundary falls. Others in the family are expected to honor boundary divisions and not intrude unless invited.

For these subsystems to function well, each has specific needs that must be met. We believe that it is difficult to parent well if your marital relationship is not working well. At the same time, the demands of parenting can take a heavy toll on marriage. Unfortunately, some of our beliefs about marriage can make this more difficult. Couples often hold onto certain myths about marriage and parenting which make it even harder to be effective, without realizing what they are doing. Consider some of the following myths and try to see which pertain to your situation. All of these myths can easily generate counterproductive interactions and arguments.

Myths About Parenting

As discussed in earlier chapters, myths are frequently misleading. Every myth originates in a kernel of truth, but it is expanded to have universal, mythic application to many different life situations. Obviously, thinking in all-or-nothing and/or black-or-white ways is too rigid for you and your partner. But in the emotional situations that arise in family life, if you are not careful, it easy for this to happen. You can take a myth you may have held onto for years without ever thinking about it, and, under pressure, you might apply it to a problem as if it were the unbending truth. That can be dangerous for a marriage.

Myth No. 1: A Good Parent Makes a Good Spouse/Partner

Compared to being a good partner, being a good parent takes a whole different set of skills. Sometimes being a "good enough" parent is what is needed. But it may be difficult to convince your spouse that being a "good enough" partner is sufficient. A good (enough) parent is able to provide the listening, the guidance, the discipline, and the nurturing that a child or youth needs and do so in an age-appropriate fashion.

If Jesse is eight and Susie is fifteen, a good enough parent knows how to provide each kid with what is needed according to their age, rather than treating them the same. But, as a rule, a "good enough" partner cannot be "good enough" for very long before s/he triggers resentment in the other partner.

Sometimes, you may find yourself in situations that require you to put more than your customary time and energy into them, like a time-limited work project, thereby lessening the amount of time you have available for your marriage. Most partners would understand this deviation in your routine and tolerate it for a while. Perhaps you would be expected to make up for the "lost time" with special time and activities when the job is finished. That is, if you and your partner operate on the basis of an egalitarian marriage, sharing the responsibilities of the relationship equally.

Intimacy in marriage is different than loving guidance in a parenting relationship. One role expects that the two partners are emotional equals, the other requires that the parents and the children not be considered emotional equals. Each job demands different skills and self-awareness. It is faulty thinking to expect that the skills are transferable.

Parenting requires skills for nurturing, firmness with limits and expectations, and knowledge about children/adolescent developmental needs, just to name a few. Being a spouse/partner may require some of the same skills—the ability to nurture, the ability to know oneself—but the role also requires you to build close ties of friendship and intimacy.

Myth No. 2: Responding to Kids' Needs First Makes for a Healthy Family Life (and Marriage)

If your family is composed of yourself, your partner, and very young children (i.e., aged ten and younger) then there must be an emphasis on providing nurturance and guidance to children. Emotional closeness and intense companionship between parents and children actually is necessary for children's mental and emotional development in their early years. By their middle-school years, they will need more emotional connection with their peers, a more flexible structure with their parents, and their parents' wisdom to know the difference.

Healthy family life needs to change with the developmental changes of a family's members, especially the children. As the children grow and change, the need for nurturing and taking care of your marriage increases accordingly. For instance, once your child enters grade school, that child needs increased social experiences, consistent nurturing, and limit-setting. However, the intensity and round-the-clock need for nurturing from parents begins to lessen at grade-school age. It is important to sustain the nurturing you provide for your marriage at this stage in your family's life. Young children can be extremely demanding of your time, energy, and spirit. But from your child's infancy until s/he leaves home, the nurturance you provide for your marriage actually will give you the extra energy you need to be a responsible and responsive parent.

Myth No. 3: Our Children Have No Influence on the Health of Our Marriage

Although there is not (or should not be) a causal relationship between your children's lives and your marriage, it can be said that how your children manage their daily lives affects the anxiety level in your marriage. And, as we have consistently pointed out, your anxiety and your partner's are major factors in how intimacy is sought, maintained, or avoided.

There is a dynamic in family and marital life that is called detouring. *Detouring* can occur when your anxiety and your partner's reach an unbearable level, and the need to create a triangle with another person is present. A child's problems can result in a frequent detour to a triangle when couples are experiencing a great deal of anxiety in their marriage. Similarly, children may come, over time, to fear your marital conflicts and will demand your attention, as a way of providing a new focus for your marriage. They may do this out of their own fear, out of habit, or out of the belief that they should not be ignored. The older a child gets, the more creative he or she becomes at this.

It is important to remember that children easily can become part of your marital give-and-take even when you aren't aware of it. Present or not, their names may be spoken at the most extremely anxious times by either you or your spouse. The kids in your lives have the strongest potential to influence your marriage.

Myth No. 4: When the Children Are Grown, We Will Have Our Time Together

This is an incipient trap. It starts when your firstborn is an infant, and it's so hard to leave the baby with someone else, even for an hour. Then as your kids grow, it remains difficult to carve out the time to be alone with your partner. We know people who say they can't even go out to dinner (let alone away for a weekend) because of their child-focused commitments.

Obviously you love your children. You are very aware of what they need in the way of encouragement, nurture, discipline, and teaching. The mere thought of putting your "couple time" ahead of your time for your children may seem selfish or neglectful. But the two roles you have as a partner and parent can, and should be, kept in balance. Recent findings by Wallerstein and her colleagues in a twenty-five-year study (2000) showed that the children of divorced parents valued the times when they knew their parents were with each other. Family activities are not the same as couple time.

It is a myth that you will have plenty of time to be with your partner when your kids are adolescents or out on their own. If you do not work on your marriage consistently while your kids are growing, you may find there is nothing left of the marriage when your kids leave home. Your children will become healthier individuals when their needs in the family are balanced against the needs of others, including their parents' need to be together as adults.

Myths Create Interactions

These four common myths about marriage create problems in marital interactions. They fuel expectations and beliefs. If you buy into them, you may believe that you do not have to work hard to protect and sustain your marriage. You may not continue to cultivate it as a separate entity, even while you are engaged in parenting. This is a common trap for many couples. These couples wake up in midlife when their children are gone to find that they have little or nothing left in their marriage. Unless these myths are challenged, and the importance of working on your marriage while you are parenting is made a priority, intimacy will slowly slip away.

Challenge Your Myths

Although these four myths about parenting as a couple are by no means an exhaustive list, you may find at very busy or anxious times that they influence you more than you realize. You are most vulnerable to myths like these when you are very busy or very anxious. Remember, when your anxiety level mounts, your ability to stay nonreactive and think clearly diminishes.

At this point, you may wish to consider the myths that operate for you in this special area of marriage and parenting. Which myth seems to best reflect the tension in your marriage and family? Pay attention to how your myth affects your role and actions.

My Myths About Parenting with My Spouse

1. _____

_____

_____

2. _____

_____

_____

3. _____

_____

_____

4. _____

_____

_____

Beliefs About Children's Developmental Needs

Not only are couple interactions influenced by myths, they are also influenced by the developmental needs of kids. This is an important area for couples to learn about and to share their knowledge with each other. When you function as a parent, you do so on the basis of your beliefs of what is needed for your child at the time: limit-setting, nurturance, discipline, guidance, play time, and so on. Your partner may not have the same beliefs you do about what your child needs. In fact, based upon your families-of-origin influences, you may have very different notions of what your child needs at any particular time.

You may find it useful now to think about the range of knowledge you have about the developmental needs of children. By that we mean: What amount of nurturing, socializing with peers, relating with adults, privacy, discipline, dependency, autonomy, and time with or away from the family is appropriate, given the changing age of your child? It is not uncommon for spouses to have different sets of information or beliefs about child and adolescent development. That knowledge may be from books, magazines, professionals, friends, or family. It may be accurate, or it may be partially true and based on family legend. The important fact is that those beliefs are the basis for how you parent and how you interact with your partner about parenting issues.

Developmental Needs Change

It is also important to recognize that as children move toward adolescence your joint style of parenting needs to change. Less time is needed together as a family, allowing more time for your teens to connect with peer groups. This change is crucial for healthy development, allowing youths to stay connected to their families while moving out into the world. Your parenting also requires that you stay clear about your values, and remain flexible about your daily expectations. Rules about acceptable behavior should stay intact over the years, but not every problem with a teen has to be a battle. One of the top rules for parenting adolescents is to *pick your battles carefully*. Don't waste your energy fighting the small ones. However, deciding which battles are the important ones should be an important couple decision. The interactional styles identified earlier in this chapter may make that discussion quite difficult.

You and your spouse can benefit by working in sync about which battles to sidestep without sacrificing your values. If Jerry comes home thirty minutes late from a school function because he lingered to talk to his friends, that's not the same as when he comes home thirty minutes late from the movie theater, which is five miles from home. You may know what you want to say or do, but does your partner know what you're thinking? Possibly not. So, you might be better off if you talk with your partner after Jerry comes home late, before you talk to Jerry. Remember to keep your anxiety at a manageable level. Quick decisions and actions may not be the best choice when it comes to parenting. A little waiting, thinking, and discussing with your partner will help to reduce your anxiety level. It will also do Jerry some good to sweat it out until you decide to discuss it with him.

Beliefs About Priorities

Each family of origin teaches by example and word what is important for the children in that family. These might be called the family priorities. They can differ from family to family. The priorities may be physical safety and comfort, or the need for education, or social opportunities, or athletic opportunities, or even performing arts opportunities. What is essential is that couples understand and know *together* what their priorities are and how to negotiate with their children.

To complicate matters further, what if your partner is focused on accompanying your son to a football scrimmage for his high school team, while you have been feeling deserted by your spouse the whole past week due to work demands? If your spouse suggests that you both go watch the scrimmage, you may feel conflicted about the invitation. Although your partner may think that being together as a couple is the same as being together as parents watching your son's scrimmage, you know that your needs will not be met because you won't have your partner's undivided attention. Whose priorities win out? It is difficult to balance priorities when you have couple needs as well as busy family needs.

Putting a Boundary Line Around Your Marriage

Whenever we ask couples what they routinely do for entertainment together, we often hear "We all go out to dinner," or "We all go camping," and so on. The "we" means the entire family. Family life may be amply nourished, but when is the marriage nourished? Where do you fit in your quality couple time? It is very important to make regular time for your marriage. Even at times of family or parenting crises, taking the time to be friends and lovers with one another will preserve a foundation of care and trust needed for the tough times. It is invaluable to view your adult relationship with your spouse as a place where only the two of you belong. Be careful to keep your parenting struggles separate from your couple time for recreation and pleasure. When this rule is not observed, it takes very little effort by a child to intrude into your couple time thereafter, especially if your child is adept at misbehaving and acting out.

If you believe that your marriage need not have a boundary line around it, while your spouse believes otherwise, then that is a significant difference in beliefs which should be explored and resolved to the satisfaction of both of you. This belief difference may be due to your families-of-origin influences, which are often the model for this particular issue. We believe that keeping such a boundary in place is essential if you want to keep your dual roles of spouse and parents functioning well.

Either of you may have come, for instance, from a family where the parents were fully absorbed in their own pleasures, without any regard for the care of their children. In families such as those, children are, at best, an afterthought. Their physical and emotional needs frequently receive little healthy attention. Coming from such a background, you might then be so dedicated to your current family that little time is given to your marriage. That can be a problem, even though your actions are motivated by genuine love and concern for your kids. The balance between your roles of spouse and parent and the time you spend in each role is very important.

Beliefs About Roles

How are the roles handled in your marriage when it comes to parenting? In your marriage, you may want a feeling of equality when it comes to sharing responsibility for affection, communication, money and home management, and sexual relating. But you may end up with a more traditional division of labor in your parenting relationship.

On the other hand, you may want to be the primary parent with only backup support from your husband or wife. Or you may be tired of carrying the major load of parenting and want your partner to take it over for a few years while you support his/her decisions with the kids. These beliefs about how roles should work in regard to parenting are very important, and should be discussed thoroughly by couples who are also parents.

Some of the differences in parenting roles, as well as the roles in your marriage, may be determined by your *ideas about gender,* too. What you learned while growing up about a woman's role as a wife in marriage, as well as a parent, may be quite different than what your spouse learned when growing up.

For example, your spouse may have come from a family where the mother died when the children were young, and they were raised by their father. Different expectations and ideas about what men and women are capable of, or are willing to do, fuel your thinking. Too often, couples accept without question traditional gender-based roles when it comes to parenting. Over time, this can lead to a great deal of frustration. If the husband assumes he can pursue his career, and that his wife will be completely responsible for the kids, the wife's resentment may grow. In addition, role issues can detract from a sense of partnership, thereby negatively affecting marital intimacy.

Beliefs About Your Partner as a Parent

Besides gender-based belief systems, there is also the important area of what you believe your partner is capable of doing as a spouse and parent. How much do you trust your partner as a parent? Issues of competence, or your perception of incompetence as defined by your beliefs, can surface, especially around the handling of kids and their needs. Or you may question your spouse's competence as a husband, even though he is a good parent. These are all part of your dual role relationship.

Parenting Together Requires Trust

If you do not believe that your partner is a competent parent, you easily may fall into one of the interactional patterns we have described. For example, if you do not think your spouse is involved enough with the kids, you may begin to pursue and nag to try to force your partner to become more involved. If you believe that your partner overreacts to your adolescent, you may overcompensate by being too lenient or forgiving of your teen's misbehavior, and you may be very lax at maintaining good discipline habits. Or you may overfunction and try to do all the parenting yourself. Any negative belief about your partner's parenting skills will fuel counter-productive interactional patterns, which will only make matters worse.

Now, before moving on to the next section, take a few moments to review. What are some of your belief systems about parenting? Where do your beliefs about parenting conflict with those of your spouse? Make a list of some of your belief systems. Then, make it a point to compare notes with your spouse.

_____

_____

_____

_____

_____

_____

Family-of-Origin Influences on Your Parenting

How often have you said, "I will never be the kind of parent my parents were!" Yet, without realizing it, you may use your family of origin as your model of how to, or not to, work together as partners in the task of joint parenting. This is quite common. Many people who come from troubled family situations have little to rely upon for guidance in this regard. They lack good models. You might come from such a background, or you might have been lucky and had parents who were able to work together rearing their children and maintaining their marital intimacy.

Either way, the family you grew up in influenced your beliefs about how to be—or not be—a parent. While you were growing up, you learned about parenting by watching the interactions of your parents. They were your model. And part of the model used by your family was based on their unique family constellations.

Family Constellations

Family constellation refers to the actual membership of the family, the rank of influence due to age or skills, and the interplay between the members, as well as the roles assigned by birth order. Much of your early experience was affected by the family constellation you were part of as a child. Was it an intact family with two parents and their biological children? Was it a remarried family constellation? Was it a single-parent constellation, with or without a significant other in that single parent's life? Did a grandparent, uncle, or aunt live in your home and influence how parenting and child care were conducted? Did you live with a foster family, or a series of families, perhaps leaving you with a variety of atypical examples of how parenting by spouses takes place? Each of these types of family constellation provides different models for different types of parenting.

Birth Order

Birth order can suggest a variety of belief systems that may have been modeled in your family of origin. For example, you might have been taught that the eldest child should carry more responsibility than younger children. And the belief systems in a family constellation die hard. There are people in their fifties today, who were the youngest children in their families, and who are still referred to by all of their family-of-origin relatives as "the baby"!

If you were the eldest child in a family of four children, while your spouse was the youngest in a family with two children, there are likely to be differences between the two of you regarding your expectations about responsibilities due to others, leadership and initiative, and possible uncertainty as to how much autonomy and/or dependency to expect from each other.

Gender

Adding the factor of gender to family constellations makes the mix even more complex. What if you were the eldest and only daughter with three younger brothers in a family where Dad worked two jobs and Mom was partially disabled? You most likely grew up receiving limited adult attention as a child. You may have been expected to be a junior adult, attending to the needs and care of others at home.

If your spouse had an older sister, and his father worked outside the home while his mother was a full-time homemaker, then he might have been raised with two women taking care of his needs. He may never have been given any responsibility for attending to anyone else's needs. Furthermore, he may expect help attending to his own needs.

Different family constellations generate many different expectations of marriage and parenthood. On the one hand, you may assume your partner shares your expectations. On the other hand, s/he may come from a very different type of family with very different expectations. It is extremely important to compare your different sets of expectations.

Other Powerful Influences

There are other influences that affect what you believe and how you act as a spouse and a parent than just your family-of-origin's constellation and structure. Was there alcoholism or substance abuse/dependence by a parent? Was there domestic violence between your parents, thereby blocking any healthy parenting, given the unsafe setting? Was there chronic mental illness, which certainly affected not only how your parents related to each other as marital partners but also their ability to coparent you and your siblings? Did a relative, like a grandmother or grandfather, live with your family? If so, that had to have had an impact on how you were raised. Your model and your beliefs about how parents work together, or do not work together, largely come from such memories and experiences.

It Wasn't Like This Growing Up: Fred and Jean's Struggle

Fred and Jean have been married for eighteen years. They have three children from this marriage, a son, fifteen, a daughter, thirteen, and another son, ten. Jean works as a registered nurse at the local hospital emergency room. Fred runs his own computer sales and service business from their home. Their children are all active in school-related extracurricular organizations and teams. Their daughter takes private flute lessons and their eldest son has a paper route in the morning.

Because of Jean's varied schedule she and Fred frequently have to scramble at the last minute to arrange transportation for the kids, meal preparation, and so on. Fred experiences a lot of anxiety over all these chores. He had never had to witness much stress or irregularity in his placid family life as the youngest of three sons, with a stay-at-home mother. His father had worked at a local factory, with predictable hours, and his mother had done all the homemaking and chauffeuring for her sons.

Jean, on the other hand, came from a family with a mother who had worked two part-time jobs, while managing their home and all of the parenting of Jean and her younger brother. Jean's alcoholic father had lived at home while he moved from job to job almost every two years. Obviously, both Fred and Jean came to their marriage with different expectations about the roles they would play, as well as different sets of belief systems about the dual roles of spouse and parent.

In their current family structure, by necessity of their schedules, Fred often turns to his daughter to help with meal preparation. She has become his right-hand helper at home, especially when he has to attend to his business in the afternoon. Fred appreciates her help and grants her special favors from time to time, such as money to go to the movies with her friends. His sons do not chip in to help the way their sister does, and they complain to Jean that their father never gives them spending money. When they complain to Jean, rather than fight with Fred about money, she usually gives her sons some spending money.

The structure that Fred and Jean have developed in their roles has created triangles, with an alliance between Fred and his daughter around home tasks, sometimes to the exclusion of the two boys. This puts a strain on the sons' relationship with their sister, as well as their father, as they are jealous of her special role with their father. Similarly, Jean has a distant relationship with her daughter because of the small amount of time they spend together and the emotional closeness that Fred has developed with his daughter.

The dynamics become quite heated whenever Fred forgets to confer about schedules with Jean and talks instead with his daughter about meal preparation and helping the youngest son with homework. Jean can become furious at being ignored by Fred, just as she was hurt as a child being ignored by her father. As a result, their parenting style is beginning to put a large strain on their marriage.

Jean and Fred illustrate the different dynamics and structures that can evolve in a family, and the impact of family-of-origin messages and models on that structure. Now, think about the type of family structure you grew up with. How were roles handled? How much time was set apart for the marriage? How did it affect your expectations as a parent? In the space below, try to summarize what you learned from your family about parenting.

_____

_____

_____

_____

_____

How Did Your Family Teach You to Parent?

As a child and a teenager, you watched both of your parents. Perhaps in your family of origin neither parent spoke directly to you about "This is what a mother is supposed to do...," but it is likely that there were examples of parenting that you witnessed regularly, as well as examples of how spouses behaved with each other.

For instance, your father may have come home from work while your mother was preparing dinner. He might have walked over to her grumbling about his boss a little, and then reached for her to kiss him, pulling her away from the counter where she was preparing a salad. In response, she might have sternly said, "Not now, Russ! I've got to get this dinner ready so that Billy can get to his game in time!"

This brief attempt at expressing affection would have taken only thirty seconds. But you as Billy, or Billy's sister, would have seen your father's affectionate gesture shunned, and your mother steadfastly placing dinner preparation as her top priority, right behind the priority that Billy had to get to his game on time. Such an affectionate act would not have held up anyone in the short time it would have taken. But the underlying beliefs were clearly being demonstrated.

Your observation of this type of interaction would have been filed in your memory bank. The message was as clear as it could be. It was an indirect message about balancing the roles of spouse and parent and very clear about which has first priority. "A mother in this family should place parenting and providing for the children's needs way above time for marital affection, even above a quick kiss in the kitchen."

Keep this example in mind as you consider how family beliefs about spouses as parents affected the standard roles that your parents played in your family. Was your parents' relationship as parents modeled on "Mom the caregiver and Dad the disciplinarian"? The "Wait until your father comes home!" model? Or was your mother the nurturer and disciplinarian, with your father focused on earning the money, paying the bills, and mowing the lawn? Did your dad work nights so that he could be home when you came home from school while your mom worked a daytime shift? Was it his or her responsibility to check your schoolwork and provide study help? Or did your dad work at his job, come home, read the paper, fall asleep in front of the television after supper, and never really interact with the family ... while your mom did her day job, made supper, cleaned, and helped you with your schoolwork?

You might have been raised in an intact family, and then later in your life in a remarried family, thereby experiencing more than one of these patterns before your adulthood. There are attitudes about parenting by spouses that you developed just by living in your family of origin. These attitudes may not always be discernible to you, while others may stand out all the time.

Gender-based actions are one area in which attitudes reveal themselves quickly. For instance, you may believe that boys learn best from their fathers about life, proper behavior, and so on. Similarly, you may believe that girls develop greater sensitivity for others by associating more with their mothers than with their fathers. With those attitudes, nurtured over time in your family of origin, there might be some rigid expectations about how your children should be parented and how that parenting may interfere with your marriage, too. There are many other attitudes about parenting that you learned from your family of origin that, because of space constraints, we cannot discuss here.

So, What Did You Learn?

Growing up, you learned a lot about the roles of spouse and parent, and how to balance the two. Although your parents probably never taught you directly, you learned from watching their modeling, and from the beliefs they demonstrated both directly and indirectly. It is important to understand what you learned about parenting from your parents, as well as to share this learning with your spouse. Remember, both of you come fully equipped with parenting maps from your own histories.

The Role of Your Anxiety—The Catalyst for Action

A basic element in defining your "self" is understanding all that you learned from your family while growing up, and not remaining captive to it, or becoming extremely reactive to it, as discussed in chapters 7 and 8. To be self-defining means being able to choose nonreactively what you want to keep from your family models and what you want to change. To do this, as we said in chapter 8, demands a differentiated or well-defined person, not only in relation to your parents, but also in relation to other significant persons in your life now. Your spouse and your children are in this category.

Throughout this workbook we have discussed the need to define yourself nonreactively, and to find ways to sort out all the influences from your own history. Unfortunately, your anxiety, that sense of whirring and swirling inside of you when things are tense, or when you feel uncertainty mounting within, can easily cause you to react. Anxiety can cause you to be reactive to your kids or to your partner. Anxiety may stir you to pursue your partner to dialogue about something bothering you, even while your partner is trying to exit, either through the door or to a television show. On the other hand, your partner's anxiety level may diminish when s/he distances from you upon encountering your tension. Anxiety can motivate you to overfunction. It can motivate you to avoid conflict. In essence, anxiety can cause you to fall back easily on less thoughtful or less defined ways of relating. Nowhere is this more evident than in parenting.

Family members share and connect with each other in patterned ways. The anxiety within each person at any given time is the catalyst, the gasoline in the tank, for reactivity to come into play. That reactivity might be to seek solace alone in the bathroom, the only room in the house with a door and a lock. Or it might manifest itself in exploding at one of the kids, or cause you to give your partner the silent treatment because of his/her parenting style.

Anxiety can make parenting even more complicated than it need be. Your beliefs about family, what children should receive and deserve, how they should be raised by a mother or a father, and how mothers and fathers should work together for the common good can all create tension and increase the growth of anxiety over time. Whenever you feel anxious as a parent/spouse, it may be because what you learned while growing up is no longer working. Or you may not know how to work with your spouse at raising children together, even though you believe it is a good idea to do so.

Holding onto and defining yourself may require that you give yourself more time to reflect about your parenting patterns. Or you may need to give yourself an opportunity to relax a little *before* you confer with your partner about how to discipline Jerry for his third night out past his curfew. It may also be important to recognize that your spouse has his/her own anxieties in these areas.

Talk and listen often to your partner, while clarifying your beliefs frequently to yourself and with your partner. Compromising and finding a middle ground between your family-of-origin beliefs about parenting and what is needed now in your family are valuable processes, but they sure can stir up your anxiety levels. Increased self-understanding followed by many dialogues with your partner is a great beginning. As always, begin by focusing on your own actions when you become anxious.

Triangles and Kids

The more anxious things become within a family, and the less differentiated a person is, the more his/her life decisions are based on reactivity to important people. In keeping with this line of thinking, the more you behave based on your reactivity to someone else (like your child), the more you and that person may act as one unit rather than as two separate people with your own separate sets of thoughts and feelings. If there's enough anxiety swirling within you at the time, it will become impossible for you to make thoughtful decisions.

As discussed in the last section, your anxiety can be a guide. Begin to watch yourself when you are anxious. What you do? Do you complain to your child about your spouse? Do you share too much personal frustration with your child? This damages both your children and your marital intimacy. Your child, especially when s/he is of school-age and still wanting to be close to you, may feel like a valuable confidant. But, although the triangle you construct with your child may meet some of your needs, it does so in an extremely unhealthy fashion. The closeness of confidants should take place only at the same generational levels (adults with adults, children with children).

How Can You Change Your Parent Role to Improve Your Couple Interaction?

- Take time for yourself regularly. Nurture your own spirit and soul with activities you enjoy doing.

- Initiate and arrange time together with your spouse on a regular basis. Cultivate rituals that allow you and your partner to have time alone apart from your children. Make this sacred time. Protect it from interruption.

- Take regular time to confer with your partner on parenting issues. Compare your belief systems. This should be initiated on a planned basis, when things are calm, not just when there is a pressing issue facing you both today. Tell him/her how you think you are doing in managing the roles of spouse and parent, and invite your spouse to comment. Try to comment less about your spouse and more about what you are doing to improve yourself.

- Let your kids know how important your marriage is to you. Be clear about it often, with words and with time taken to relax and play together, with demonstrated affection.

- Let your kids know how much you cherish them by making time to be with them just to talk about how they are, not only about what they are doing. Invite your partner to join you in these talks. Kids love to have the undivided attention of both parents, not shared with other siblings.

- Remember that families are designed to change and have the children grow into their own lives apart from you. You and your partner are likely to be with each other after the kids grow up and join the circus, so stay cozy with each other. Don't become strangers.

Now, in the space below, summarize what you can do by yourself to enhance your dual roles of parent and spouse with your partner. Remember, you can't change your spouse. You can change only yourself.

CHAPTER THIRTEEN

Remarried Couples: Mixing Families

This chapter focuses on the complex task of building a new marriage following the loss of a previous marriage. It examines the issues of loss, difficult interactional patterns, as well as the complications introduced by the presence of children. Recent studies (Gottman 2000; Wallerstein 2000) have noted that the divorce rate has been unchanged for the past twenty-five to thirty years. Fifty percent of all marriages eventually end in divorce. Within seven years after divorce, most men and women have remarried or have begun another serious relationship. Among those who remarry, the current rate of divorce for second marriages is around 70 percent. That's after less than ten years of marriage for those who fail in their second marital attempt. For many, this is a surprising statistic. After all, don't we learn from our mistakes? What is it that makes remarriage so difficult?

Why Is Remarriage So Difficult?

Certainly, media portrayals of remarried families, beginning with *The Brady Bunch* years ago, do not help. Television presentations make the extremely difficult enterprise of remarriage seem completely feasible, even simple, in thirty-minute segments, which we know are far from the reality. Creating a healthy remarriage and remarried family life means creating something that most remarried adults never even had models for in their earlier lives. When this is so, how can they—and you—know what is healthy?

In chapter 12 we emphasized several factors to consider in your quest to achieve a healthy marriage *and* parenting relationship. We stressed one point in particular: that the quality of your couple relationship sets the tone for the rest of your family. This is particularly true for a remarriage involving kids. The vitality of the marriage itself is the lifeblood of a remarried family, not just the source of stability.

It is extremely difficult to create a successful remarriage and raise healthy children, especially from two prior intact families. It is a mammoth task. Allow no one to convince you otherwise. It demands so much from you in terms of energy, stamina, flexibility, creativity, hope, patience, and clarity of thought. These qualities are very hard to come by if you have experienced defeat, a sense of failure, and hopelessness in your prior marriage.

There are many issues to consider regarding remarriage. What we discuss in this chapter is relevant to any remarried couple relationship. Although we may refer to your remarriage as your second marriage, the same considerations apply if you have remarried a third or fourth time. The difference is that matters become ever-more complicated each time you remarry. In all remarried situations, however, there is one experience in common. That experience is loss. Whether your marriage ended with a divorce decree or the death of your spouse, loss is the common denominator for everyone whose marriage has ended.

The Central Issue is Loss, Loss, and Loss

It is hard for all of us to face loss in life. It is doubly difficult if that loss is accompanied by guilt, bitterness, sadness, regret, or betrayal. When two adults divorce, each person may experience any one of these emotions, or all of them. Invariably, you wish to move past the pain of your separation and/or divorce, yet your emotional world stays with you. Even when you try not to think about your sadness, or try not to obsess about how bitter you feel, those feelings creep in whenever you're not busy.

Whether your loss was triggered by divorce, or your spouse's death, there may have been many questions and emotions that remained unsettled when you decided to remarry. You might be well into your new marriage now, yet you still may feel a lot of discomfort around your new spouse for reasons that you don't quite understand. Feelings of uncertainty about your current spouse are often due to unresolved emotions from your prior marriage. Until some of those emotions are named and worked through, your current marriage will be severely handicapped.

There will be great benefit for your new marriage if you can achieve emotional closure from your previous marriage. By closure we mean a settling and understanding not only of what went wrong, but also an understanding of the dreams that never materialized in that marriage. Understanding how you were wounded is essential to healing. What most people do not understand is that when you allow yourself to grieve for your lost dreams, you become more capable of being emotionally vibrant and healthy in your remarriage. For this reason, it is important to understand fully your own contribution to the failure of your prior marriage.

Take some time to go through the following questions carefully. They are designed to help you flush out unresolved issues that you may have shunted aside. There is a good likelihood that there are other questions we have not asked, so look at this exercise as just a starting point. Identifying the issues will outline the areas in your past that you need to understand better, so you can nurture yourself in the coming months and years. These questions are designed to clarify issues that may be lying under the surface now, but are likely to reappear prominently in your current relationship. So, answering these questions will expand your self-understanding, identify points for resolution, and aid you on your path to a healthy remarriage.

1. What initially attracted you to your former spouse?

_____

_____

_____

2. Did the traits that initially attracted you become irritants for you during your marriage?

_____

_____

_____

3. Name five things you liked about your former spouse.

_____

_____

4. Name five things you disliked about your former spouse.

_____

_____

_____

5. Why do you think your marriage ended? What did you contribute to the marital problems?

_____

_____

_____

6. List the major topics you and your former spouse routinely (at least once a month) argued about.

_____

_____

_____

7. How did you feel when you were with your former spouse's family? Did you feel good about yourself when you were with them?

_____

_____

_____

8. How did your former spouse treat you when you both were with his/her family? Did you feel that s/he was more attentive to her/his family than to you?

_____

_____

_____

9. What qualities were you looking for in another spouse before you remarried? Were they present in your former spouse? What did your "fantasy new spouse" look like?

_____

_____

_____

10. What was your fantasy of what marriage could and would be?

_____

_____

_____

11. When you think about how your former marriage ended, what saddens you the most?

_____

_____

_____

12. What was your deepest hurt? What was your greatest loss?

_____

_____

_____

13. How have you tried to mourn what you lost in your former marriage?

_____

_____

_____

14. Given how your former marriage ended, how could that history now contribute to troubles in your current marriage? (E.g., if you and your current partner both met while you were still married to former spouses, then dated, and then your marriages ended, you might have feelings of mistrust that your current partner may have an affair with someone.)

_____

_____

_____

Answering these questions will take some time. You may find it beneficial to come back to the exercise a few times before you complete all the questions. What you will have when you are done is a good start for understanding yourself, what you longed for in marriage, and what role you played when that dream came up short for you. Working through loss requires you to know what your losses were. Be as forgiving of yourself as you can, yet be mindful of any unrealistic expectations that may have been embedded in the dynamics of your earlier marriage.

The Baggage Car Is Always to the Rear ... You Just Don't See It

As you probably sensed during the last exercise, *none of us enters into marriage without some baggage.* Entering a second or third marriage involves more baggage than you may be willing to acknowledge. Even though you may try to convince yourself that you have already learned from your prior marriage what you need now, are you aware of what was good about your prior marriage? Are you aware of what you were searching for when you married the first time? How do you know you do not still long for those qualities in a partner?

As you reviewed the questions in the last section, you might have realized that you need to do some more grieving to move on. Moving on involves understanding your lost dreams; letting go of unhealthy baggage (i.e., accepting the pain of rejection by one partner does not mean rejection will occur again with another partner); and establishing a clear self-focus. Having a clear self-focus guards you from blaming your previous partner for issues that are really your own, like questions of trust and fidelity. Without good self-focus your baggage can ruin your present marriage's future. Too many individuals rush into new relationships without first working through the pain and loss of their last relationship.

As you saw in earlier chapters, especially chapter 8, the ability to maintain a clear self-focus is crucial for marital stability and happiness. By adhering to this idea, you will be better able to understand your baggage from past relationships and observe how it may (or may not) play out in your current relationship. *Baggage* is best described as those myths, beliefs, and expectations from your past that affect how you interact in your marriage, usually to the detriment of the relationship.

Baggage interferes with your ability to listen, empathize with your partner, or to creatively change how you interact with him or her. The baggage car is not readily visible, but is attached to you in your journey. Self-focus allows you a good view of your baggage and the opportunity to uncouple the baggage car from your train when you are ready.

Baggage, therefore, is the collected set of beliefs and expectations associated with painful, negative experiences from your past relationships. It weighs you down when you are embarking on a new, promising relationship journey. As you develop improved self-focus, and reduce the blame you ascribe to your past partner, you will be able to see that your baggage prevents you from risking efforts at greater intimacy. You will see your baggage when you recognize the role you play in some standard relationship interactions.

Interactional Patterns in Your Current Relationship

When you find yourself focused more on your partner and his/her behaviors than on your own, there is a strong likelihood that troublesome interactions will follow. All of your insecurities and expectations, your unmet needs from prior relationships, and your unhealed wounds can influence every aspect of your current relationship, even your tone of voice, let alone how you choose to act and respond.

Mel and Trish

Mel and Trish have been married now for three years. Trish was married once before for ten years. Her two children, Sean, eight, and Debbie, six, are from that marriage and live with her. They visit their father every other weekend. He lives in the same town as Mel and Trish. Mel was also married once before. His marriage ended when he found out that his ex-wife, Sarah, was having an affair with his best friend. Mel's parents live together in a neighboring town. Trish's parents, who are also still married, live across the state about a two-hour drive away.

Trish and Mel have a frequently occurring squabble that revolves around her employment as a real estate agent. Trish is very successful in her work and she takes great pride in how highly regarded she is in her field. She often has business meetings and conferences that take her out of town. Mel works as an accountant in their hometown, operating his own business there. He has some flexibility, especially in the evenings when Trish may need to work. Therefore, he is frequently home with Sean and Debbie when Trish is showing a home to a potential buyer. Her work and its required contacts with many people, including men, is a sore point for Mel. He appreciates her success and values her substantial financial support for the family. He is, though, very jealous of the time she spends with new acquaintances.

Mel's jealousy surfaces when he and Trish become embroiled in an argument about his interactions with her children, especially when he is home alone with them. Mel's harsh demeanor and his tendency to discipline the children unnecessarily is reported back to their mother immediately when she returns home from work. Invariably, Trish rushes to wherever Mel is in the house and proceeds to give him the third degree. She questions him on what and why he did what he did as her children's stepfather. In the heat of their arguments, she often calls Mel by her former husband's name.

The insecurity that Mel feels in his marriage with Trish surfaces as defensiveness and harsh generalizations about her children. He usually winds up saying that, if she cared enough about them as their mother, she wouldn't be out working at night. At that point in the routine guilt trip, Trish usually breaks down in tears and goes to the bedroom alone. This is an interaction pattern that has played out frequently during their three years of marriage. Neither Mel nor Trish has tried to correct this interaction, or to change his/her part in it.

Mel's behavior was heavily influenced by his fear of being abandoned and betrayed. As noted above, he not only was betrayed by his former wife, but also by his best friend. His behaviors clearly come across as controlling and insensitive, despite the fact that he actually feels the exact opposite within himself—out of control within his marriage and overly sensitive to possible abandonment by Trish.

Trish, on the other hand, hasn't forgotten all the nights she spent feeling trapped alone at home when her former husband was out with his friends, and with their only vehicle. She had no relatives close by for support, neither did she have any opportunity to develop close relationships with other women. She sees Mel as stable and reliable, yet she still mistrusts him (because he is a male) to be concerned for her children's emotional well-being. What fuels the interaction described are these factors: (1) Trish's mistrust of Mel, (2) her desire to make good in her professional life, (3) her desire to make up for what she missed in her first marriage, and (4) Mel's expectation that his wife is likely to tire of him eventually, and will forsake him for other interests. And so they go round and round, with hardly a start or a stop to this circle of mistrust and blame.

As you can see, there is an abundance of emotional baggage (e.g., fears of abandonment, wounds, parental guilt, jealousy) that was carried into their new marriage by both partners. This baggage provides the fuel for their frequent arguments. Beliefs about gender and work, myths about marriage and fidelity, myths about parenting and equality all seem to surface when these two partners engage in their now chronic squabble when Trish returns home after working evenings.

Perhaps you will recognize traits from your own marriage in the description above, especially if you are remarried. As Mel and Trish discovered, the baggage car loaded with all your beliefs and myths is a lot to tow behind you, but it is very hard to cut loose. The baggage from previous relationships can cripple a new stepfamily. Unrealistic assumptions, often resulting from old baggage, can destroy a stepfamily's potential for happiness.

Predictable Flash Points in Remarried Families

There is a deep anxiety that may exist in remarriages, especially in the early months and years. That anxiety is felt both by you and by your partner. It is at least partially the result of broken dreams and unresolved pain and hurt from past relationships. It is your baggage; and as we have been saying, this baggage can create many problems in your new relationship.

From your own marriage, or remarriages, you may have recognized patterned interactions or predictable arguments taking place, even if the subject matter for those discussions changed from time to time. We have described marital interactional types in previous chapters, such as the pursuer/distancer couple, the dominant/submissive couple, and so on. But when we think about remarriages we must be mindful that the couple interaction is even more complicated because of the very likely unresolved baggage and because there are often other family members (especially children) who are part of the interactional mix.

There are three predictable issues unique to remarriages that may have an impact on your couple interaction, making it even more complex. By no means are these three the only issues that will affect your couple interactions. In fact, there are many other issues that may come to your mind after you read about these. But we have found that these are the most frequent patterns to emerge for most remarried families at one time or another. The first pattern might be called *yours and mine.*

Yours and Mine

This marital interaction is triggered by one partner's concern that his/her children are mistreated or ignored by the other partner. This interaction is very likely fueled by your baggage and your partner's, but it is activated by an event involving the perceived needs of any of your children when they come into conflict with the needs of someone else in the family. Loyalty to blood relatives and to history is at the core of this interaction.

Your marital argument maybe intensified by the yours and mine pattern over many different parenting issues. These conflicts generate great pain and the creation of distance in your marriage. In fact, they can become so intense that marital intimacy can be lost. This is certainly the case with Meg and Rudy.

Meg and Rudy

Meg and Rudy have been married four years. Their marriage is the second one for both of them. Together they have three children, two sons from Meg's prior marriage who live with them, and one daughter from Rudy's first marriage, who lives with her mother. When Rudy's daughter spends the weekend at his and Meg's house, Rudy is very protective of her.

For example, whenever Meg's sons are watching television and Rudy's daughter doesn't like the show, she complains to Rudy that the boys won't let her watch what she wants to see. Rudy never asks the children to describe what took place. So he does not find out that his daughter rarely tells her stepbrothers what she wants to see, expecting them to ask her instead. When she is not asked, they proceed to choose what they both want to see, and then she sulks and pouts and looks for her father to put matters right.

Meg is sensitive to her stepdaughter's plight, as an only child in her original family and the only girl in her stepfamily. However, Meg is also quite concerned that her sons should have some relaxed time at home after enduring years of their parents' frequent fights and arguments. She doesn't see why her stepdaughter can't just learn to speak up with her stepbrothers. Rudy worries that his daughter is ignored, much as he worries she is ignored by her mother when her mother is preoccupied with her own relationship struggles with her current "significant other."

When Rudy's daughter comes to him, he turns to Meg and demands that she should "straighten out her sons." He says that they are "insensitive" and "selfish," and that she is "failing as a mother," so long as they continue to not share the television with their stepsister. Meg routinely reacts with outrage whenever Rudy speaks about her sons in this manner. She retorts that his daughter is a "spoiled princess" who can't speak up for herself and "needs her daddy to fight her battles."

As they shoot barbs like these at each other, Rudy's daughter stands speechless watching them and listening to them fight. She still feels left out and insecure because of her father's marriage to Meg. Rudy and Meg have never tried to find a way to settle this family problem as a couple. Instead they hold on tightly to their separate parent identities, which is much easier for them. As a result, their intimacy as a couple is rapidly disappearing.

Meg and Rudy need to change their counterproductive parenting styles and the resultant arguments by means of open family discussions. After all, this isn't an adult problem, neither is it a "yours versus mine" problem. It is a family problem that could be helped by a family discussion between all five people on how the children might get along better. Helping each person to speak for himself or herself would be an important step forward. Meg and Rudy could thereafter spend some time reviewing the questions you were asked to answer earlier in this chapter, so that each of them could determine how their baggage is preventing their marriage from improving. They are in great danger of increased marital conflict unless this is resolved. Their rapid-escalator style is veering out of control.

You're No Different

As we said above, there are two other predictable, important interaction patterns in remarriages. The second one can be called *you're no different*. This is the interaction that predictably heats up when you and your partner find yourselves mired in an argument. The pattern is fueled by unresolved baggage either of you still carries from a previous marriage and how either of you may still feel abandoned, uncared for, or neglected.

Invariably, the partner who feels that s/he is losing ground in an argument in an intimacy struggle about closeness and distance needs will invoke this statement, "You're no different from _____ (the previous husband or wife)!" It usually follows after one of the partners, rightly or wrongly, has tried to define himself or herself by clarifying what he or she wants to do, either alone or as a couple.

What the partner wants to do may remind you of your previous spouse, or the manner in which the partner states his/her wishes may seem similar to you. But the effect is the same. Your partner's statements create a tension, requiring you to define yourself. If you are not ready to do that, you may find yourself trying to reel in your partner closer by claiming, "You're no different!" thereby cranking up your partner's anxiety that you will end the relationship. Your partner can then pursue you through critical comments or by minimizing his/her statement in such a way as to indicate that s/he is ready to compromise with you, or your partner can choose to continue the argument.

This predictable interaction can also play out when your partner has habits that raise your anxiety levels intensely, habits like alcohol abuse, underfunctioning at home or work, poor parenting, and so on. This is especially true if these were problem areas in your previous marriage. Your spouse's habits may so alarm you that you may seriously wonder whether you have chosen the same partner again, except that this one looks different and has a different name.

He (or She) Is Still Their Father (or Mother)

Finally, a third unique pattern in remarriages could be called *he's still their father (or mother)*. This predictable interaction often takes place between spouses following a dispute over your children's relationship with their other biological parent. It is fueled by the baggage of unresolved feelings of loyalty within yourself toward your former spouse who is your children's other biological parent (and always will be).

For instance, suppose you and your partner have an intense discussion about finances and you each realize that the support payments you receive from your children's father are pivotal to the family budget to make ends meet. What happens if those payments have not been made in a timely fashion? What happens if, because money is tight, a check bounces for lack of funds in your joint account? Or what if your children's father has a habit of changing the days he wants to pick up the kids for his weekly visit? All of this agitation and anxiety will create a great strain in your new relationship. At some point, your new partner will begin to complain about how unreliable your former spouse is and how s/he should have her/his visitation schedule changed by a court order.

At this point in the interaction you may invoke the "He's still their father!" (or mother) comment. It comes up unbidden when your own anxiety has risen to intolerable levels, your own unresolved baggage about having chosen your former spouse still haunts you, and your irritation at your current spouse's financial complaints has reached the boiling point.

Rather than stating that complaints about your children's father's irresponsibility will not help either of you to solve your financial problems now, you may make a pronouncement validating your children's father's right to see them. But this is not really the issue, and it detours you both from resolving your financial problems.

In each of these three typical interactions, yours and mine, you're no different, and he's still their father, there is old baggage at work, as well as your own anxiety about the durability of your current marriage. It is hard to avoid the fear or uneasiness that you might be in the wrong marriage when you have lived through the pain of other relational failures.

Each of these interactions can take place in any marital couple type, as outlined in chapter 12. To avoid replicating any of these interactions, as well as to change your marital type, it is once again important to continue to work through the baggage you brought to your remarriage with you. Take a look at the myths and beliefs that influence and fuel your interactions. Then review for yourself what changes you can make to those myths and beliefs so that your role in your couple interaction will shift, thus allowing you to feel less anxiety and to experience greater self-focus.

Remarriage Myths

Just as there are patterned interactions that are unique to remarriages, so, too, there are myths unique to remarriages. Perhaps you will recognize some of these myths in your own thinking. It may be difficult to acknowledge that some of these myths operate both in your thinking and in your behaviors with your partner. Be honest and ask yourself which of these myths you believe. Become more aware of how these myths influence your behavior. Your tone of voice, your scowls, your inflexibility in problem solving all may be signs of a myth's hold on your thinking.

As we explore the roots of these myths, or half-truths, you may come to realize why they are very hard to let go of and release. Usually, myths about marriage, especially remarriage, have to do with our difficulty in accepting loss and with the unrealistic expectations to which we cling. The strength of these myths may also be due to the popular culture that surrounds us. Myths originate in various sources. They are maintained by your acceptance of them as true, and they may handicap your ability to forge better health and greater intimacy in your current marriage.

Myth No. 1: Remarriage Provides You an Opportunity to Correct All That You Missed in Marriage Before

It is certainly invaluable to understand what went awry in your former marriage. Most important, it is crucial that you assess and comprehend all that was happening emotionally within you when you chose your former spouse, let alone what took place during your former marriage. But it is folly to consider a second marriage as your opportunity to "get it right." First of all, that places an unnecessary pressure to succeed on you and your partner, pressure that either or both of you will crumble beneath. It is unrealistic and unhealthy because this myth will block you from healthy mourning for your failed marriage.

Myth No. 2: Any Man (Woman) Who Loves Me Must Also Love My Children

This myth is a big one, and we often hear it in remarried families. Your new partner has chosen you and feels affection for you. Hopefully, s/he fully comprehends how your children will be affected by your love for one another. But make no mistake about it, s/he is marrying *you*. S/he is not required to love your children to your standards. To expect that is unfair to your new partner, unfair pressure to put on your kids, and very unrealistic for yourself.

You can have a healthy stepfamily if you and your partner love each other, treat each other with care, and your partner treats your children with respect. Your partner not only doesn't have to love your kids for this to work, s/he shouldn't even be placed in the role of being a parent to them until years later, if at all. If s/he hasn't developed love for them (and it may take years for that to happen), how can you expect your partner to parent them?

You and your new partner chose each other for your relationship. If your new partner tries to be a respectful friend to your children, that is enough. Although your children are a necessary and valued part of your life, your partner is marrying you, not your children. By so doing, s/he is accepting and respecting that your kids are important and central in your life. Supporting you in your parenting tasks need not require that s/he also love your children. If you accept this, it will lessen any pressure you, your kids, and your partner feel about this issue. That kind of pressure can be the death knell of your marriage. It has been exactly that for many other remarriages.

One common misconception that new partners have in the early year(s) of remarriage is that there should and can be instant love in a remarried family. This arises out of the need to re-create the feeling of an intact family. However, there can never be instant love. Love is a feeling that grows with proper nurturing, and which can wither under pressure.

Love should not be expected to arise between people, adults or children, who have been thrown together by chance, not choice. The research on remarried families over the years all indicates that families blend and reconstitute *over time*. Time is needed for love to develop. What is needed are respect and low expectations for any parenting responsibilities by your new partner. These will allow your kids, and you, to keep your parent/child relationships steady, while helping the stepparent to ease into the lives of the children with less pressure.

Myth No. 3: Because My Children's Other Parent Is So Ineffective or Irresponsible, My Current Partner Must Make Up for That Parent's Shortcomings for My Children's Sake

Your new partner is in your life because of you, not because s/he loves your kids. Therefore, you need only ask and hope for a respectful friendship to *develop* (not to happen instantly) between your partner and your children. There are no magic solutions for the shortcomings of your children's other parent. Your children need to reach their own conclusions about their father/mother, rather than be sheltered from disappointment through the magic pill of a "new dad" or a "new mommy."

If your partner is a good friend (read that as "friend" not "parent"), your children will not lose anything as they grow and develop. Unlike the common lore that holds a child needs a "good male role model for a father," it is far more meaningful for your son or daughter to have whatever kind of relationship they can have with their other biological parent, in addition to having a supportive friendship with an adult who loves you.

Myth No. 4: The Important Relationship in a Remarried Family Is the Parent Relationship, the Remarriage Will Take Care of Itself

We examined a version of this myth in chapter 12. But in a remarried family it is especially true that your energy must be applied to your marriage's development. As discussed in myth no. 3, your relationship with your new partner is a marriage; it is not a parenting relationship. You or your partner may have children from your previous relationships. But they are not the children of your new marriage. Marriages never just take care of themselves. In a remarried family, the parenting of children from previous marriages is best done by the biological parent of those children.

This concept that the biological parent of a child in a remarried family should be the "hands-on" parent is an idea with which you may have to struggle. We have found that other parents have a lot of trouble with it at first. But it is important to understand that, for your child to resume healthy psychological development, s/he must have as much continuity as possible in the face of all the changes your remarriage has introduced to the child' life. If s/he harbors resentment toward either you or your former spouse for the breakup, that resentment will escalate if you ask the child to permit an unrelated stranger to parent him or her.

The process of creating family bonds in a remarried family is one of time, patience, and flexibility. You must view this as a reconstituting process between the members of two former families. They all need to retain their memories and customs from their previous families for the healthy new family configuration to arise from the two sets of former families. It's a remarried family, not a blended family. Boundaries need to be more flexible. There cannot be a sense of being an intact family yet, because there must be emotional hinges to allow for constant change in expectations, customs, and the varied grieving process each family member will go through. This entire process can take five or more years to unfold.

Myth No. 5: My Family-of-Origin Relatives Will Shift Their Love From My Former Spouse to My New Spouse Automatically. My Children Will Love and Respect My New Partner, Too, Because They Know I Love Him/Her

This two-part myth posits a set of assumptions and expectations that are both unreasonable and impossible to achieve. Your family of origin feels a sense of loyalty and allegiance to you. Some relatives may have developed their own satisfying relationships with your former spouse. But just as loss is a major issue for you and your children, it is also an issue for some, perhaps all, of your family relatives. For instance, your divorce may be not only hard for them to accept, it may also perplex them how to stay supportive of you while not being willing to sever their friendships with your former spouse. Divorce is hard on everyone in the family, and it is helpful for you to be as sensitive as you can to everyone's loss.

Some of your relatives may be able to shift their love and loyalty from your former spouse to your present spouse. Others may be unable to do that. This does not mean they are abandoning you; it simply means it is a struggle for them.

To an even greater degree it will be very hard for your kids to open themselves emotionally to your new partner. Making room for him, or her, while remaining in a parent-child relationship with your former spouse will take a lot of time. Some kids can't do it. Others do it rapidly, only to feel tremendous guilt later on about their choice.

No one can force them to open themselves emotionally to someone whom you selected to be in their lives. The only person you have that kind of control over is yourself. Time, patience, and flexibility are the elements that count for your kids to learn how to respond in an emotionally open way to your new partner.

What may motivate you to subscribe to this two-part myth is the desire to leave your baggage, your unpleasant feelings, completely behind. In your anxiety to do this, be careful not to put enormous pressure on your kids and your family. Again, your kids should not be expected to stop loving their other parent and begin loving your new partner. They need to have their own emotional relationship with both of their parents, along with having their own type of respectful friendship with your partner.

To summarize these myths, take note of how these half-truths actually fuel your marital conflicts and interactions. Believing in myths can cause you to try to change your partner to conform to the myth. If your partner complies with your myth about what should happen in your remarriage, then each of you will have roles that you play out consistently. Your part in each of these myths is the role you play. The role is defined by your statements, your requests, your times of unreasonableness and inflexibility. One of the hallmarks of a successful remarried family, the kind of family that over time truly develops into a new family, is flexibility. Without it, you are ruled by myths that will ruin the marriage.

Beliefs About Your Partner

Believing in these myths easily fuels powerful beliefs about your new partner. These beliefs can leave you feeling hopeless and depressed. You can start to worry that your partner doesn't care about your kids. It is extremely important to challenge these myths so they do not become powerful negative beliefs about your new partner.

Family-of-Origin Beliefs About Marriage and Remarriage

Your parents and other relatives undoubtedly influenced how you think about marriage, let alone how you think about remarriage. Comments like, "The preacher said, 'til death do us part' didn't he?" may have been commonplace when your relatives gossiped around a holiday table, and talked about the ups and downs of various marriages in your extended family or among the neighbors.

Unstated family-of-origin beliefs about marriage can be just as subtle as those that are stated clearly. It all depends on the experiences of the generations before yours. However, when it comes to remarriage, there have been few good, long-lasting models of how remarriage can be successful. There may have been a successful remarriage somewhere in your family, but remarriage is not something adults openly discuss around children, the way your first marriage was grist for everyone's mill. This reluctance to talk about remarriage may be because remarriage suggests starting over. Starting over can be as frightening as it is uncertain. Family members don't usually gossip openly about frightening issues within family relationships, but they whisper about rumors and take sides in quiet but intense discussions to vent their anxiety.

When you were growing up, what did you believe was acceptable? What did you think your options were? What would have been shameful? Was divorce even voiced as an option for decent people to consider? Or was divorce something that only sinful people did? Surely your relatives voiced their beliefs about emotionally laden topics like domestic violence, substance addiction, or infidelity. You even might have received an unsolicited lecture from a parent, uncle, aunt, or cousin about "making your family proud," when you embarked on your first marriage.

Now, we would like you to complete the following exercise to help you sketch these early influences in more detail. Fill in each incomplete sentence with words that accurately describe your family history and belief system.

1. When you marry someone you love _____

_____

2. Divorce is _____

_____

3. When your spouse dies you should _____

_____ for the rest of your life.

4. Children who are in a family that divorces _____

_____

5. Women who marry more than once _____

_____

6. Men who marry more than once _____

_____

7. In marriage, love is _____

_____

Read and review what you wrote. Assess whether your comments and beliefs came from your upbringing or from your recent adult experiences. Those influences that came from your family of origin will be important to attend to as they may be very alive and present in how your relatives respond to you and your new partner. You can change your beliefs, but you cannot directly influence those of your relatives. All you can do there is recognize their biases and prejudices and decide whether they are any longer true for you. Holding onto yourself nonanxiously and nonreactively should be your goal when you are around your family-of-origin relatives.

The Influence of Beliefs from Your Family of Origin

As you completed the sentences in the previous exercise, it may have become clear to you that some of the beliefs that bind you in your current marriage come from your family of origin. Your beliefs can restrict your ability to be open to new ways of thinking and acting in your new marriage. If you believe, for instance, that your current wife will be likely to deceive you if she finds an interesting fellow employee at work, then you will be mistrustful with her whenever she goes to work. You may even believe that you should insist that she not work away from home, and that you can earn enough for the family by yourself. But can you be honest and vulnerable and share with her your fears of losing her? Probably not, if in your past marriage you were betrayed and hurt, even if your family of origin never provided you with beliefs to mistrust a spouse's fidelity.

That's one example. There are countless others that could illustrate how your thinking about marriage has either changed, or only confirmed what you grew up believing about matters of fidelity, trust, needs sharing, commitment, affection, intimacy, parenting responsibilities, and the role of gender. Can you really trust a woman? Can you truly rely on a man to be a steadfast companion for you, as you age? Can you count on your spouse to help you parent your shared kids, and support you in your parenting of your own?

As you have been in marriage before, and may be in a new marriage now, all these beliefs have been put to tests over time. It is likely you need to know what you can count on because your dreams have changed due to your experiences and losses. In time, we do change many of our beliefs, as well as challenge the beliefs we absorbed from our families. Similarly, you may hold beliefs that are really outdated. Beliefs that may have been true in your prior marriage, or in your parents' marriage, but do they still fit your marriage today? Hopefully, you have been able to recognize the beliefs that affirm you and your marital efforts.

Reclaiming Yourself in the New Mix, and Letting Things Go

The challenge of remarriage is an enormous one. You have your beliefs and biases. Your new partner has his/her beliefs and biases. Your children have their emotional wounds. Your children's father (mother) has his or her issues and involvement in your life. Your families (perhaps four—-his and your former in-laws, yours and his former in-laws) have their losses to resolve. And even your friends may have changed with the changes in your marriage. These are a lot of changes and losses to deal with over the coming years.

And, yet, the one constant is you. Reclaim yourself, that is, continue to develop self-focus and self-definition. By better understanding your baggage, your expectations, your beliefs, feelings, and behaviors you are better able to help your marriage. You can do this by changing what needs to be changed in yourself. In a remarried family, especially one that is trying to blend, it is more difficult to retain self-focus. But without that kind of change, the future for your remarriage is shaky.

Self-focus in remarriage is essential, yet for most people it is more difficult than in a first marriage. That is because in a remarriage you have more relationship history with others. You have added pain from broken commitments, added anguish from unmet expectations. Your task is to sort out your old baggage and old myths and figure out what should be scrapped as part of your effort to achieve self-focus. There is just more of it to do. And it is likely to be done in a new geographical location, with new friends, possible faltering loyalty from family or friends, and doubts about yourself.

Self-focus under such circumstances requires steady attention to yourself, and the need to be flexible and forgiving. Being gracious to yourself will allow you to find increased self-focus in your remarried life. It will keep your attention on your own growth, and thus you will engage less in efforts to control the others around you. The efforts to influence and control others, so prevalent in remarried families, largely exists because the adults don't want the marriage to fail again. Yet trying to influence and control others almost ensures that it will.

Frank's Story

Frank has been married now for two years. This is his third marriage. His first took place when he was eighteen and on leave from the Navy. His first wife, Charlene, was seventeen. Before a year was over, Charlene had filed for divorce. She had developed an intimate friendship with a male neighbor while Frank was at sea. Frank was devastated when he learned of her affair and the divorce filing.

He met Julie two years later and fell head over heels in love. She was everything that Charlene had not been. Julie was steady, responsible, wanted a family, and was dedicated to Frank's choices in career development. In a year they were married, and five years later they had three children. Julie worked hard as a mother at home while Frank labored at his electronics job. He made just enough money to support his young family, but he never worried about Julie's faithfulness while he was at work.

By the tenth year of their marriage they had four children, aged nine through two, and Frank was feeling overwhelmed. He never found time to have fun with Julie, neither did she ever have any extra energy to spend time alone with him. Before long, Frank befriended a female colleague at work. He had an intimate relationship with her that lasted six months before Julie learned of it. When she confronted Frank, she gave him an ultimatum: be faithful to her, or leave the family. Try as he might, Frank couldn't relinquish the excitement of his affair and how alive he felt again. Eventually Julie filed for divorce. Frank moved out and dutifully paid child support to Julie and maintained regular visits with his children.

His lover, Elaine, soon put pressure on Frank to marry her. His fear of marriage was trumped only by his fear of being alone. Frank and Elaine married within a year of his divorce. He now has been married two years and is confused about why he mistrusts Elaine, feels bored with his life again, and frequently argues with his wife.

Frank's task now is to unpack all his baggage——his beliefs, his family-of-origin beliefs which likely prompted his marriage at such an early age, and his fears of being alone. He needs to look into his own beliefs and see how they fuel his anxiety when he is with Elaine. He will need to see and accept his role in their conflicts before he can change his part. His improved self-focus could do a lot to make this marriage healthier, although he and Elaine have a tough hill to climb with all the betrayal and pain that have been at the heart of their relationship from its beginning.

This example of a tough situation is not, however, one of impossible odds. Frank can develop a self-focus. In fact, increased self-focus is his only way of rescuing his marriage. Unfortunately, he wrongly believes that if Elaine would only change how she treats him and how she flirts with others at work, then their marriage will right itself immediately. In essence, Frank wrongly believes that the hope for his third marriage's success rests on his wife's behaviors.

In fact, Frank's happiness rests on his own self-definition process, not in what his wife can do to lower his anxiety. Perhaps in the same way, you may now be starting to see what you can do to help define and focus yourself as a way of lowering your anxiety in your complex family situation. You can change only yourself. Changing how you are and what you do will change how you feel. It will also change your marriage for the better.

CHAPTER FOURTEEN

Money and the Use of Power

Money issues are rarely only about money. Rather, for couples, money becomes a symbol of trust, power, and control. These issues, rooted in deeply held belief systems, result in some very complicated couple interactions. It is only when the couples' belief systems are clarified and discussed that healthier dialogues about money can emerge.

Fran and Richard

Fran was rushing to get ready for work. She was dressed and ready to leave, but she remembered that she had planned to stop at the grocery store on her way home later in the day. She rushed to the desk drawer to get the checkbook. As she walked to the door with it, she curiously checked the register's pages. Noticing that a check had been written to her mother-in-law for fifty dollars, she suddenly felt the blood rush to her head, and she shouted out Rich's name.

"*Richard!* What's this check for to your mother? You never said anything about it to me! I didn't even know you had seen her. Where are you? I'm in a hurry and I want an answer!"

"I'm here," Rich muttered slowly as he walked toward her from the back room. "What's the big deal? She needed some money to get through the week. We've helped her out before."

"I know and that's what's bothering me!" Fran shouted. "I never know what's going on with you and her, what you are discussing, or what she's doing. You share more time with her than you do with me! I have to go now, but I need to talk with you about this tonight!"

Rich looked at Fran with contempt. "There's nothing to talk about. We argue all the time just 'cause you get so damned insecure. What do you think, I'm going to go live with my mother? Man, you sure are twisted!"

Fran bolted to the front door in tears, opened it hastily, and rushed out to the car, not bothering to close the door behind her. Rich shook his head, waved his hand at her in disgust, slammed the door shut, and returned to his newspaper.

Today, people who fight about money like Rich and Fran probably can be found in thousands of homes all across our country. The struggle to maintain a family, combined with the additional strain of being a dual-career couple, is very hard for many couples. In the midst of this stress, money, its usage, and all that it represents, can become a significant issue and a major source of conflict.

So, What's the Problem?

From the example above, we could say that the problem is all about money. But why is a fifty-dollar check such a toxic matter? We might say that it's all about overinvolvement with the family of origin. Or we could say it's about power and influence. Money can represent many things. We have found that of all the problems that couples routinely argue about, including children, in-laws, work, and sex, money is often a consistent bone of contention for conflict. We believe that this is so because *money is a medium for managing influence and power in the marriage.*

Typical Money Problems

In listening to hundreds of couples argue about problems with money, we hear a variety of financial issues. For some, it is the tension that emerges between the partner who wants to spend and the other who wants to save. Other couples have variations of this discussion. One wants to live frugally and save for retirement, while the other wants to spend now, before inflation makes their money worth less. One obsesses about the kids' college fund while the other wants to take expensive vacations. In all cases, the polarization between the partners results in greater tension and more battles for control. One constant is that all the parties involved try to convert their partners to their own points of view.

In some homes, the debate is similar to the conflict between Fran and Rich. That is, these couples argue about how much money is spent on family-of-origin relatives. The spending can take the form of gifts and/or loans to parents or siblings, or even helping out a more distant relative who is going through hard times. This can become particularly tense if your spouse believes your family members are irresponsible and should not be helped, while you want to assist them financially as much as you can. How does the decision about helping them get made? Is it reached independently, even secretly? Or is it made through compromise and dialogue?

Couples often argue about how much independent spending each person is permitted to do without checking with the other. It may be one thing to have the cash to buy Starbuck's coffee every day, or to go out for lunch with colleagues from work. But what if you want to buy a new suit or an expensive dress? Are these decisions made independently or separately? Are the purchases charged on credit cards, paid for by a check from your joint checking account, or do you keep separate checking accounts? Obviously, there is no right answer. The more important question is this: How do you arrive at a conclusion together? What is your couple dialogue like on these subjects?

Money and Children

Then there is the issue of kids, not to mention stepkids. How much money should be spent on soccer, dance lessons, or Tae Kwon Do? Should you buy designer label clothes or just what is on sale at Penney's? How much should be saved for college, and for what percentage of that should your kids be held responsible? What about allowances? Should kids earn their allowances doing chores? Or should they get a certain amount of spending money, without having to do anything for it?

Some couples believe that adolescents learn the value of money best by receiving a set amount every month. From that, the kids are expected to budget for their school supplies, clothing, movie admissions, CDs, etc. If they want to buy something, and they haven't budgeted properly, they are out of luck.

But again, the most important issue is this: How do you and your partner make decisions together about how much to spend on the kids?

In reality, none of these issues is simply about money. We have heard many well-off couples argue about very small amounts, even how to split a grocery bill. There are also those couples who, while having the financial means, argue over whether to pay ahead on the mortgage, that is, whether to strive to be fully debt free, or to save for college tuition. In this case, both partners want to plan ahead, but for entirely different reasons. Are these arguments fueled by the absence of money? Obviously not. Something else is going on.

For most couples, money is symbolic of something else. Whether you are arguing over spending versus savings, giving money to your kids or family members, or making all of your "big" purchases together or separately, money is always symbolic of something else. As a result, your financial discussions can become very intense.

Money as a Symbol

Quite often money is a symbol of how power, influence, and control are apportioned and managed in a relationship. Money is also about trust, and about how you view your partner in terms of finances. Obviously, the less you trust your partner, the more you will try to control, influence, or manage his/her spending or saving habits. Trust pertains not only to each person's financial savvy but also to whether you can allow yourself to be vulnerable to your partner's money expertise.

As you can see in Rich and Fran's situation, money can be a means of maintaining a parent-child connection. It also can be about power. For example, the person who writes the checks maintains control of the money that is spent. That's a form of power. Money can also provide an arena in which communications break down completely.

Rich felt that he could not be candid with Fran about his desire to help his mother from what was essentially his and Fran's shared checking account. To avoid conflict, he tried to help his mother secretly. Furthermore, money was the subject matter for a clear triangle to emerge among Fran, Rich, and his mother. It is not hard to see why the anxiety about complex money issues can be tremendous. In the end, though, the anxiety is rarely about money itself.

When You Don't Have Reason to Trust, Anxiety Fuels the Need to Control

Throughout this workbook, we have made it clear that learning how to manage your own anxiety will help you along the road to improved self-definition and thus toward empowerment in your marriage. The more anxious you become, the more you will deal with money in one of the counterproductive interactional styles we have described elsewhere.

For example, if you become anxious, you might pursue your spouse as a way of controlling his/her spending. Or, if you believe your spouse is spending too much, you might try to be more domineering and try to dictate precisely how much your partner can spend.

Anxiety can lead one spouse to adopt a more conflict/avoidant style. The tighter your finances are, the more you might be afraid even to talk about money. If you and your spouse have ever tried to write a budget—and live within the constraints of that budget—you have a beginning sense of what we mean. How money is spent, saved, hoarded, given to charity, and so forth originates in your family myths and belief systems. All of your discussions about money are intensified by your belief systems.

How Do You Talk About Money?

Now, stop and think for a while about how you and your partner talk about financial issues. Try to visualize one of your financial discussions. Who raises concerns about whether there is enough money saved, whether you should each have your own money, or whether one of you has secret debts that the other has just learned about? How are the types of financial issues outlined above discussed? More than likely, your financial discussions fall into a predictable interactional pattern. As you read the next section, figure out which type of interactional pattern best describes your typical financial discussions.

As noted above, when anxiety about money increases, your financial interactions become more intense. Your beliefs about money increase your anxiety, as well as the anxiety that is generated by problematic and difficult interactions concerning money. These beliefs and concerns generate a variety of marital interactional patterns that make it difficult to solve financial problems.

Pursuer/Distancer Couples

In this type of interaction, the pursuer anxiously pursues, nags, and pushes for more discussion while the distancer slowly withdraws. When things become difficult financially, the pursuer is the one who anxiously worries about money, wants to develop a financial plan, and/or wants to find out more about the spending habits of her or his partner.

The distancer says, "Chill out and relax. We'll be okay. Don't worry so much," and then goes back to watching TV. Of course, this has the paradoxical effect of leaving the pursuing partner even more anxious than ever. In some extreme cases we have worked with, some distancers refused to reveal even how much money they earned, and where and how they spent it. Some distancers even keep several saving accounts active, accounts about which their partners know nothing. The more their partners try to pry out financial information, the more distant and secretive they become. As this type of interaction intensifies, it becomes more and more difficult to resolve the original financial issue. The interaction itself becomes the problem.

A variation on the pursuer/distancer pattern is the person who emotionally distances from his/her spouse, spending hours and hours reviewing spreadsheets, budgets, and investment portfolios. How can their partners complain about how they spend their time? They "need" to stay on top of the finances. In reality, however, they are using finances to gain distance and space from their partners. Money is their vehicle.

Dominant/Submissive Couples

With dominant/submissive couples, the dominant partner tries to control and influence the submissive partner's spending. S/he wants to know exactly what has been spent on each purchase. S/he might scrutinize the checking account and offer countless "helpful" suggestions to help their partner become more frugal. S/he may check receipts to see how much has been spent. The submissive partner appears to give in to the dominant person's control. Often, however, they "forget" to record checks, "lose" receipts, or hide credit card bills. They may even have impulsive shopping sprees. In the end it is never clear which partner really has control over their joint finances.

Jeanne and Mike

Jeanne and Mike are a classic example of a dominant/submissive couple in the way they handle their money. Mike works diligently to control the family finances. He gives Jeanne an allowance with which to buy groceries, clothes, and school supplies for the kids. He demands receipts for all of her purchases, and, at times, he challenges her to be more frugal. Jeanne appears to be quietly submissive. She rarely fights back. Yet she routinely "forgets" to record checks, and occasionally goes on shopping sprees and then hides the credit card bills. Mike was horrified to find that their VISA bill was approaching their $10,000 limit.

Conflict/Avoidant Couples

As we have said, money can be a symbol for many things. In some relationships it can become a toxic issue. Often a couple's "solution" to this toxic issue is simply to avoid talking about money at all, to avoid yet another argument. The implications of this interactional style, however, are frightening. The couple could wind up without any financial plan at all, or even experience a financial disaster. Because these couples become too anxious about their finances, they avoid dealing with them at all.

Over/Underfunctioning Couples

When handling money issues, this couple moves in a predictable pattern. As anxiety grows, or as money gets tight, one partner assumes too much of the financial responsibility. "Just leave it up to me. I'll find a way out of this mess," says the overfunctioner. The overfunctioning spouse contains the anxiety for both partners. S/he takes on too much responsibility, and does not expect much help from her/his partner. In the long term this creates a great deal of resentment. At some point, the overfunctioning partner asks, "Why am I doing everything? Why is it my responsibility to balance the checkbook, pay the bills, and establish a long-term financial plan?" Balance and dialogue are missing from this couple's interactions.

Rapid-Escalators

Robert and Joan are a good example of rapid-escalators. Robert loves to shop and believes in buying only the best. His partner, Joan, is just the opposite. She believes in saving for their kids' education and for their own retirement. She goes shopping only when there are good sales. Their differences are obvious. One day when Robert came home with yet another new coat, Joan blew up. "Are you addicted to shopping? You now have four good coats, what are you thinking about? We have three children to put through college, not to mention retirement." In response, Robert also exploded. "Who made you my mother? Don't tell me what to do with my money. I work hard for it, and I will do what I want with my own hard-earned money!" They were off and running, escalating the argument rapidly, with little hope of resolution. The issue about the new coat was completely lost in the escalation when they both began blaming and criticizing each other. The more these arguments escalate, the less likely the issue will ever be resolved.

Now, in the space below, describe the pattern that best illustrates the way you and your partner interact around money issues:

_____

_____

_____

In all of these interactional styles, there is an attempt to solve a problem. It may be to write a financial plan, create a better balance between a saver and a spender, establish a savings account for college, get out of debt, or buy a vacation home. No matter what the issue is, when anxiety increases the intensity of the interactions, the problem becomes impossible to resolve. The interactional pattern, initially aimed at solving the problem, takes on a life of its own.

Furthermore, these interactional patterns are made even more intense by the belief systems to which you and your partner subscribe. You have beliefs about money, about your partner, and about gender. These beliefs fuel the intensity of your discussions and interactions and underlie many of the issues that have become too toxic to discuss quietly.

Belief Systems About Money

What do you really believe about money? Do you value savings over spending? Investing versus spending it now? Are you able to defer gratification or do you give into impulse spending? How should the money for taking care of your kids' needs be spent? Should they have designer label clothes paid for by their parents, or should they use their own money to purchase what they need? What do you believe about credit card usage? About savings? About keeping a budget? How much should be spent on vacations, or entertainment, or saving for your kids' college education? Does money represent satisfaction and security for the present, for the future, or can it be both?

How much do you worry about money? For some, money, or its lack, is a source of enormous anxiety. Some people worry that financial disaster is just around the corner. Others believe that, no matter what happens, "the universe will provide." Obviously, whether you realize it or not, you have a set of clear beliefs about money. Unfortunately, they may not be the same beliefs as those of your partner. In fact, have you and your partner ever taken the time to discuss what you both believe about money? Have you ever told each other what your financial priorities are?

Beliefs About Your Partner

At the core of your beliefs about your partner are trust issues. *Do you trust your partner's way of handling money?* Or do you see your partner as an impulsive shopper who never thinks twice about using a credit card? If so, you may anxiously try to control his/her spending. On the other hand, do you see your partner as "cheap" and always "saving for the rainy day that never comes"? If so, you may believe that your partner is always trying to control you. As a result, you may hide bills, or even create your own secret cache of spending money. Are you able to be honest with your spouse about your views and beliefs about money? Or do you sometimes withhold information that you think will make your partner angry?

Obviously, your beliefs about your partner may fuel painful interactions. For example, if you believe that your partner spends impulsively, you might try to be domineering and controlling, or you might pursue in a lecturing, nagging way, offering countless lectures on the need to save to deaf ears.

On the other hand, you might believe your partner wants to control your finances and oversee all of your spending. If you believe that, then you may work at avoiding conflict, and become dishonest about your own spending and your own views.

Now, in the space provided below, list your beliefs about your partner and money:

_____

_____

_____

_____

Beliefs About Gender

For couples, the entire area of finance is laden with cultural assumptions and expectations. Many of the beliefs that couples buy into were promulgated by the media and the work world. Most of us grew up in a world where the "captains of industry" and other business leaders were always male. Only in the last two decades has the business world seen the emergence of female leaders.

But these changes have been slow to trickle down into the everyday lives of families. Today, many couples still accept uncritically the gender-based models of handling finances they witnessed when they were young. Rather than defer to the partner who has an interest in and a knack for managing the day-to-day bills and investing, many couples force themselves to adhere to the cultural template that dictates men are better at handling money than women are. Or they operate within the configuration of their parents' money management procedures.

In contrast, healthy couples discuss who should be responsible for managing what, and they may even choose to do the bill paying, checkbook balancing, and investing together on a regular basis. This type of balanced financial planning requires relationships that are basically egalitarian. Such a relationship assumes that each person is fully capable of handling money, and is built on a foundation of trust. Gender biases, however, can make balanced or egalitarian relating on finances difficult.

Here are three widespread examples of gender-biased beliefs we have all heard: "All women live to shop (or spend)." "Men are dictatorial, controlling, or irresponsible." "Men are much better at working with numbers than women are." Now, think about some of the gender-based beliefs you may hold. What do _you_ truly believe about gender and money?

Often your answers were shaped by your family-of-origin beliefs. Take some time to review what you really believe about gender and money. Write down your thoughts and review them with your partner. Ask yourself if these views really fit your relationship, or whether it is time to create some new models of financial partnership.

_____

_____

_____

_____

This is an important conversation to have with your partner. What if s/he has a different set of beliefs than yours? For example, suppose your partner was raised in a family where the father was an accountant, the mother a commercial artist, and they both agreed that he should handle all the finances. And suppose you come from a family where your father was a hard-working long-haul trucker who was gone all week, and your mother had no choice but to do the bill paying and banking between going to her job and taking care of the children? You might have the money and the mathematical skills, your spouse might not be able to add a column of figures and arrive at the same total twice, but s/he may believe firmly that only the man should do the finances because that's what worked for his/her parents (and it is the man's "domain"). Do you hash it out and compromise, or do you defer to the gender-based rationale?

Family-of-Origin Influences

As you reflect on your beliefs about money, about your partner, and about gender, it is probably obvious where those beliefs originated. While you were growing up, you learned many lessons about money both directly and indirectly. Your parents may have been clear and direct and even may have taught you how to budget or save. They may have given you an allowance and taught you how to take care of your own clothes. They may have expected you to pay for your own car insurance or even to save for college.

On the other hand, they may have given you everything you needed and not expected you to save. Or, they may have given you nothing and expected that you would work for anything you received. No matter what your experience was, and whether you learned it directly or indirectly, you absorbed many of your beliefs about money from your family.

Your Family Legacy

The way money was handled between the generations in your family may also have influenced what you were taught in a variety of ways. For example, if your grandparents, or great-grandparents, lost everything in the Great Depression of the 1930s, this is part of your financial legacy. You may have been taught to save and to live simply in case another financial disaster of that magnitude ever happens again. The value of saving money for a rainy day is obvious. In fact, the need to save is rooted in the anxious expectation of imminent financial disaster. It represents not just security, but perhaps the preservation of life.

Many immigrant families modeled similar lessons for their children. When they immigrated to this country they often started with very little, living simply and working long hours to provide for their children and grandchildren. In such a legacy, we see three important core values: hard work, simplicity, and saving for the future. Those elements of such a legacy can be passed on to several generations.

On the other hand, if your parents received a large inheritance, and, consequently, had a surplus of money, an entirely different set of values may have been transmitted to you. There might have been an emphasis on extravagant spending and very little attention given to saving and simple living. Knowing more about both of your families' financial legacies can be an important step in understanding how your and your partner's attitudes about money evolved.

Money and Control

You also learned important lessons from your family about the relationship between money and control. Who controlled the money in your family? It was not necessarily the person who earned it. Did your father hand over his paycheck and receive an allowance from your mother? If she controlled the spending and the budget, how did your father react? Or did your father control the money, claiming that he was the one who earned it? Was your family a single or dual-career family? How did that influence the control of money? Again it is important to understand what you learned *indirectly* about money and control.

Money and Anxiety

Who in your family worried most about money? When that person worried, what did he or she do? Lecture other family members on the need to spend less, yell, become domineering, or simply work longer hours? Were there any financial crises in your family? Who took charge? How did they turn out?

Most families goes through times of difficulties and financial stresses. During such times, more anxiety is generated than usual. Everyone in the family feels it. During such times, who took charge? Did one person overfunction and create a solution? Did one person become extremely controlling as a response to anxiety? Or did the family problem solve together, and work together until the financial crisis was resolved?

The Value of Money

Money can be a conveyor of meaning and value. It can lead to present-day comfort and security, something that you might have missed out on as a child. Some people who grew up in poverty, or without financial security, may have vowed to establish financial comfort and security in their adult lives. For such people, money holds a very high value in their scheme of things.

Conversely, there are those who grew up with plenty of money who now place a higher value on simplicity and freedom, rather than giving primary value to a large paycheck or a portfolio of high performing stocks. They may choose to earn less money so they are free to pursue artistic or scholarly or activist goals. Twenty years ago, a sociologist invented a term for such people, they are *downwardly mobile*. That is, they choose to be less affluent than their parents were.

Money can also convey to you and your partner a sense of future security—perhaps in the form of a comfortable retirement fund—which your parents might never have achieved because of the loss of a pension, or never having had quite enough money to save for the future.

Money can be a symbol of how much you value your independence and security. It can become a symbol of self-worth. This can be especially true if you watched your parent or parents work at jobs they hated just to survive and make ends meet. As a child, you may have resolved that you would never live that way, that you would have enough independence to work at something you enjoy. If that was the case, and if your partner does not understand how important these issues are to you, there can be much misunderstanding about financial matters.

So, What Did You Learn?

Many of your beliefs about money emerged from the lessons learned in your family of origin. Now, take some time and write down the important lessons you learned from your family about money and the way it is to be handled. Share these insights with your partner.

_____

_____

_____

_____

Money and Finances: A Crucible for Trust

Money is a symbol of trust in marriage. The financial health of a couple and their children is very important. It is not something that can be casually disregarded by the couple without generating some degree of anxiety as it involves the basic security needs of food, shelter, and so on. Establishing trust requires you to have the ability to change your interactions, as well as to understand your beliefs and family-of-origin experiences. To build trust in regard to money, it is important to change your role in counterproductive interactions. Often, this is very difficult.

For example, when you mistrust your partner's judgment when it comes to spending money, it is difficult to trust that partner's ability to handle any other monetary issues. How do you tell your partner that you do not trust him/her when it comes to money? This can be a very difficult matter to discuss.

However, if the issue is not dealt with, you may feel that you must adopt the role of overfunctioning partner to compensate for what you believe your partner may do. This overfunctioning can occur in a number of ways, including hoarding cash from your joint income, so there will be emergency funds in case your partner overdraws your joint accounts. Or you may keep a hidden balance in your checking account, unknown to your partner, to cover any checks written on insufficient funds.

The list of secret behaviors could be endless if you choose to overfunction rather than discuss your feelings of mistrust and unease with your partner. But do you really want to create that kind of secrecy in your marriage? By definition, it would be harmful to marital intimacy. Finally, mistrust also can be demonstrated in regard to one partner's fear of being managed by the other partner. Charles and Carol's story illustrates this point quite well.

Charles and Carol

Charles and Carol have been married for twelve years. He is in his late forties and this is his first marriage. Carol is in her mid-fifties and this is her third marriage. Carol's two prior marriages were both very abusive, physically and psychologically. Money was always a toxic issue in both previous marriages. Her former husbands had tried to control all of her spending, and had often been verbally abusive, accusing her of wasting money or of hiding it for herself. Frequently, she had been left with no cash at all due to their rigid controls.

Not surprisingly, Carol grew up in a violent family with much physical abuse. Money had always been a toxic issue for her family, who lived from paycheck to paycheck. Her father had been a compulsive gambler. But anyone who challenged his gambling habits was subjected to a barrage of verbal and sometimes physical abuse. When Carol met Charles she saw that he was clearly not interested in controlling her. Her assessment has proven correct.

However, Charles was raised in a family of alcoholics. Prior to his marriage to Carol, Charles had had an addiction to marijuana for many years, but since then, he has remained sober. He does, however, prize his independence and is not eager to spend much time together as a couple. Charles gives Carol a set amount of money to run their household from his weekly pay, and he keeps the remainder for his own use to buy whatever he wants. This was the way his parents handled their finances, despite the fact that his father spent so much money on alcohol.

Carol doesn't know what Charles's income is, neither does she know what his other expenses might be. However, with the weekly check he gives to her and her own income she is able to pay for all of their joint expenses. She has agreed to do this because he has stated that he will not agree to joint accounts. Because Carol has very little money left for herself after paying the bills, she has covertly assumed the role of overfunctioner in exchange for their arrangement.

That arrangement provides her with a sense of independence, of not being controlled by a man who abuses her and does not recognize her abilities. Charles does defer to Carol on most couple matters, yet there is an absence of a true connection between them because he so fears losing his independence (a family-of-origin issue and myth for him).

There are a number of important issues in the way Charles and Carol handle their money. In looking at their *interactional style* it is clear that Carol overfunctions by handling all of the household's money. It is also clear that this couple avoids conflict by not ever discussing their finances. These interactions, in turn, are supported by their strong *belief systems*. Carol does not want to be controlled or hurt, so she avoids conflict. Charles prefers to stay distant, and believes it is important to keep most of his finances a private matter.

Both partners had powerful *family-of-origin experiences* that strengthen their beliefs. Charles is simply replicating the financial pattern his parents used. Carol went through so much conflict about money in her previous marriages that she is relieved by their present arrangement and does not resent the need to overfunction. Although it is unfair, she does not challenge it because it is a peaceful arrangement. Neither partner is unhappy with their arrangement, but their marriage suffers from a lack of intimacy. If they wanted to improve their marriage, they would have to change their patterned behavior around money. But to change their pattern, they would have to work hard to change their interactions, their beliefs, and their family-of-origin models.

Change Your Role in Financial Interactions

Changing your role in your interactions around money and intimacy is a process that must be done with slow, steady, and nonreactive steps. We have found that keeping a journal that records how you feel when you deal with finances, with or without your partner, can be quite useful.

If you cannot maintain a true journal, try keeping a mental journal. That is, when dealing with money issues, try to pay attention to all of the feelings that come up for you. Try to *name* the feelings that come up. That kind of self-aware self-monitoring will allow you to stay nonreactive, even when you are feeling anxious about money, rather than distancing from your partner or pursuing him/her regarding financial issues.

Staying calm is preferable in most situations. It also allows you the opportunity to think through your beliefs about money management. Staying calm involves understanding your role in your financial interactions, as well as your belief systems and family-of-origin experiences about money.

Steps to Create Change

Step 1. In order to create change, first "watch the videos" of your discussions about money. Pretend your most recent financial discussions had been videotaped. If you could watch them, what would you observe? What happened? Whether it was talking about a budget, dealing with debt reduction, or paying for your kids' college education, something "happened." What was it? What happened when you got anxious? Did you try to control or pursue? Did you distance as a way of avoiding conflict? Or did you and your partner rapidly escalate the discussion? In general terms, how do you interact with your partner when you feel mistrust and anxiety? In the space provided below, answer the following two questions:

(a) Can you describe your role when you are feeling anxious?

(b) Can you describe what happens between you and your partner when you talk about money?

_____

_____

_____

Step 2. Review and discuss your powerful beliefs about money and what money symbolizes. For example, do you believe in saving or spending? Should finances be managed jointly or individually? Do you trust your spouse as a full financial partner?

(a) My beliefs about money are these: _____

_____

_____

(b) My beliefs about gender and money are these: _____

_____

_____

(c) My beliefs about my partner and money are these: _____

_____

_____

Step 3. Review the influence of your family of origin on your belief systems and interactional sequences. Talk with your partner about both of your family-of-origin legacies. It may also be important to talk to your kids about money, and concern yourself with what you are teaching the next generation.

_____

_____

_____

Step 4. Learn to hold on to your anxious reactivity. Let yourself feel, but do not react. Work on slowing down your anxious, or reactive, responses to your partner. Practice the strategies that were outlined in chapters 7 and 8.

What I can do to hold onto myself?

_____

_____

_____

Step 5. Move toward change. *Decide what the problem is.* Is it about overall trust, or about budgeting? Is the problem about creating a long-term financial plan, or about paying off debt? Decide what you want to change *with* your partner in your plan together. What is the most immediate financial problem that you, as a couple, have?

_____

_____

_____

_____

Step 6. Continue interacting with your partner about money and hold back your own reactivity.

This is the challenge. It is essential to recognize how you feel, what you think, what you want to propose as a plan, and to hear what your partner proposes. Then, it is essential to remain in dialogue with him/her (not criticizing, not shutting down, not abruptly leaving) until a compromise agreement can be fashioned together.

These are the key questions to consider:

- What points are you willing to negotiate?

- What points in your money plan are fixed and inflexible, as far as you are concerned?

- How can you stay on the topic and change your beliefs to allow yourself to hear your partner's proposals?

- How can you listen and not react to your partner is a disparaging way?

_____

_____

_____

_____

_____

_____

_____

_____

_____

_____

_____

CHAPTER FIFTEEN

The Journey of Long-term Marriage

If you have taken the time to work your way through this book on marriage, it is more than likely you have done so because you want to achieve a happy long-term marriage with your partner. You are not simply hoping to avoid becoming a divorce statistic, rather, you want a fine quality marriage that will last throughout your lifetime. Perhaps you have witnessed the joy of a couple at their fiftieth anniversary party, or you have seen an elderly couple strolling down a beach, hand in hand, in the autumn of their lives. You admired their friendship, comfort, and ease with each other, and wondered about their shared history over so many years. Growing old with someone you love and are committed to is a powerful and wonderful idea.

The fact is that, although most people would love to have a long-term relationship marked by love, friendship, caring, and shared history, few actually get there. As you have undoubtedly figured out by now, the journey is not easy, and it is filled with complications. Throughout this workbook we have tried to provide you with proven principles and ideas to help you on that journey. But, as you have already discovered, putting these principles into practice takes lots of energy and work. It is easy to become discouraged, and, at times, it may seem that there is just too much to think about during the process of creating change.

As you continue on your journey to improve your relationship and to change your role in that relationship, keep in mind five important principles that will help you along the way.

Principle No. 1: Commitment

The first principle required to build a long-term relationship seems almost too obvious to put into words. It is the principle of commitment. Although it may seem simple, it is anything but that. Commitment involves taking the longest view of marriage that it is possible to take, and not focusing on the short term.

Creating change is not a short-term process. Those who value instant gratification will not last on this journey. If you do not take a long-term view of the process, you will never accomplish your goal. In chapter 2, we described many popular myths about marriage. Many of these culturally sanctioned myths suggest a short-term view of marriage. Unfortunately, both life and committed relationships experience too many ups and downs to survive short-term, instant gratification points of view. Those couples who make it survive challenges, problems, crises, and sometimes heartache on that journey. Their long-term view sustains them.

Close the Exits

An essential part of a long-term view of a long-term commitment, means you have to close the exits. If you think about separating or starting over every time you hit a serious problem, you will not do the type of hard work you need to do. It is like beginning a new workout schedule, and two weeks later checking to see whether your body looks like a new physique. Then, if your body has not changed much in two weeks (and it is unlikely that it will), giving up on your workouts in discouragement. Change takes time.

We have worked with too many couples who have one foot in their marriage and one foot out. (Doing the split is never very comfortable.) That is, they never really leave the marriage, but they never really commit to putting all of their energy into making the relationship work. Because they do not close off the possibility of exiting, they do not fully commit to making their marriage work.

Making a full commitment, of course, also means finally putting away the fantasy that someone else might make you happier. This fantasy, called myth no. 8 in chapter 2, is the myth of the ideal soul mate. This is the notion that you can solve your problems and have an ideal marriage if only you could correct your mistake and find Mr. or Mrs. Right. Not only is the myth wrong (witness the statistics; second and third marriages fail more frequently than first marriages do), it will also keep you from doing the work you need to do on your present relationship. Your fantasy of finding the right person will prevent you from taking the steps that you need to take in the present.

What If I'm Not "Feeling in Love"?

The heading directly above, "What If I'm 'Not Feeling in Love'?" is a fairly common question. It stems from the myth of romantic love also described in chapter 2. This myth suggests that love is a feeling that you have little choice about. You "fall in love" and you "fall out of love." In both cases, you are passive and love either happens to you or it doesn't. So, if you have fallen out of love, or are no longer feeling "in love" with your partner, you may believe that your relationship is doomed. If you believe this myth, all you can do is wait for love to return, or leave.

Remember, love is a verb. Rather than wait for the feeling to return, be proactive. Try being loving toward your partner in the way that your partner defines love. Don't worry if the feeling is not there at the present time. Rather, focus on changing yourself and your role, as well as engaging in loving behaviors toward your partner. Imagine that your marriage was exactly what you would like it to be. How would you treat your spouse if things were great? Try pretending, and treat your partner in a loving way in the present. You might be surprised at what happens.

Commitment Means Integrity

Although the word *integrity* is used often these days, it is sometimes difficult to find examples of integrity in the people around us. At its core, integrity is being who you say you are. It is doing what you say you will do. It is defining yourself clearly, and then being that person.

Integrity involves being clear about boundaries and agreements and keeping your word. It is having the courage to be yourself no matter where you are, or with whom you are spending time. It means being clear with yourself and your partner about who you are, and always being honest.

Integrity is about honesty. If, to avoid conflict, you give up parts of what you want or who you are, you will compromise your integrity and wind up being dishonest. If you are afraid to tell your partner about a purchase you just made, and you hide the credit card bill, this is a form of dishonesty. You are compromising your integrity to avoid conflict. If you "forget" to tell your partner about having lunch with someone because it might cause tension, again, you are compromising your integrity to avoid conflict. Integrity is built on a foundation of honesty in all of the little things, as well as the big ones. Trust is based on integrity. This kind of trust knows that your partner will always be who he or she says they are, and that you always will be who you say you are and you will always do what you say you will do.

Principle No. 2: Life Is Difficult

Scott Peck (1998) introduced that simple yet profound sentence in his bestseller *The Road Less Traveled*. Life, in fact, is one darn problem after another. That thought contains a lot of wisdom, especially for marriage. Ask couples who have been married for a long time if their road was easy or carefree. Most couples would tell you about the struggles they have been through. They might describe their struggles with parenting, or the pain of caring for a sick and aging parent while simultaneously raising their own kids and keeping their careers on track. They might tell you about financial problems, stress, disappointments, and tragedy in their journey together. No wonder the old marriage vows contain the words "in sickness and in health, for better and for worse." Those old vows knew that life is unpredictable and is, in fact, "one darn problem after another."

There is, however, a very important principle contained in that simple statement. The statement encourages couples to take the long view and not surrender to discouragement in the moment. Those who really believe that life and marriage should be easy are in for a tough time. We have heard many couples say, "We thought that everything would get easier after the adjustment of the first year." What they did not take into account is the fact that family life is never static. It changes constantly. Careers change, kids come and grow and change and leave, parents get sick, age, and die. In the midst of these life cycle issues and crises, couples must do the best they can to adapt and continue to love and grow.

Remember that time should always be set aside to nurture the friendship of your marriage in the midst of all of these changes, and in spite of them. Your marriage won't stay on cruise control. That is why we believe it is essential for you to keep reviewing the material in this workbook, to examine your role in the problems that inevitably will arise in your relationship in the midst of life's predictable crises and changes.

The Need for Adaptation

If life is one darn problem after another, then adaptation is essential for health. People who are rigid and unchanging will have a very hard time. Couples who assume that if they work out the kinks of marriage in their first year together, they then will have a stress-free marriage for a lifetime, could not be more mistaken.

Successful couples have a large capacity for dialogue and communication. They also have a healthy appreciation for the anxiety that emerges when life changes. The anxiety caused by predictable life crises can make it easy to fall back into old ways of being. It can cause you to pursue, to distance, to do battle, to try to change your spouse, to avoid conflict, and/or to avoid changing.

Successful couples can move through their anxiety without regressing back to old, unhealthy patterns of behavior. They can adapt and change and expand. They recognize when they are getting anxious, or becoming caught in old patterns. They know how to focus on themselves, and how to change their responses. Rigid individuals resist change and adaptation, and often fail at their relationships because of their rigidity.

The Need to Celebrate

Since life *is* one darn problem after another, take the time to celebrate the good days. Slow down, live in the moment, and celebrate your small successes. Each time you are able to accomplish something you wanted to do as a couple, or each time you adapt or take on a new challenge as a couple, take the time to celebrate. Celebrate your parenting successes, even in the middle of a stressful time. Celebrate when you reach a goal. Celebrate your children's accomplishments. Celebrate getting through another stressful week by going out to dinner. Celebrate what you admire in your partner. Don't allow the difficulties of life to diminish the joy in life. Celebrate the moment whenever you can.

Principle No. 3: Self-Focus and Self-Definition

By now, you must be tired of hearing about self-focus. We have emphasized this principle throughout this workbook. We have discussed focusing on your role in your interactions, focusing on your belief systems, and focusing on the baggage you bring with you from your family of origin. We have described how you can pretend to watch yourself interacting with your partner on videotape, and focusing on changing your role more creatively.

At the same time, the principle of self-focus is essential to creating a long-term marriage. It takes discipline, focus, energy, and the process is often frustrating. Many people find that self-focusing is very difficult. But, if you find yourself after an argument saying to yourself, "What did I contribute to this argument?" then you know you are on the road to self-focus. When you begin to talk with your partner about how the baggage you brought from your family of origin might be affecting your marriage, self-focus is emerging. When you are able to take responsibility for the way your belief systems may have caused you to misinterpret something your partner said, you are on the road to self-focus.

Applying self-focus to your problems is a lifelong principle that is essential for your marriage to flourish and grow. Self-focus does not appear quickly. It takes time. As your marriage encounters the predictable problems of life, tensions are bound to be felt. Old, familiar arguments and patterns can emerge all too easily. These arguments can be caused by sex, parenting, money, by just about anything, and then they turn into patterned, predictable interactions. What is essential is to continue to focus on changing your role in these interactions. It will be much more tempting to focus on your partner and try to force your partner to change. That strategy, however, will only make matters worse.

Self-Focus Is Built on Self-Definition

As explained in chapters 7 and 8, self-definition is essential to self-focus. It is difficult to hold onto who you are, especially in the midst of anxiety, if you don't know who you are.

Integrity and trust are built on self-definition. If you cannot hold onto your sense of self when things become difficult, then trust will become difficult. If, for example, you try to make yourself into someone more like what your partner wants you to be, or you do whatever your partner wants you to do, then it will be more difficult for your partner to trust you. Your partner will think that if s/he can force you to change, then maybe someone else can get you to change, as well. If who you are is not solid and well-defined, it will be difficult to build a lasting intimacy in your relationship.

Intimacy

As we explained in chapter 10, real intimacy can come about only when you are clearly defined. If you are afraid that your partner is trying to change you, or turn you into someone he or she wants you to be, you will have difficulty with intimacy. If you find yourself becoming anxious and distancing when your partner moves toward you, you probably are not confident of your self-definition, and your ability to hold onto your sense of yourself. In the same way, if when you are anxious, you pursue your partner for greater emotional closeness, or if you find yourself avoiding conflict, or even escalating arguments, the problem again is most likely to be that you are not differentiated fully enough (see chapter 8). Even sexual intimacy depends on movement toward differentiation.

So, principle no. 3 suggests that for building a long-term marriage, you must work constantly on self-focus and on defining yourself. Furthermore, you must be able to do this work in the midst of anxiety.

Principle No. 4: Be Proactive, Not Reactive

In Steven Covey's classic book, *The Seven Habits of Highly Effective People* (1989), he suggests that effective people are always proactive, never simply reactive. This is especially true for couple relationships. Reactivity, as we have explained, is the opposite of self-focus. When you are reactive, you find yourself responding automatically, motivated by the anxiety aroused by the particular situation.

The danger is that your automatic response may be triggered by belief systems, myths, or family-of-origin themes. This combination can produce a counterproductive couple interaction. Reactivity inevitably results in becoming stuck in counterproductive arguments, and certainly it never moves toward a deeper understanding of yourself or your partner.

Being Proactive Means Watching Yourself

On the other hand, being proactive results in moving toward increased self-focus. It causes you to step back from interactions and arguments and ask, "What did I contribute to this argument?" Being proactive means using the techniques outlined in chapter 3 to watching yourself in an imaginary video of your interactions, and then to change your role.

Being Proactive Means Taking the Initiative to Change

Proactive people do not wait for change to come to them. They do not create full-blown fantasies of their partner changing or taking the initiative to change. They initiate change themselves by working on changing their role in their interactions. They carefully assess their style. They understand what they are likely to do when they are anxious: They know whether they are likely to become defensive, pursuers, distancers, avoiders, escalators, overfunctioners, whatever. As they better understand their responses to anxiety, and to difficulties in their marriages, they work on changing their responses. They take the initiative to work on themselves.

Being Proactive Means Moving Toward Your Partner

To be proactive means to check in constantly with your partner. It means asking if your partner feels understood. It means in the middle of an intense discussion, asking your partner if he or she feels that you are "getting it," or whether you are totally missing the point. It means sharing more of yourself with your partner, as part of defining yourself.

Being Proactive Means Making Repairs

Finally, proactive people never allow a conflict to end without checking in with their partners. After a conflict or misunderstanding, proactive people move toward their partners and say, "How are you doing? We had a difficult conversation last night, and I want to know where you are today with it." Rather than hope the conflict is over for good, proactive people make sure they move toward making repairs and mending the damage that may have been done.

Principle No. 5: Acceptance

We hope that, by this point, you have given up the fantasy of changing your partner. You may by forming a long-term view of marriage, and you may have recommitted yourself to the process. You may be actively working to change your role in interactions. And you may be making progress on your own self-definition. But in the end, being truly loving is being an accepting person. It is not just giving up on changing your partner. Being accepting means accepting your partner for who s/he is. Down deep isn't that what *you* crave? The experience of being accepted simply for who you are?

Long-term marriages are built on acceptance and friendship. Personalities do not change much. Extroverts do not become introverts, and introverts do not become extroverts. Cognitive people do not suddenly learn to communicate based on their feelings, and emotional people do not learn how to communicate without feeling. For the most part, what you see is what you get. No matter how hard you try, your partner is not going to change much. Interactions can change. Your role in interactions can change. But people do not change much.

Does that mean you must accept unacceptable behavior? Of course not. Accepting abuse (or addictions) is never okay. But, most often, that is not what you are trying to change. Too often, what you are trying to change is your partner's personality. You must work at seeing your partner in context. Try to see him/her as a child being shaped by their family-of-origin. See him/her for their strengths and weaknesses. Reinforce their strengths, and constantly tell them what you appreciate. Be patient with their faults. Accept them for who they are. Work toward offering your partner the greatest gift possible. Acceptance is what many religious traditions call "grace." Almost always, genuine intimacy and long-term marriage follow your increased acceptance of your partner.

References

Beavers, Robert W. 1977. *Psychotherapy and Growth. A Family Systems Perspective*. New York: Bruner/Mazel.

———. 1985. *Successful Marriage*. New York: W. W. Norton.

Beck, A. T. 1976. *Cognitive Therapy and the Emotional Disorders*. New York: International Universities Press.

———. 1988. *Love Is Never Enough*. New York: Harper & Row.

Beck, J. 1985. *Cognitive Therapy: Basics and Beyond*. New York: The Guilford Press.

Bowen, Murray, and M. E. Kerr. 1988. *Family Evaluation*. New York: W. W. Norton.

Bray, J., and E. M. Hetherington. 1993. Families in transition: Introduction and overview. *Journal of Family Psychology* 7:3-8.

Carter, E. A., and M. McGoldrick, eds. 1980. *The Family Life Cycle: A Framework for Family Therapy*. New York: Gardner Press.

Clinebell, H. J., and C. H. Clinebell. 1970. *The Intimate Marriage*. New York: Harper & Row.

Covey, Steven. 1989. *The Seven Habits of Highly Effective People: Restoring the Character Ethic*. New York: Simon & Schuster.

Dattilio, F. M., and C. A. Padesky. 1990. *Cognitive Therapy with Couples*. Sarasota, Florida: Professional Resource Exchange, Inc.

Friedman, Edwin. 1985. *Generation to Generation: Family Process in Church and Synagogue*. New York: Guilford Press.

Glick, P., and S. Lin. 1986. Recent changes in divorce and remarriage. *Journal of Marriage and the Family* 48:433-441.

Gottman, John. 1999. *The Marriage Clinic*. New York: W. W. Norton.

———. 2000. *The Seven Principles for Making Marriage Work*. New York: Three Rivers Press.

Jacobsen, N. S., and M. Addis. 1993. Research on couple therapy: What do we know? Where are we going? *Journal of Consulting and Clinical Psychology* 61(1):85–93.

Jacobsen, N. S. 1984. A component analysis of behavioral marital therapy: The relative effectiveness of behavior exchange and communication/problem-solving training. *Journal of Consulting and Clinical Psychology* 61(1):85-93.

Lewis, J. M., W. R. Beavers, J. T. Gossett, and V. A. Phillips. 1976. *No Single Thread: Psychological Health in Family Systems*. New York: Brunner/Mazel.

O'Hanlon, W. H., and M. Weiner-Davis. 1989. *In Search of Solutions: A New Direction in Psychotherapy*. New York: W. W. Norton.

Peck, Scott. 1998. *The Road Less Traveled*. New York: Simon & Schuster.

Schnarch, D. M. 1991. *Constructing the Sexual Crucible*. New York: W. W. Norton.

———1997. *Passionate Marriage: Sex, Love, and Intimacy in Emotionally Committed Relationships*. New York: W. W. Norton.

Wallerstein, Judith. 2000. *The Unexpected Legacy of Divorce: A Twenty-Five Year Landmark Study*. New York: Hyperion.

Watzlawick, P., J. Bavelas, and J. Jackson. 1967. *Pragmatics of Human Communication: A Study of Interactional Patterns, Pathologies, and Paradoxes*. New York: W. W. Norton.

David Olsen, Ph.D., Executive Director of the Samaritan Counseling Center of the Capital Region of New York, has been a practicing marriage and family therapist for over twenty years. A teacher, consultant, workshop leader, and presenter for the Menninger Continuing Education Program at the renowned Menninger Clinic, Dr. Olsen is the author of the classic *Integrative Family Therapy,* and the coauthor of *When Helping Starts to Hurt.*

Douglas Stephens, Ed.D., is Director of Training at the Samaritan Counseling Center of the Capital Region of New York. A marriage and family therapist with over twenty-five years of experience, Dr. Stephens also gives workshops and teaches family therapy.

Some Other
New Harbinger Titles

Thinking Pregnant, Item TKPG $13.95

Pregnancy Stories, Item PS $14.95

The Co-Parenting Survival Guide, Item CPSG $14.95

Family Guide to Emotional Wellness, Item FGEW $24.95

How to Survive and Thrive in an Empty Nest, Item NEST $13.95

Children of the Self-Absorbed, Item CSAB $14.95

The Adoption Reunion Survival Guide, Item ARSG $13.95

Undefended Love, Item UNLO $13.95

Why Can't I Be the Parent I Want to Be?, Item PRNT $12.95

Kid Cooperation, Item COOP $14.95

Breathing Room: Creating Space to Be a Couple, Item BR $14.95

Why Children Misbehave and What to do About it, Item BEHV $14.95

Couple Skills, Item SKIL $14.95

The Power of Two, Item PWR $15.95

The Queer Parent's Primer, Item QPPM $14.95

Illuminating the Heart, Item LUM $13.95

Dr. Carl Robinson's Basic Baby Care, Item DRR $10.95

The Ten Things Every Parent Needs to Know, Item KNOW $12.95

Healthy Baby, Toxic World, Item BABY $15.95

Becoming a Wise Parent for Your Grown Child, Item WISE $12.95

Stepfamily Realities, Item STEP $16.95

Why are We Still Fighting?, Item FIGH $15.95

Call **toll free, 1-800-748-6273,** or log on to our online bookstore at **www.newharbinger.com** to order. Have your Visa or Mastercard number ready. Or send a check for the titles you want to New Harbinger Publications, Inc., 5674 Shattuck Ave., Oakland, CA 94609. Include $4.50 for the first book and 75¢ for each additional book, to cover shipping and handling. (California residents please include appropriate sales tax.) Allow two to five weeks for delivery.

Prices subject to change without notice.